Geprüft

GEPRÜFT

FRANCES ZAGNI

THE REMARKABLE
SECOND WORLD WAR LETTERS
OF PRISONER OF WAR
JOHN VALENTINE AND HIS
WIFE URSULA

Bomber Command Observer John Valentine, Lido, 1942.

Ursula.

Published in 2018 by Fighting High Ltd,
www.fightinghigh.com

British Library Cataloguing-in-Publication data.
A CIP record for this title is available from the
British Library.

ISBN – 13: 978-19998128-1-2

Designed and typeset in Adobe Minion 11/15pt
by Michael Lindley. www.truthstudio.co.uk.

Printed and bound in Wales by Gomer Press.
Front cover design by www.truthstudio.co.uk.

Contents

Chapter One

Setting the Scene

This is the story of the first few years of married life for a young couple, my parents John and Ursula Valentine, as depicted in their letters to each other from 1940 to 1945. The letters chart the effect of the Second World War on their lives, and on those of their generation. John came from a Scottish family and was the eldest of five children, followed by his sisters Bunty (married to Stewart), Irene, Leslie (in the Army) and much the youngest, Ann. The family home was in High Barnet, north London.

John went to Christ's College, Finchley, and left school in 1929 after matriculation. He was then articled to the firm George A. Touche (later Touche Deloite) to train as a chartered accountant. (There is a photo of him aged eighteen at the firm's Christmas party.) John continued to live at home and was given just enough money each day to cover his bus fare, and the purchase of a daily paper and a bun. This was not the career that he would have chosen, but by the time he was fully qualified, in the mid-1930s, jobs were scarce and the future was uncertain, with war seemingly inevitable. However, John determined to follow a different path later on, agriculture being the preferred option. While training with Touche he became close friends with another articled clerk, Roy Cowdry, who had also been placed there by his father although he had a vocation to follow in the Church of England. (As a result of this his nickname was 'Bish'; as soon as he qualified he began training for the Church and later in life became a bishop in South Africa where he had moved as a result of poor health.)

John's father, Arnot, was Managing Director of Balfour Beatty. He was a difficult man, prone to take offence very easily, as becomes apparent in the letters (where he is often referred to by his initials A.S.V.). In addition to the family home in Barnet, the parents bought a second property, Gable End, in Priors Marston, Warwickshire, and this house features regularly in the correspondence. John's sister Bunty had married in 1937 and had two children (Muriel in 1938 and Robert in 1940). Her husband Stewart was in the Army and, as they had no property of their own, Bunty acted as housekeeper for her parents and she and her children lived in Gable End throughout the war.

Ursula was the second of three children; Barbara (also known as Ba), the eldest, trained in domestic science and photography. She drove ambulances in London during the early part of the war, and later worked in catering on a bomber station in Huntingdonshire. Ursula attended North London Collegiate School, winning a series of scholarships to fund her place there. She was a linguist, and after leaving school studied in Germany, Italy and France. Before her marriage she worked as a secretary, offering shorthand in both English and German. Peter, the youngest sibling, trained as an electrical engineer. Their parents, Frederick and Gertrude Griffin had spent most of their married life in India. Frederick became Chief Public Health Engineer for Bengal (which then included Bangladesh) and later spent some years in Delhi before retiring to England in 1943. They owned a property in London, Lido, Tenterden Grove, Hendon, which became John and Ursula's first home. The house was also home for Barbara and Peter, and Ursula acted as housekeeper.

John and Ursula met in 1938 and became engaged on 29 October 1939. They married on 6 January 1940 in St Mary's Church, Hendon, with Leslie as best man and Ann as bridesmaid. Ursula's father was still in India so the wedding was hosted by her mother and she was given away by her uncle, Arnold Cliff. After the wedding Gertrude returned to India until 1943.

The newly-weds spent their honeymoon in Scotland at the Bridge of Lochay Hotel in Killin before returning to London to take up residence in the Hendon house. John's application to join the RAF was accepted in May 1940, and he was called up October. Ursula had become pregnant with their first child in July and bombing of London was a regular occurrence, causing John much anxiety for her safety.

John's letters during the three months of basic training are long and funny, reflecting the chaotic conditions prevailing as thousands of young men were called up. He spent two weeks in Uxbridge, a month in Bridgnorth, three weeks in Grantham and two weeks in Stratford-upon-Avon. It was in Grantham that John met Norman Bowack, a farmer. They continued most of their training together and became close friends. Norman was married to Vera who was also pregnant. (Norman was killed on 29 May 1942, the day before John was shot down, although it was months before the Red Cross confirmed his death.)

Just after Christmas 1940 John was posted to Aberystwyth, where serious training finally began, and he managed to persuade Ursula (and their dog Jane) to join him there. The long journey by numerous trains, heavily pregnant and with a dog, cannot have been easy but she duly arrived on 1 February 1941. Finding accommodation for a pregnant woman and a dog was difficult enough to solve, but problems presented after the birth proved almost completely intractable. John was due to be posted to Scotland for the next stage of his training at the beginning of April but was allowed to delay because of the baby's late arrival (11 April) and he finally left on 26 April. The Sandford family, with whom Ursula had stayed before the birth of the baby, agreed to let her stay with them for a few weeks while she searched for a long term home outside London. Ursula had just decided to return to Hendon when the Howie family with whom John was billetted in Monkton, Ayrshire, agreed to take her in. The couple regretfully decided that travelling with a dog was one thing too many, but fortunately the Royles, the family who had been looking after Jane in Aberystwyth since the birth of the baby, were keen to keep her and she remained in Wales while Ursula and baby Frances joined John towards the end of May. While in Monkton John qualified as an air observer navigator (the course running from 23 April to 19 July 1941) and they remained with the Howies until he was posted for the next stage of his training to the Isle of Man at the end of July, when Ursula then returned to Hendon.

John took the ab initio bombing course in Jurby (28 July to 24 August) flying in Blenheims and Hampdens, and then the ab initio gunnery course (25 August to 20 September) in Blenheims. This was followed by seventeen days' leave, after which he was posted to Upper Heyford, Oxfordshire, for his final training before going on operations. Ursula remained in Hendon until John managed to find digs for her in Stoke Lyne, near Heyford, at the beginning of January 1942 where she moved until his training was complete on 15 March 1942. Then they both returned to Lido and after a short leave John was posted to No. 49 Squadron in Scampton, Lincolnshire, to begin operational flying. Ursula stayed in Hendon.

After flying eight operational flights from 6 April in Hampdens, John then transferred to Manchesters on 26 April. There was a short period of training on the new plane before operations began again on 4 May. Further sorties took place on 9 and 30 May; on the latter his plane was shot down over Cologne as part of the 1,000 bomber raid. John and most of the crew parachuted to safety but the pilot, Philip Floyd, stayed at the controls to give the crew the chance to escape and was killed. The front gunner also failed to escape. After eleven operational flights, John spent the rest of the war as a POW.

John and Ursula's letters to one another reflect their deep mutual love and their belief that Britain would win the war, but also the knowledge that, once John was operational, his chances of survival were slim. 'Out of a total of 125,000 Bomber Command Aircrew who served (British, Canadian, Australian, New Zealanders and others) 55,573 were killed, 8,403 were wounded and 9,838 taken prisoner. In simple terms it meant that 44.4% of those who flew, died. The real picture was rather grimmer. Many of those included in the overall aircrew figure were still training when the war ended and never saw action. According to one study the true figure is closer to 65%.' (Bomber Boys *by Patrick Bishop, published in 2007 by Harper).*

During John's training period the series of letters to one another have many gaps; John's letters only run from 18 October 1940 to 25 January 1941 and none are then extant until he became a prisoner. Ursula's letters cover the periods of January 1941, the second half of April to mid-May, and 26 July to 30 December 1941. After John was posted to No. 49 Squadron, Scampton, Lincs, at the end of March 1942 her letters were continuous.

However, once John became a POW almost all letters survived until towards the end of 1944 when understandably postal services became erratic. All Ursula's correspondence from December 1944 failed to get through and were returned to the UK, but no letters of that time from John ever arrived until he was liberated. So I have no direct evidence from him of the appalling conditions in the camps in the closing months of the war and am dependent on accounts given in three books: The Sergeant Escapers *by John Dominy (Ian Allan Ltd, 1974) and, more particularly,* No Flight from the Cage *by Calton Younger (Frederick Muller, 1956). They were both in the same camps, and Calton Younger came to interview my father for the book and he is briefly mentioned in it. A later publication,* The Last Escape *by John Nichol and Tony Rennell, published in 2002, gives a harrowing account of treatment meted out to the upward of quarter of a million Allied POWs in the last months of the war.*

There are 224 letters and postcards from John and 305 from Ursula, with a further 73 written to him during his long periods of hospitalisation after his return. Once John was a prisoner the content of the letters was severely circumscribed. Neither was allowed to comment on politics and the state of the war, and in spite of great care, many of the letters, particularly John's, were censored. But photographs were allowed and Ursula sent many to her husband, almost all of which came back with him. Another POW made a camera and one photo of John reached Ursula. He was only allowed to write on postcards or official forms, which were quite small, so his letters are necessarily short and they had to be written in pencil. Ursula typed most of her correspondence on both sides of a single sheet of thin paper. John was anxious to hear of every little detail of her life, since these letters were the main solace for him during the years of captivity, so they really are a daily diary. Because mail took a long and variable time to reach the recipient there is quite a lot of repetition to make sure essential information arrived. The same POW who had taken the photo of John in 1942 also took over 200 photos of life in the camp and the ex-prisoners were able to acquire copies of them. Two other prisoners (R. Anderson and D. Westmacott) were professional cartoonists and their book Handle With Care *was published in 1946. In their introduction they say:* 'Some of the sketches were taken by the Germans and had to be re-drawn. Others were damaged in transit from camp to camp. During the last big Allied Push the book was so bulky that it had to be left with a friend in the Camp sick bay and we hoped never to see it again. However, it finally turned up in England, and after going astray in the post for 14 days, once again fell into our hands.' *I like to think that the friend was my father, who features in at least two of the sketches.*

John and Ursula's wedding, St Mary's Hendon, 6 January 1940.

Chapter Two

1940

During these first few weeks of basic training John wrote long and often very funny letters to Ursula. In letter 2 (20 October 1940): This morning at 9 o'clock we paraded for Church. The common or garden C of E – chiefly those who had not sufficient imagination to think of anything else – were drawn up in two large squadrons. R.C.'s formed another but much smaller group, while the rest of us O.Ds. (other denoms) *(John put 'nonconformist' as his denomination in the Volunteer form)* were drawn up into the fourth and smallest squadron. All fellows in our block paraded at first immediately outside the building. Our own Sergeant, a very good fellow, told all those who were not C of E to fall out into a separate batch and after sending elsewhere the R.C. blokes, he checked over the rest of us asking each his pet persuasion. There were Congs. Meths (not spirits) Prests etc. When all the answers were given he said 'What! Ain't there no bloody Spiritualists?' Then he handed us over to our Corporal and told him to lose us somewhere. Being full of resource the Corporal marched us off to another block hoping to palm us off on another Sergeant. The latter said 'Nothing doing' and the Corporal marched us back to our own Sergeant. When we reappeared his face flushed with strong and ill concealed emotion and he told the poor little Corporal in no uncertain but very rude and unrepeatable terms just what he thought of him and us. Having a certain flair for bad language myself, I rather gathered that he didn't want us and the unfortunate Corporal had to march us back again to

the place he first thought of. Upon our arrival he moaned to the
Sergeant there 'What am I to do with these bloody odds and sods?'
Thereupon they went into a huddle and decided to march us on to a
remote corner of the parade ground and leave us to our fate. This they
did and one by one other misfits from other blocks joined us and
soon we had a real useful Sergeant and Corporal all to ourselves and
under their direction we played a minor part in the grand parade –
complete with band and march past.

*A week later, in letter 3, John described his return to Uxbridge after a
weekend's leave:* No sooner had I got to Wembley Park than an
Uxbridge train came in. We had a little excitement at Eastcote. The
train had just come to a standstill when we heard the now familiar
sound of bombs coming down and I was flat on the carriage seat in
two shakes. There were two or three large crumps and when the noise
had died down I poked my head out of the window. The first thing I
saw was the engine driver and a pal crawling along the platform on
their hands and knees and then we saw an awe inspiring firework
display. A bunch of incendiaries had fallen about 100 yards ahead just
by the side of the track. They burned furiously with a curious hard
silvery flame sending up clouds of white smoke and intermittent
sparks. After a second to two one of them exploded and showered
lumps of flaming metal all over the place. It was just like any Guy
Fawkes display without the coloured effects and the whole affair was
extremely vivid and quite eerie. The train was very crowded and all
passengers came on to the platform and watched the show in absolute
silence. Before we saw the sparks flying the railway men thought that
the ghostly white light was caused by an H.E. on the track followed by
a short circuit of the conductor rail. Then they thought that one of
the fire bombs might have fallen on to the track and burned through
one or some of the many rubber cables that always run alongside of
any electric railway, so the train had to stay in the station while
patrolmen were sent ahead to inspect. Before they returned the
flames had subsided but soon a more ominous dull red blaze started.
However, the patrolmen returned to say that the track had been
missed, most of the bombs had fallen in some allotments and had

burned themselves out and one had set fire to a small wooden shed which was the cause of the red flames. This too soon died down and after a total delay of not more than 20 minutes the train restarted and we arrived here without further incident.

At the end of October 1940 John was sent to Bridgnorth for the next stage of his basic training. In letter 4 he describes the enormous camp: There are literally hundreds of single story wooden huts giving the effects of a vast oilwell as seen on the screen or a town such as is usually depicted when a gold vein is discovered in the back of beyond. The huts are well made, though, and there is a general impression of cleanliness. The food is incomparably better here and is really excellent. There are, however, two great snags, one of them being <u>cold</u>. We live in little wooden huts holding 30 chaps, but we are not allowed to light fires until after 4.30 so that it is quite late in the evening before the temperature of the room is at all bearable. The other snag is that the washing place is separate and is not blacked out. Consequently, as we get up at least an hour before dawn, we have to wash and shave in total darkness. The washing is fairly easy but of course shaving isn't.

Yesterday was a most miserable day. After the dreadful business of ablution in darkness there was a bright period of good breakfast. Then we went back to our rooms for a few instructions on various points but as it was bitterly cold outside and we had no fires in our hut we soon became horribly chilled. We stayed there for an hour and then had to stand outside for another 30 minutes then we were marched off to a large unheated lecture room where we were read a lecture by our Flight Sergeant. After that while we were still growing colder and colder our C.O. came in and said a few kind words. Still colder. Then a Padre preached to us and when we were really like ice we were taken outside only to stand there for 30 minutes. By this time paralysis set in and we were marched off to the unheated camp concert hall where we sat for over an hour listening to a lecture on the facts of life. That occupied a whole morning of unrelieved frigidity which lunch only temporarily alleviated. After lunch we went back to our freezing room and spent the whole afternoon there being inspected by our Commanding Officer and getting instructions on matters

relating to kit. After that 3 of us, all frozen, decided to restore the
circulation by walking the 3 miles to Bridgnorth and to come back
early before total darkness. So that we might walk quickly we didn't
wear great coats but after walking for a mile it started to pelt with
rain. We didn't waste any time in the town but nevertheless we were
soaked right through before we got back!

*None of Ursula's letters to John survive for this period. She was four
months pregnant at this point and very anxious to do something to assist
in the war effort. Her sister, Barbara, had been an ambulance driver ever
since the beginning of the blitz on London and John was horrified by
Ursula's suggestion that she might go on duty with her sister:* I am
always thinking of you, wondering if the bombs are falling anywhere
near you and praying that you are not hurt or upset by anything. I am
not very keen on the idea of your going on duty with Barbara. If you
want to do so, you must be the judge, but I don't think that it would
be at all wise. Hendon is safer than Euston and even if you are in a
shelter you are much more likely to be upset because of the greater
probability of bombs near you. Furthermore as it gets darker earlier
and light later you are more and more likely to have to travel during
A.A. barrages. That in itself is unpleasant and I know what London
travel can be like nowadays.

*One facet of John's life that constantly recurred was clothes washing and
he regularly sent parcels of dirty socks and handkerchiefs back to Ursula.
The other was shortage of money. In letter 5 he wrote:* Reluctantly – very
reluctantly I am going to ask for money. I have got only 3/6 to last
until Thursday and it is obvious now that I shall have to borrow. Will
you send me a few shillings – not more than 5/– so that I will be able
to repay and not start with my pay reduced for that purpose. I bitterly
regret having to ask for money but I have no option now. Perhaps if
the RAF start paying me the full rate of 1/6 a day instead of the paltry
9d I may be able to live on my earnings. *And in letter 6:* Yesterday your
parcel arrived safely and most acceptable it was too. You have no idea
how I love getting something from you – it is such a real comfort to
me to know that I have your love and to hear that you are well and

what you are doing with yourself. The cake is excellent – how glad I
am that you sent it. I am afraid that the cost of postage was a bit high
– 10d. It is going to be quite a problem if we are to send much one to
another. To cut down the amount to be posted I think I will try to
wash all my socks except those that require darning. Will you give
me a few hints as to what to do, and if you could let me have the
appropriate soap or flakes I would be grateful. *A further recurring
theme was boots!* Another annoying thing is the way we have to use
our boots. As you know, we have two pairs and I started by wearing
them on alternate days. Here, however, we have to keep one pair in
reserve for our passing out parade. We have to polish this pair ad
infinitum so as to have a surface like patent leather at the end of our
month. The result is that we are unable to use this pair, whereas our
everyday pair was thoroughly soaked long ago and gets no chance
of drying. *And later in letter 6:* I am now in a very chastened mood.
When I finished writing to you I started polishing my ceremonial
boots in an effort to get warm but that didn't prove very successful.
Dinner is at 12.15 and at about 10 mins to 12 I thought I would have a
bath. I had a gorgeously hot soak and feeling much better for it
arrived back at the hut just as the last man left it for dinner. Knowing
that if I went in then I would have to wait at least 10 minutes before
being served I stayed in the hut for that time cutting my moustache
and brushing my boots again and then went over for the meal. I had
no sooner got into the canteen than a voice from the centre of the
room roared 'Come here – you.' It was the hell cat of a Warrant
Officer. He asked me why I was late and when I told him he just about
exploded. Using every swear word known to me he told me exactly
what he thought of me, then he took my name and number and has
promised to find a really dirty fatigue duty for the week end. That
means that I shan't get out of the camp and will probably be peeling
potatoes all Saturday and Sunday. *However, on Sunday:* I had to act as
sidesman at the Church parade, take the collection, count it and then
put 1,000 chairs away – with one or two others. We had to count the
cash in the Vestry and I forgot where I was and that the Padre was
standing behind us and I swore violently when I upset a pile of
pennies. I regret to say that I used the word that astonished you when

I was mending a puncture on our cycle tour at Easter! However he said nothing. …When we started putting away the chairs most of the helpers silently stole away …*when only John and one other were left …* we too thought it was time to disappear but had only got a few yards before we were called back by the Padre. Reluctantly we obeyed thinking that there was more work to be done, however, he gave us an invitation to tea that afternoon from some ladies in Bridgnorth …*these were part of a number of ladies willing to entertain any two airmen to tea on Sunday afternoons… .*Our hostess was a very sprightly widow of 86 and she had a companion of about 50. They were exceedingly hospitable and gave us an enormous tea of white and brown bread and butter, jam and cake. It was a delightful change to get into a decent warm room and to feel like gentlemen. The dear old soul had even bought a packet of cigarettes for us to smoke and after tea the companion played and sang to us. She asked us first if we could do either but we shyly said that we couldn't. Her effort was appalling, she only played about 1 note in a dozen and that merely for the purpose of correcting her voice. However, we managed to preserve straight faces and to express polite appreciation of her efforts. *In letter 7 John wrote to Ursula:* I was one of a party of 8 chosen on account of our height to put 1,000 chairs in place in the gym for Church Parade tomorrow. The same 8 have to act as ushers, take the collection and then put away the 1,000 chairs. They have issued us with boiler suits for all dirty work including fatigues. Mine of course was made for a fellow 12 inches shorter and I look just like a bunny in a panto in a tight fitting skin. While at Uxbridge I was told to have a haircut, but I received a similar order here. However, a haircut has to be a haircut – no musicians locks are allowed and they shoot at sideboards. I had to go to the camp barber and you should see me now. The barber had electric shears and ran them from my neck upwards stopping just short of the pate. Then with scissors he removed most of the top hair and tried to even out the sharp line left where the shears had stopped. My head (God how cold it is) is naked almost up to the top and on that is a little short cropped stubble. Unfortunately nothing less will satisfy the raging Warrant Officer and I had no option but to submit.

John's letters continued and the same subjects regularly recurred: Thank
you very much for the soap flakes, I felt very guilty when I saw the
cost of the postage for them. I suppose the flakes themselves must
have cost much less than that – I really ought to have bought them
myself. I have now washed 6 pairs according to your instructions but
I think that after all I shall have to send the future dirty pairs back
to you because the last two I washed have been stolen while drying.
There is a drying room here but the pipes in it are never more than
lukewarm so that it is a matter of a day or two before such things as
socks are dry. I looked in the room today only to find it empty – my
last two pairs which I had left having disappeared. One of the missing
pairs was your first pair and I am terribly disappointed because they
are my most comfortable ones. ... Under threat of dreadful punishment
we now have to devote quite a large portion of each evening to
polishing and re-polishing our stupid ceremonial boots – blast them.
... I am at the moment engaged on a 12 hour fatigue – 9am–9pm, a
punishment too, for a most minor and entirely innocent offence.
After duty on Friday a few more names were required for weekend
fatigue duties but as I had already done a gardening one (planting
cabbages) I was strictly speaking immune from any more for some
days. The Corporal, however, didn't think of taking the names of
those who hadn't been on fatigues but without any warning they
inspected our hats. You may or may not remember that I had put a
few stitches in the centre of mine to prevent it from opening too
much when on my head. That apparently is an offence of which we
had been given no warning. Six fellows who had tried to improve their
appearance were caught in this way and given various fatigues as a
punishment. Actually mine isn't an awful one – I am Wing Runner
for 12 hours and my duties are to stay in the long office and run any
errands that become necessary during the day. I have had only a few to
do but one of them was unusual. The Sergeant in charge of the camp
hospital rang up to say that he had two dead German Airmen on his
hands and he wanted a copy of Air Publication 130 paragraph X?,
which apparently contains instructions as to disposal of same. It
appears that a German plane was brought down very near here the
other night and that two of the crew were brought to our own hospital.

My job was to find a person likely to have a copy of this particular publication.

Towards the end of November Ursula, Ba and Jane (the dog) visited Bridgnorth. John's time there was nearly over and he expected the final days to be preparation for the passing-out parade, but We paraded expectantly as usual at 8.15, brushed and polished only to receive the order to get into overalls and report to the cook house for a morning's fatigues. I spent a fairly varied time there starting with the boiler room scrubbing party (boiler being enormous cast iron saucepans or vats in which half a hundredweight of veg at a time can be boiled). This job was very wet, greasy and dirty and occupied us until 10.30 when we were given a mug of tea. Thereafter I transferred my attention to a meat mincer and alternately with a fellow sufferer I fed the machine or turned the handle. The monotony was to some extent relieved by a WAAF from the next table cutting cake, who periodically surreptitiously slipped a slice into my hand. Having disposed of the meat I was instructed to render a few thousand slices of bread into crumbs for fish cakes. This job too had its compensation for I had to work at a bench on the lower shelves of which were stored the tins of cake cut up by the WAAFs. It was extraordinary how many slices of cake appeared to spring from the piles of sliced bread and I put 'paid' to the accounts of quite a few. I then graduated to pot washing for the remainder of the morning, which was completed by a 'fatigues dinner' which is supposed to be the reward for our labours. It really was a blowout and I left the cook house feeling like a balloon. …

In the afternoon we had the first inspection of our ceremonial boots, mine exciting no comments from Hell Cat who has now returned from leave. He proved to be in a thoroughly good frame of mind for he took us for half an hour's arms drill and then dismissed us with instructions to spend the rest of the afternoon polishing again and again our boots and buttons. I have no qualms about the Passing Out parade except that I am more than a little worried about arms drill. Our hut has been particularly unfortunate nearly every time the Flight has had arms drill because we have either been on a fatigue, or in disgrace, or arrived at the rifle store after the other huts only to

find all the rifles taken. So that we have had to put up with broomsticks.
As a broomstick hasn't got a trigger or any of the other parts of a rifle
it is very difficult to memorise the drill because there are quite a
number of different movements in the whole of the syllabus. ... After
lunch we had 30 minutes to shave for the second time today, change
into our best pants, polish our boots (ordinary ones) for about the sixth
time and our buttons for the second time – all this for an inspection
by our CO in preparation for the real show on Thursday. After that we
were all told to have a haircut irrespective of the length of our whiskers
and so my scalp has been shaved again. I haven't been in the RAF for
six weeks yet but already I have been shorn four times. Three of them
here. However, this last one is for Thursday's display and thereafter I
ought to be allowed to grow a little more wool to keep the draught out.

There are numerous minor catastrophes. Our washing is sent to a
laundry at Birmingham and gossip has it that the laundry has suffered
a fate similar to our furniture. *After they were married Ursula and John
bought furniture for their future home, but in mid-November Ursula
wrote to say that the warehouse where they had stored some of it had
been destroyed by a bomb.* This hasn't been confirmed yet so that we
don't know what they will do about replacing our losses, if any. If the
'usual channels' are employed to produce fresh issues of pants shirts
etc we shall positively 'stink' before they arrive. I myself sent shirt,
towel, pants and vest and as we have only two of each and my existing
ones have been in service for over a week already, I shall soon be
unable to go anywhere without advertising my presence. ...We are
still anxiously awaiting news of our washing. It hasn't turned up yet
and another story is circulating that the laundry itself has not been
bombed but the water supply to it was hit last week. If this is true,
though mind you I don't believe it any more than any of the myriads
of rumours that float about, we ought at least to get our things back
even if they are unwashed. I hope so, because the situation will soon
be very serious; my present shirt for instance has seen at least ten days
service. ...

Our passing out parade at Bridgnorth was a complete farce. There
must have been 500 men on it with the result that the stock of rifles
was inadequate and much to our relief we went on to the parade

without arms. We were lined up on the square before the Commanding
Officer of the Camp arrived. He was new to the Camp and our NCOs
had been very worried about the extent of his examination. All he did
was to march at breakneck speed up and down our ranks, followed by
a cortège of breathless junior officers and NCOs. He hardly seemed to
look at us at all and when he had finished he took his stand on a small
beflagged dais to take the salute. This meant our marching past him
with eyes to the right and left on our return journey but I am sorry to
say that the marching was atrocious, there being about 20 different
steps in each column of men instead of one. However, we 'passed out'
and after it bitterly regretted the hours spent on our ceremonial boots
at which he hardly cast a glance. …

*On 30 November John was posted to Grantham. His view of the RAF, not
very high after Bridgnorth, fell further! In letter 16 he wrote:* Our
unanimous opinion of the RAF is just about rock bottom now. The
waste of time is positively incredible while there appears to be no
cohesion whatsoever in the activities of various departments.
We commenced our last morning at Bridgnorth by rising at 4 am
with breakfast at 4.30. We were then given rations and paraded, many
hundreds of us, in the large gym at 5.15. There we were herded into
sleepy groups according to our respective destinations and led outside
to form a long column of men. Luckily large lorries were in attendance
to relieve us of our kit bags and after depositing these we stood
awaiting developments for nearly an hour. It was a bitterly cold
morning, with a thick deposit of frost and ice on all puddles and
streams which abound in Bridgnorth camp. Then we moved off for
the station where another wait ensued before we boarded a special
train for Birmingham. Arrived there, we changed stations now
carrying our kit and forming a disgustingly ragged column while
we marched through the main streets of the city. London has little
to show Birmingham in the way of bomb damage for we saw a great
many nasty looking wrecks during our march. Having reached the
station we had another agonising wait, crowded in hundreds on one
of the smaller platforms. We managed, despite dire threats from our
NCOs, to buy a cup of tea at one of the refreshment rooms which

partially restored the circulation and temper. They did not want us to leave the platform for fear that our next train, already much overdue, should leave during our absence. However, it did at last come, and we literally had to jam ourselves into the very limited room at the disposal of the RAF. I was unfortunately unable to get away from the door of one of the Pullman type of carriages and, there being no heating on, became exceedingly cold during our journey through Derby to Nottingham.

At the latter station we had to change stations again and as before we must have presented a sorry picture straggling through the main streets of the city (holding up all the traffic) burdened with our kit bags and forming an uneven column of men none of whom was in step with any other. At the new station, too, we had a wait of over an hour until the train for Grantham picked us up and deposited us there at 4.30. Again we waited while an RAF van came down for us but shortly after 5 pm as dusk was falling we reached this camp. It was a perfect evening, clear as a bell, while the sun set with a gorgeous display of crimson what time we waited and shivered, for it was really cold, until we were led off for a meal. It was now 6 pm and apart from our rations given us at Bridgnorth, we had eaten nothing since 4.30 am. Nevertheless our meal consisted of a thin slice of cold mystery sausage and some bread and jam – nothing to drink. When we had swallowed this snack out into the cold again we went and by now it was pitch dark. However, waiting meant nothing to us now so we managed to endure another hour and a half in the hope that at least someone knew of us and even thought that we might like a bed for the night. Eventually someone did come along and his solution of the problem was to comb the camp in search of a bed belonging to someone on leave and to deposit one of us there for the night. I landed in a barrack tenanted by cooks and butchers and I slept in the bed and sheets of a butcher on leave. He must have been a tough customer for he had only three blankets and I spent a very uneasy night trying to forget the cold and doing my best to snatch an hour or two of sleep. … Oh yes, there is one silly thing to tell you. One of our fellows has got 5 days leave. Yes, five days and what for – to go home for his trumpet AND he was given a railway warrant too. While we

were waiting as usual this morning an officer passed. Seeing us he
said 'Are you the new arrivals?' Receiving an affirmative answer he
then enquired if any of us played in a dance orchestra in civil life.
This particular fellow said that he was a trumpeter so the officer said
he could go home for his instrument if he wished and enquired if
48 hours was enough. The chap had the sense to say that, although he
lived only at Richmond, travel through London was very difficult
nowadays. Whereupon the officer gave him 5 days leave. Can you
bloody well believe it? Five days leave for a trumpet while I with a
nice wife, five months gone, can't get anything. That's all now dearest
– will resume tomorrow.

This morning was gorgeous but cold. There was a very severe frost
last night and any amount of ice was knocking about in the early part
of today when we resumed our waiting. After breakfast we trooped
over to the Medical Dept. where after 90 minutes' wait we had an FFI
and then began the longest hold up since our arrival here. We had
fondly imagined that someone would know that we had come and
would be deputed to house us, provide us with blankets, sheets and
toilet paper, tell us of our duties, times of meals, the hours we would
work and answer any questions we might like to ask. Yes, we imagined
all that but what did we get? Nothing! Absolutely nothing. After the
FFI we asked an NCO at the Medical Dept. what was the next step.
He said he hadn't the slightest idea, but suggested that we went to
the Camp Warrant Officer. This we did and found our irritable Flight
Sergeant to whom we addressed ourselves. His irritability was matched
only by his lack of interest in our plight but he did condescend to say
'Get into ranks of three and wait.' This was precisely what we had been
doing for days but nevertheless we obeyed. After some time a Clerk
opened a window from a nearby room and took down our names,
numbers etc. and while each of us in turn went up to the window to
give this information gusts of lovely warm air issued therefrom into
our cold and pinched faces. When this operation was concluded the
window was shut and we went on waiting. In time a Sergeant came
out and called the names of 8 of us (not mine) who formed into a
separate little squad. The Sergeant then disappeared and both squads
of us started waiting again. Then another Sergeant came out and said

'You spent last night in the married quarters didn't you?' We said 'No' and after goggling at us in a rather nonplussed fashion he shook his head in disgust and took himself off. We, of course, went on waiting. After half an hour more had elapsed he re-appeared, put the same question, got the same answer, again looked as if he didn't believe us and again disappeared. Still we waited feeling very, very chilly especially about the feet. Finally out he came once more and bid the remainder of the original group to follow him, leaving behind those eight whose names had first been called.

We were led to the newest of the Married quarters, rows of little immature brick built maisonettes. MQs aren't used for their proper purpose in war time but they are still building them here. We were ushered into one only just finished, in fact it had been slept in about one night. There was no coal or central heating and no electric light. H&C water is laid on but the H functions only if coal is available. Having parked us, our guide made himself scarce while we were left without any further instructions about what we were to do and when, or what not to do and when not to do it. It was by now, of course, lunch time and we had spent the whole morning idle and neglected standing in the open air stamping our frozen feet, and swearing violently, so we hastened to the canteen for some corpse reviver in the form of cooked food. After dinner, we returned to our billets to see what could be done about heating them. They were newly built and there were others still in course of construction so that there was plenty of builders' material lying about in the form of planks and wooden posts. We had no axe, of course but we managed to scrounge quite a considerable stack of wood of all shapes and sizes and somehow we were able to break it into a size more or less useful for the purposes of a fire.

The rooms in these quarters are small, the one in which I have been placed accommodating only three but I have got the two nicest of the whole bunch of fellows as my room mates so that if we three can stick together when we are moved I shall be perfectly content with my companions. One of them is a farmer, Bowack by name and an exceptionally pleasant fellow, quiet, conscientious and sensible with quite a cheery personality. He is married, seems to have plenty of

money and is followed (sometimes preceded) everywhere by his wife
in their car. A Sergeant came and left hurricane lamps because, as the
billets are not blacked out, it is impossible to use anything but candles
or hurricane lamps. It is by the light of this lamp that I am now
penning this. … I am afraid that the RAF, or at least some sections
of it, is in an infernal muddle. No one seems to have had the slightest
idea of what to do with us here, why we have come, where we are to
be housed or what we are to do for keeping ourselves warm during
day and night. The married quarters in which apparently we are to
live have beds and 4 blankets only, but no coal, no light, no sheets, no
pillows, no blackout facilities, no wood, no brooms for sweeping out
the place and no materials for cleaning basins and sinks, no hot water.
Some of these things are 'on the way' we understand but no promised
time has been given. However, we have scrounged a lot of builders'
planks etc. for wood which we have broken up by hand. We have been
given hurricane lamps and we stick a blanket over the window for
blackout purposes. Of course the rooms are bitterly cold during the
night and 4 blankets are really not sufficient. A further worry is the
fact that all our spare clothing is still at the bombed laundry to which
we sent it at Bridgnorth. My shirt of course is filthy but I shall just
have to wear it until my other returns from Bridgnorth or I get issued
with another.

We have been here for three complete days, but so far I, myself, have
not done the slightest stroke of work although a few have done all-
night guard duties. However, this morning we were taken on a tour of
all the gun posts of the 'drome and I gather that we are to be split into
parties to man these posts. When that is done we shall do 24 hours on
duty and 24 off, but on the 'off' day we will be confined to camp until
4.30. When on duty we will sleep by the guns in our clothes. All guns
are in the open air and the crews of four of the posts sleep in tents.
The men on the remainder sleep in dug outs and although they look
cold and wet I hope I get one of them. The thought of sleeping in a
tent at this time of year just doesn't attract me. The discipline of this
camp is far more lax than that of Bridgnorth and we have been
described as the smartest squad to arrive here for many a day. I am
dreadfully afraid that we shall slack off, though, for with baths

difficult and no supervision of uniform and no means of cleaning out the billets it is not easy to maintain a high standard of cleanliness.

I am in disgrace again and really it is all your fault. When writing to you on Saturday night I had to counter the very poor lighting provided. To do this I hung the hurricane lamp just above the fire and sat very close to it so that I could be as warm as possible and get the maximum light. I don't remember doing so but I must have crossed one knee over the other and hung the toe of one boot too close to the fire. At any rate, the following morning I found a chunk of the welt of my boot missing. The only possible explanation which occurs to me is that I must have dried the boot until the leather was stiff and then in the blackout stumbled over something and broken off the missing piece. I took the boot in for repairs today but the official looked very dubious and said that he would have to consult with the boot repairer before letting me know if they could do the repair. If they can't I shall be called for an explanation of the damage and possibly put on a charge for negligence. I shall learn tomorrow.

Letter 17 written on 4 December was not quite such a marathon as No. 16: We had a little excitement yesterday when a Junkers 88 visited us. It was a day of continuous fine drizzle with low cloud at about 3,000 feet. The warning went in the afternoon and those of us not on guns (myself included) were sent to shelters where we sat for 20 minutes or so. The All Clear sounded and we left the shelter only to hear the warning signal about 2 minutes later. Several of us thought that it would prove to be another fiasco so we hid behind our shelter where we couldn't be spotted by officers. In a few minutes the drone of an aircraft could be heard and then we saw him. What a thrill! He was just about cloud level so he kept on appearing and vanishing as he flew out of and into the lowest clouds. Of course, he was quite low and flying in a straight line dead over the 'drome and camp. However, he appeared to take no notice of it and the camp guns (of which there are quite a number) withheld their fire for fear of disclosing anything of their positions or the nature of the thing they were guarding. We grew quite excited and shouted to all and sundry to open fire. However, when he had passed the camp, guns opened up from all

quarters and we saw him surrounded by little puffs of smoke. Then
suddenly he disappeared and all was quiet for a few seconds. Then he
came into sight again over Grantham and flying in our direction. Guns
opened up once more and the plane went into a shallow dive. Then
we saw three bombs leave the aircraft and a few seconds later columns
of smoke shot up from the ground. After completing his dive, he
opened up his engines and roared towards us, rising all the time.
The noise of gunfire was now terrific, the most thrilling sight being
the hundreds of tracer bullets shooting past him and all around.
However, although we shouted encouragement to our gunners,
Jerry disappeared finally into the clouds, apparently unhurt. We have
heard today that he was hit, and being unable to maintain his height,
crashed a few miles away. We await confirmation of the story before
believing it. One bomb hit a brewery but did little damage, another
fell near a large factory and again was comparatively harmless while
the third, a DA, exploded today killing the officer in charge of the
bomb disposal party. It was my first sight of real action and has given
me quite a bit of excitement.

Living conditions, however, remained very poor: We still have no
sheets, pillows, lighting etc. and the coal delivered yesterday is already
exhausted. It is almost impossible to read or write for long in the light
of the hurricane lamp, so apart from writing to you I spend a lot of
time staring into the fire which we manage to keep going with wood
scrounged from somewhere or other. I am developing a horror of
filth. My shirt, underclothes and handkerchiefs almost sicken me and
I have to shut my eyes whenever I use my towel – it is absolutely black.
Today I had my first bath since arriving here and there being no HW
at our billets I went over to one of the barrack rooms. The water was
merely tepid while the bath looked as if it had coped with 1,000 men
since its last cleaning. On account of the coolness of the water and
dirtiness of the bath I performed my ablutions in the erect position,
sitting down only for a hurried rinse at the end of the operation.
Was it a wretched bath or was it? We haven't yet been provided with
brooms or materials for cleaning our basins etc. so the quarters are
rapidly becoming too dirty for my liking and as we never have hot
water our hands are assuming the appearance of those of a chimney

sweep. Nobody loves us, nobody wants us, nobody has anything for us to do, nobody is in charge of us, nobody … etc. We see nothing but a blank wall of ignorance about our prospects and it is obvious that we are not required and only a bloody nuisance to the Ground Defence Staff on the Station.

Incidentally that Staff must be the most inefficient body of bloody boobs ever told to do a job which is really quite an important one. 75% of them are on guns which they haven't the slightest idea how to use. They are never given instructions, the posts are never inspected, their uniforms and boots are disgustingly dirty, they wear odd scarves and gloves and sometimes no ties. The other day a Corporal visited a post. At least one member of the crew should always be on the lookout but instead some were asleep and the others all writing. When the Camp patrol is on duty at night time the guards call into gun posts for cups of tea and a chat instead of marching up and down the 'drome boundaries. When the guard changes, all the patrols congregate at a central point in the camp, thus leaving the whole camp and 'drome unpatrolled while the changing of the guard takes place. Ursula, it is so inefficient that I am thoroughly ashamed to be a part of it. Yesterday four of the guns were taken away and are not to be replaced for some days, but the posts are still manned by 4 fellows per post for 24 hours a day. Incredible isn't it?

Today has been a fairly interesting one for we have spent the whole of it having a lecture on the Lewis Gun, interrupted only by a full-scale Gas practice this morning and an Air Raid warning this afternoon. For some extraordinary reason, I have yet to do a duty on Camp patrol or at a gun post. All the other fellows have now done one duty, and some have even done two but my name hasn't been called at all. I must admit that I am not at all keen to be up all night patrolling the 'drome or to spend 24 hours in a remote corner of it sitting in a turf dug-out or spending my off hours sleeping in a tent so I am not going to point out to my superior officers that as yet I haven't done a single stroke of my real work. Tonight our conditions in the billets are worse than ever for when we returned in the evening we found to our horror that all the hurricane lamps had disappeared. It is early closing day in the town and it was therefore impossible to buy candles but after an

anxious half-hour we managed to borrow one by the light of which
I am writing this. Unfortunately, it is only a 'Woolworths cheapest'
and gives a poorer light even than a hurricane. Infuriated by the
requisitioning of our lamps, Bowack and I sallied forth at dusk
determined to scrounge something that would give us a good fire
even if adequate lighting were impossible. We took a tin with us and
headed for the coke dump. We had previously noted that the very
ample coke stocks were kept in their place by wire fences and that,
at the back of the heap, a lot of coke had fallen through the fence.
No one was about so we were able to gather enough coke for at least
two evenings' fires, the first of which is now warming us beautifully.
We should get a little hot water from it too for our fire heats the
system in the house. Up till now, having had only wood for fuel, we
haven't been able to generate sufficient heat to make much impression
on the HW tank.

*An overriding concern of John's was Ursula's health and safety. Ursula
was acting as housekeeper at Lido as it was home for both Barbara and
Peter as well as herself; and in letter 18 this concern is voiced:* As regards
your removal from Hendon to a less alarming part of the country, you
know I am all in favour of it and that it is only through your own wish
that you stay there. If at any time both before and after Baby's arrival
you want to move I would be more relieved than by any other news
(bar the cessation of the war). I am constantly worrying about your
safety, even this week when I had to wait a day or two before hearing
from you I kept imagining all sorts of accidents or disasters that
might have occurred. *Finally on 6 December John received a parcel of
clean clothes from Ursula.* How grand it was to have on clean clothes
while the joy of blowing one's nose into a clean handkerchief is one
of the few pleasant discoveries that the RAF has yet allowed one. I
think now, that I have as many clothes as I can comfortably wear, no
matter how cold the weather. The shirt, you darling, was really a
heavenly surprise. I had anticipated getting my undies from you
sometime, but I feared that I might have to spend yet a few more
weeks in my already filthy shirt pending recovery of the lost one or
a re-issue. I haven't tried the cake yet, but I look forward to doing so

this evening – come and have a slice with me!! I have today sent you
rather a large parcel of washing. I am sorry for it, my dear, but owing
to the loss of clothes my existing ones got into a bit of a mess, as
I have told you. I hope that I shan't have to send you the towel or
shirt again – will hankies, socks and pyjamas be alright? Don't
bother to return the pyjamas or tea cloth until I ask. We have little
storage room in our quarters and I don't want to increase the
danger of loss by theft unnecessarily. The remainder could I have
back at your earliest convenience. (Blast you John) especially the
handkerchiefs. By the way, be very wary of those, THEY STINK I
am sorry to say.

Finally John did his first turn of guard duty. The first watch started
at dusk and was brilliantly moonlit. We had to patrol a side of the
'drome which we did without incident. Two gun ports were on the
beat and I pitied those poor devils who do a 24 hours duty – 2 on
and 4 off. Off duty they sleep in a tent and on they are confined to an
exposed square in the centre of which stands the gun. The bitter wind
yesterday must have made it hell's own job to keep oneself warm.
I think it is a crying shame that at an established camp like this there
should be 10 gun posts, the crews of all of which have to sleep under
canvas throughout the winter months. We stopped for a short chat
whenever we passed these posts but the fellows there seemed quite
cheerful. Luckily it was free from rain and the cold and the howling
gale made it rather exhilarating. Coming in at 8.30 we had supper of
cold fried fish and baked beans and iced cocoa (more by accident than
design) but fortunately the guard room was beautifully warm and had
ELECTRIC LIGHT. We were then despatched to our billets for two,
given a bed and 2 blankets and told to be quiet. We could either read
or sleep in full kit ready to be out at a moment's notice. I slept –
restlessly. We were roused at 12.00 and sent out on the second patrol.
The beat was different and the moon had disappeared. The wind still
remained while the sky was clear and starlit. Our beat this time
included the bomb and petrol dumps and reserve stores. They are
very keen on netting for camouflage here but in the gale much of it
had been blown loose and was trailing all over the place. Several times

my rifle and bayonet became awkwardly tangled with flapping masses
of netting, making it rather a difficult job to extricate in the darkness
and wind. … I have found a good spot for writing at last. If one comes
on a Saturday afternoon and evening to the NAAFI writing room it is
almost deserted. True one 25-watt lamp only, lights the whole room
but that is better than a flickering candle or a hurricane lamp. Many,
many thanks for your lovely letter and the two parcels of surprises.
Tomorrow is your birthday – I shall phone you many happy returns
if I can get through. All my love, John.

PS May I have a battery for my torch sometime please?

PPS We've been given sheets at last. No more hairy blanket tickles.

PPPS We've been given a sack filled with straw for a pillow.

PPPPS Our hurricane lamps have been taken away.

PPPPPS There is a shortage of candles in Grantham so we can use
only one at a time (this is not a hint – we three have feathered our
nest well).

PPPPPPS I love you x x x x.

*The next posting, on 14 December, was to be Stratford-upon-Avon,
which delighted John except that his friend Norman Bowack was not
being posted there. Life in Grantham had improved, however:* I shall
miss Bowack & Grant enormously – all four of us are sorry that the
quartet is being split in two. The conditions here have shown one or
two improvements lately. Sheets arrived and pillows – the electricity
was switched on (but we had to buy our own bulb) and we managed
to scrounge some coal dust and coke to supplement the wood stolen
from the builders' yard. Good lighting plus a more durable fire than
that provided by wood have combined to make life a little more
cheerful. I am now going on guard duty regularly with Grant which
makes the job as pleasant as it can be. Luckily we haven't had a single
wet night yet and the cold doesn't now worry me with all the extra
clothes that you sent. I am getting quite used to prowling about the
'drome at all hours of the night. The most startling noises are made
by the canvas draped over the cockpit and engines of the planes which
flap in the wind against the wings and fuselage making a most weird
and eerie hollow sound. The planes in scores are left at night time

scattered all over the 'drome and one hears the ghostly noises coming to one from all quarters when there is anything like a wind blowing. The planes, too, sometimes look like grotesque animals or birds when you catch a glimpse of their outlines from certain angles.

Just before leaving Grantham, John once again referred to Ursula leaving Lido and joining him: Until baby arrives you ought to come to see me whenever possible. My reasoning is not entirely selfish because you know as well as I that the wisest thing for you to do is to get away from London as soon as possible. As for reconciling other family claims, surely we have been doing this ever since 6th Jan last for we had Peter with us for the first six months of our married life; subsequently we lived by ourselves it is true, but not in our own home and of course since 17th Oct. you have not seen me except for those precious 40 hours whereas all the married chaps in my party have had their wives with them for at least several days. We have only just over three months available, darling, until our own precious little infant comes along after which you must of necessity be considerably more tied than at present. So please dear, I implore you, that if any opportunity of our being near to one another should turn up, to do your best to take the fullest possible advantage of it. In common with many thousands of other newly married couples we embarked upon our new life with many horrible disadvantages owing to the war and in addition have been denied the privilege of being completely on our own for 8 out of 11 months since we took the plunge. I was very relieved to hear that the biggest recent raid on London had not troubled you too much. I had read of it in the press and seen the German claims as to the amount of H.E. and Fire bombs dropped and was quite worried until your letter arrived. These lovely moonlight nights give me the shivers for I know from my own experience what bright moonlight can bring with it.

The move to Stratford took place in mid-December and with it the news that they would only be posted there for a short time. Ursula, Barbara and Jane (the dog) visited for a few days, staying in the Falcon Hotel. Your stay here was a period of the most positive form of joy that

I have ever experienced. I shall always love Stratford for those few
walks in such lovely weather by the placid river with its trees, lawns
and swans; for those almost clandestine meetings in the cafe after my
meals; for the exquisite pleasure of waking you in the morning and
kissing you in bed; for the glorious lazy hours by the fireside of the
Falcon puzzling over the chess board, and for the final night of bliss
sleeping together – marred only by Jane barking at the sublime
moments when I was about to pass from the heavenly consciousness
that you were by my side to what I hoped would be untroubled
oblivion. However, we shall be able to give Jane a sedative or knock
her on the head on future occasions, if any. *Some wartime humour also
crept in:* Three spots of humour – at least they strike me that way. 1) A
corporal seeing a lot of us standing idle on a street pavement bawled
to us 'GET FELL IN'. 2) Hitler was about to pay a visit of inspection to
a lunatic asylum and in anticipation the inmates were given repeated
instructions, to raise the right arm in the Nazi salute and to shout
'Heil Hitler' as soon as the Führer entered their respective wards. In
due course Hitler entered a certain room and everyone obeyed orders,
with one exception. Hitler of course was furious with this man and
shouted and roared in his usual way asking for the reason for the man's
failure to salute as the others had done. The reply he received was
'I am a doctor, sir, not a lunatic.' 3) and: Hitler slinking up to Goering
and trying to keep out of sight of a passer by. He says to Goering
'Get that man locked up. I once decorated his house for him'.

*John's parents now had their country home in Priors Marston in
Warwickshire, and there were suggestions that Ursula might go there
for Christmas with John joining them just on the 25th, but, as so often
happened in her relations with her in-laws, problems arose so she
decided to join John in Stratford. John managed to find accommodation
for Ursula over Christmas. As ever communication was difficult:* I tried
to phone you again this evening for third night in succession, but alas
it was of no avail, only priority calls being accepted. I think it must be
that this line from here to London goes via Birmingham so that there
is always a lot of heavy traffic at all times of day and night. I have at
last got a room for you on Tuesday night (haste the time until then).

I started my enquiries about 1 pm and with intervals for dinner and tea it was nigh on 6 o'clock before I managed to book something. I must have tramped miles and called in at least 25 places (no exaggeration) before the lucky hit came along. It is much more 'umble than the Falcon but I think that you will be fairly comfortable. I do hope that it is good enough for my darling wife, but I do think that is the best going. The good lady in charge struck me as a charming soul anxious to do something for me in my plight and waived her objections to Jane. I told her that I might get a sleeping out pass but she said that she couldn't reserve a double room on chance. However, she has definitely booked a single bed for you dearest and she has a double vacant at the moment. Isn't this an odd Christmas! Usually at this time of year, the shops are ablaze of an evening and packed to capacity with scurrying mortals carrying innumerable brown paper parcels. This year is quite different. Christmas might never exist for all the hints that we in the RAF have of it. Very few of us will get parcels owing to the constant changes in our location and the danger of sending anything. We have no money to buy others what we want, we shan't even be at home and unless we are as lucky as I am to be, we shan't have our loved ones (if any) with us. Blooming odd, I calls it.

This first Christmas of their marriage suggests rather spartan Christmases in John's past: I returned to the billets to find your parcel awaiting me. I was in two minds about opening it, but I thought it might contain a letter of explanation about our Christmas arrange-ments, and so I took the plunge. What a galaxy of surprises greeted my eyes – you darling. Mind you I haven't opened everything but I will tell you what I have seen. First the bags. When on earth did you have time to do these? They are just what I want and I do thank you with all my heart. When I mentioned them to you I thought that you might do them sometime in the New Year in a leisure moment. But no, you must have rushed home, dropped me a line and then settled down to sew sacks like any old convict in order to oblige hubby. The figs next – they were uncovered so I couldn't help seeing them. Somehow I was unable to control myself and I tasted one – gosh was it good. A second one was in my mouth before I could stop myself.

Handkerchiefs next, how lovely they are on the nose. The cake and apples I couldn't help seeing but they are untouched. The rest of the lovely parcel is still wrapped in mystery and coloured paper and will stay so until I open the various little packages with you. The way you think of me my dear and study my comforts and take all the hints I drop as to things I would like really amazes me. I have never had such treatment in my life so it is a glorious sensation for me to be waited on. I have told you a million times that I love you and I can't improve on the expression and can only say that I love you more and more every day and am unable to tell you how much I appreciate the things you sent and even more the fact that you think of me so. I am very curious as to the contents of the other parcels you sent me and am trying hard to contain myself. I wish that I could treat you to the same kindness that you have showered upon me ever since I joined up. In your present state, you ought to be the recipient of every possible consideration, no matter how small, instead of being only the giver! And I am terribly sorry that I can't return like for like.

After Ursula's second brief visit to Stratford for Christmas, John was posted to Aberystwyth on 28 December. This proved to be a very different posting: The whole station seems to be really well organised but very, very strict. We are now entitled to wear a white 'flash' in the front of the forage cap, a privilege granted to enable us to be distinguished as 'Air Crew under Training'. We are obviously to be allowed very little chance of developing bad habits for the place abounds with rules and regulations and we have a very full timetable which is adhered to strictly. The course lasts 8 weeks and we ought to be granted a 7 day leave upon completion. We have about half a dozen exams during the course. This station is incredibly different from any that I have been at yet – its organisation is quite beyond reproach. We have been given a programme which occupies every single hour of duty for the whole eight weeks of the course and they adhere to it very faithfully. It is very strict indeed especially on such points as promptitude, smartness, behaviour and implicit obedience. Nevertheless there is a complete absence of the bullying attitude that was so objectionable at Bridgnorth. If every day is like today I shall be very happy here (except that I miss you terribly) for I love getting on with the job instead of stagnating as I have been doing for so many weeks. All the fellows in my Flight are exceedingly keen (at the moment) but I don't think that many will slack off later on. I have done a few hours swotting this evening. Fortunately we have at last a fairly suitable room for studies – not ideal but better than any we have met hitherto.

John was delighted by Aberystwyth itself and the surrounding countryside, and his letters are full of its beauties. He also extolled its suitability for Ursula for the last few months of her pregnancy. What has been on my mind today more than most things is the big raid on London, fuller details of which appeared in today's papers. Having very vivid recollections of the big fire we saw together when serious raids first started, I can only visualise the weekend Nazi visitation. I am worried for you dear. It is hateful to think that you, as you now are, should be so much nearer to horrid dangers than I who am supposed, in my new vocation, to be a unit in the fighting forces. If I can get any assurance or even a well informed forecast that I am more likely to be here in March/April than anywhere else, would you consider moving down here as soon as possible – subject to our finding suitable digs and nursing home. If you are to endure many more serious raids the worry or even fear that they might cause might in time have an effect upon your health. This on the other hand is a lovely spot, it is beautifully quiet and peaceful and appears to be so healthy.

John, Ursula, and Frances, at Lido, Hendon, Christmas 1941.

Chapter Three

1941 and 1942

The new year began with John voicing his concerns about Ursula remaining in London. The baby was due on 4 April and his current course was due to be completed by the end of March, after which there was the expectation of a week's leave. But he was quite unable to gather any information as to where he might be posted afterwards to continue his training. There was even the possibility that he might be sent overseas. For safety's sake John wanted Ursula to leave London and join him in Aberystwyth and he also felt very strongly that they should be together whenever they possibly could. Their letters to and fro constantly debate the pros and cons of her moving to join him.

None of Ursula's letters to John so far have survived, but from now on they were mostly kept. John had problems with ears, nose and throat, which steadily worsened (particularly once he became a prisoner of war). In her second letter Ursula sent him some patent medicine. Herewith the fish-balls – please for my sake do take them regularly, they are small, unobtrusive and quite palatable and cannot fail to do you good, strengthen you to withstand whatever is coming to us. Three a day is the dose I believe. *To which John replied:* Yesterday your packet of tadpoles arrived (how is the congealing and tailing done). You little darling – bothering about me like that. As an obedient husband I shall swallow one after each meal three times a day for $33^{1}/_{3}$ days. Will you make the necessary funeral arrangements, for with your superior

knowledge you will be able to forecast my early demise with
considerably more accuracy than I. *Letters continued, discussing the
possible move with Ursula and in her letters to him making light of all
the possible problems that John foresaw.* If you could get any assurance
about being in Aber. for March and perhaps beginning of April, that
alters things a lot and I should simply love to come to you. On the
other hand, the raids haven't been heavy round our part of the world
recently, and altho' I know it must be worrying for you, you really
needn't be very anxious on my account, and I don't think they will
have any adverse effect on my health unless I get snuffed out altogether
by a direct hit. But the fact remains that I should love to be near you,
even if I did only see you in the evenings and at weekends. I'm getting
fed up here, everything has frozen up again, hope to goodness it
doesn't last like last year. So glad you liked the cake – the new reduced
meat ration is going to increase house-keeping problems here! *In spite
of her light-hearted comments the risk of bombing was high and
firewatching was taken very seriously by some of the residents:*
The meeting of the Tenterden Grove Fire Squad last night was as
parliamentarian as ever, Mr Greenish in the chair. This time, however,
it was enlivened by Mr Pope (Gabriel's father-in-law) who has now
taken up residence next door with his wife and 2 daughters. He is
very deaf, and there was a good deal of comic byplay and bellowed
repetitions which made the meeting quite jolly! The upshot of all
the discussion was that the available inhabitants numbering 15 (not
counting the Neal children, Barbara and old Mrs Pope) will take 2
hour shifts all night every night, warning or no, and this works out at
2 hours every 4th night. I am starting off tonight with the worst shift,
4–6 am. The Popes do the first 3 shifts between the three of them and
then knock me up. We are not expected to go out, but only to keep
a constant look-out, back and front, through windows or doors, and
if there is any sign of incendiaries, ring the fire-bell like mad and get
the whole squad out. It is really a good idea and means you can sleep
peacefully on your nights off. I'm afraid I always have slept peacefully!
It is very nice to think that when I'm away they will be looking after
Lido for us. I'm sending the new pair of Mother's socks to which
I added new toes last night, by knitting by forced marches; also 4

pairs of civilian socks as stop gaps. The other two pairs you sent I will return when mended or re-toed. Did my first night duty on Monday–Tuesday night (4–6 am); it wasn't at all bad. There was no warning on, so I was able to finish off my green shantung smock which I am now wearing. I am on from 2–4 am on Friday night and will get on with your socks then. Darling, I hope the fishballs will help you to get thro' the flue [sic] epidemic (which seems to be all over the place) without succumbing. All my love, Ursula.

John's letters continued on the subject of Ursula's move, but also on the intense training that he thoroughly enjoyed but said how much Ursula could help him with his swotting, particularly aircraft recognition, if she came; however, he included one funny story: Did you hear the story of the Commercial Traveller who when passing through a certain town, called at his customary hotel and asked for his usual room. The hotel was very full but as the proprietor knew the traveller well he said that if he (the traveller) liked he could share a room with his small son. The Traveller consented to this and was shown into the small boy's bedroom only to find the child kneeling at the side of his bed apparently praying. Not wishing to make the small boy shy in any way, the Traveller immediately fell on his knees at the other side of the bed. Whereupon the small boy said, 'You won't 'arf cop it from Pa in the morning. There isn't one that side.'

As ever, Ursula took a positive view of the whole plan: As regards Jane I should of course like to have her with me until I go into the home, since I shall be largely on my own, and she will force me to go for healthy walks. Could you enquire from the publicity office about boarding kennels locally? It seems to me that would be the easiest and cheapest arrangements for her to be boarded out from April 4th (or so) till I am ready to return to London. If necessary as a last resort she could be sent down to Gloucestershire straight from here for the 3 months or so but I should hate it, so would she, and it wouldn't be cheap. An easier solution for me, if we could manage it, would be for me to return to the digs for a week or two – perhaps they would consent to take me with the new-born baby under the special circumstances if it was definitely only for a short time, and in a week or so I feel convinced I could travel back to London. Of course, if the blitz is very bad then it might alter things, but I think we could decide this better when I arrive. But the point is that, since I shall almost certainly be without you then, if I do stay on for any length of time I should be better off boarding with someone who does the work and cooking than in a place of my own.

Firewatching, however, remained essential for Ursula: Old Greenish popped in with the fire-watching rota which I had offered to type for him, and he stayed for nearly an hour chatting. It was chiefly about one more than usually exciting meeting on Friday, when young Evans came storming in and said the whole business was a silly waste of time and neither he nor Nancy were going to take part – which of course makes it all the worse for those remaining. I asked him whether Nancy would be prepared to take over my share when I go, so that two houses would not be thrown on to the others, and I should not feel quite such a cad etc. I hope my warning was clear to him. I must go round and see if she will really do it, as he agreed she would. They are all very sweet to me, and old Pope next door said afterwards that if I was too tired anytime he would do my shift for me, which I thought very decent of him. Actually the all-clear has gone before midnight on several occasions recently and we have now decided only to watch if a raid is on. Mr Pope has undertaken to wake me up if a siren goes during my spell of duty, which is also good of him, as I should never hear it on my own – he probably doesn't realise what a job he has undertaken! Since the defection of the Evans and the amalgamating of Helen Greenish with their maid (since Helen is considered too young and the maid too dumb to do a watch on their own), the shifts come round every 3rd instead of 4th night, but while the raids continue short and sharp at the beginning of the evening it is OK by us.

John and Ursula agreed that she should join him at the end of January, but John was so short of free time that he found it difficult to choose suitable digs for her. I am still taking your jellied eels and am feeling quite fit nowadays, except for being so tired in the evenings and I am

in good form. This new programme is a real sweat, but on the whole I
am enjoying the life here – I wish to Heaven I could see an end to this
awful war so that you and I could settle down to a really happy and
progressive married life doing what we want to do in our own way
and at our own convenience. I have next to no rights now. I am bound
to serve in a very rigid manner and get nothing for doing my duty, but
a hell of a lot of punishment if I don't. You have to live an awful sort
of life, you have no home of your own when you most want it, are
separated from me when I ought to be giving you of my best in the
way of loving care and attention and shortly you will provide a new
born babe with the most marvellous mother that any child could
possibly have.

*Meanwhile, Ursula had made arrangements in Hendon. Ba had found
digs locally and Ursula had given up the allotment that she and John
had rented and arranged for Mrs Sullivan, sister of Ursula's home help
Bridget, to take all the greens that she wanted. She had five children
and her husband had been killed at Dunkirk. Ursula wrote to John:*
I called in to see Thompson, and bought the seeds for the top of the
garden, to the tune of 4/9, which doesn't seem exorbitant if it will
keep us in vegetables for another twelve months! Of course that
doesn't included potatoes, which were the main item last year. I don't
think I shall bother with early potatoes, we have still got such a lot up
in the loft, enough for us to eat and to provide us with seed potatoes
for the main crop. There won't be room to grow so many in the
garden, but I think we ought to have some, after all they are a staple
food which will help to carry you on if all else fails next winter. I have
baked a cake which I am hoping to send off to you tomorrow, together
with Fawley's pyjamas and other sundries. The idea of the cake is for
us to eat together in the evenings, but of course if you want some
sooner, help yourself. Ba is on duty tonight – think of it, I shall only
have one more night alone in the house, on Tuesday. I shall be quite
glad, though I am often so busy that I don't notice it. But I should
hate it without Jane – funny how such a small and really helpless little
being can be a comfort to an adult human! Did you hear this crack
on the radio the other day. A farm labourer was milking a cow when

a patriotic old lady passed and asked: 'Why aren't you at the front, my man?' 'Because there ain't no milk that end, lady.'

Ursula was never very popular with her in-laws; apart from the huge failing of not being Scottish (all John's siblings married fellow Scots), it was her connections with Germany that were viewed with grave suspicion and the fact that she was a fluent German speaker. On leaving school Ursula had gone there on an exchange visit with a very musical and cultivated family called Mugden who had three sons, and she travelled there again in 1934. Ursula became very close to one of the sons, even briefly becoming engaged, although they broke off the relationship because of the imminence of war. The family were half Jewish and escaped to the USA but returned to Germany in peacetime. John and Ursula remained lifelong friends with them. One of the sons, Klaus, was a talented cellist and in a letter to me in the 1990s he said that he felt he was my 'cello daddy'.

I have heard from Mrs Stenzel (a German Jewess who was interned as an enemy alien); she is still at Holloway and I am going to visit her before I leave. She seems to think that if I apply for her release and say I will give her a job in the house there is some chance of her being let out. It would certainly be a happy solution from my point of view, and I will discuss it further when I see her. In three months the Home Office might possibly have reached a decision too. I suppose your parents would think it very awful of me to employ an enemy alien, even though a refugee from the very things we are fighting? However, times are hard, and I shall just <u>have</u> to have some help in the house when baby is here, and if can have a woman who is a lady and an intellectual companion as well as a good mother and housekeeper herself, I don't think I can do better, apart from the fact that I should be helping one who has already suffered unjustly quite enough. But maybe it will never come off. Did you hear the story of the nervous wife who started at every sound outside during an air-raid. Her husband trying to reassure her said, 'Don't get nervous dear, that's only a bus.' 'Ours or theirs?'

*A final flurry of letters to and fro and everything was finally arranged
for Ursula to join John. John had been worried that he had offended his
father, who wrote regularly on Mondays, but that had been resolved and
in his last letter wrote:* My father told me this week about the bomb
which fell through the roadway at the Bank tube station, went down
the escalator shaft and exploded at the bottom. He says that everything
fell in – road and all – and his firm have been given the job of clearing
it up. It will take months and months.

*Ursula and Jane travelled to Aberystwyth on 1 February 1941. Frances
was born on 11 April in the maternity hospital. John was posted to
Ayrshire in Scotland on 25 April (where he was once again stationed
with Norman Bowack) and Ursula's future abode was a cause of a lot of
worry. John did not want her to return to Hendon so soon after the birth,
even though the arrangement with the Sandfords was only a temporary
one. It seemed to be impossible to find people who were willing to take a
mother, very small baby and a dog; hence the suggestion of Ursula's that
she should go into a 'Mother & Baby home'. Ba also found somewhere
where Ursula could have gone and assisted in some way with the house-
work. All these proposals were repudiated by John very strongly. In the
end the problem was solved by his landlady, Mrs Howie, being willing
to take them in when her other RAF lodger, Jack, moved elsewhere. They
regretfully decided to leave Jane with the Royles in Aberystwyth. So
Ursula and Frances joined John in Monkton towards the end of May 1941.*

*Ursula's first letter to John was dated the day after he left for Scotland. It
was, inevitably, full of baby care. The Trudy King method was in vogue
at the time, which insisted that babies were NOT fed between 10pm and
6am and she wrote:* Frances is pretty well a model baby all day, sleeps
solidly from feed to feed, but her weakness is the night, she simply
cannot last through from 10 pm to 6 am, with the result that I don't
get much sleep in the early hours, so I take it in the afternoon. I shall
have to compromise over the night feeding hours, giving it to her at
11pm or so and at 5 or even earlier if she wakes, I'm sure it can't be
right for her to howl for 3 or 4 hours on end which she does if I'm
strong-minded and leave her. I'll gradually get the hours back to

normal little by little – I'm convinced they must have fed her on more than glucose and water in the middle of the night at the maternity home. *John was obviously very upset by the 'Baby home' suggestion and in despair Ursula wrote:* You really are a provoking boy. You start off by saying you won't express any opinions about my going to the Babies Home, proceed for 2 pages to express quite forceful but not very reasonable opinions, and end up your letter by saying you would be 'terribly disappointed' if I went 'baby farming' as you call it. Please try to be more constructive and helpful in your reply – I won't write anything definite to the B. Home yet. Would you object to my going there for 3–4 weeks to try it, as Miss Crow suggested? If you definitely don't want me to go there, for heaven's sake help me, think of an excuse, because I can think of no possible reason for not accepting. You know that I don't want to hurt your feelings darling, but we must consider Frances first and foremost, and I think there's no doubt she'd be better in the country than at Lido, and better in an establishment specially run for babies than made to fit into a grown-up house over which I have no control. I will pass over your remark about 'going into service' while Frances is so young and only point out that I should like to be able to do some work which helps others, especially children, in the 3 hour intervals between feeds, and that it's easier now while she sleeps the whole time than at 6 months say, when she'll need far more looking after.

By the middle of May Ursula was getting very worried about to where to go when Jack, the other 'billetee' with John in Scotland moved away and Mr and Mrs Howie were willing to accept her, so the next letters were full of travel plans and the realisation that taking Jane with her was going to be one thing too many: I went into Aber. this morning and saw Royle about Jane. I was awfully upset at having to part with her, but I'm afraid it's the wisest course. Royle says he will keep her for us in any case. *In among all the travel arrangements Ursula also commented on the wider picture:* I don't know quite why but somehow I'm feeling more hopeful about the war just now. Perhaps it's because the headlong rush of disasters has slowed up for a bit, tho' I don't suppose for a moment that it is finished. Also the night fighter figures have been so good recently – tho' I can't feel wholly glad about that, because if we've got something effective against the night-bombers, presumably Germany has or will have soon and that's not so cheerful when I think of you so soon being on active service – these next few months will surely go all too quickly. ...I've had a letter from Ba – written before the Saturday night blitz so I still don't know whether she survived it. What a ghastly business, it makes one sick to think of Westminster Abbey getting it like that. I wonder if Lido is still there? *And on 13 May:* Great excitement this morning over Rudolf Hess dropping in at Glasgow. One is tempted to jump to all sorts of wishful conclusions about internal strife, morale cracking and all the rest. I only wish someone would push old Adolf out of a plane and have done with it! *And two days later:* Haven't heard from Ba, hope she's survived the blitz. Pity you didn't shoot down Hess and have done with it. There's a deal too much fuss made of him.

Ursula and Frances lived with John at Mr and Mrs Howie's house, Fairfield Mains, Monkton, Ayrshire, until he was posted to Jurby, Isle of Man, in July and she returned to live at Lido, Tenterden Grove, Hendon. Although John wrote almost daily, none of his letters have survived. John was transferred to Upper Heyford, Oxfordshire, in October 1941, and once again Ursula was able to join him for a while, living in Stoke Lyne. When John became operational he was posted to Scampton in Lincolnshire and Ursula returned once more to Lido where she remained until she bought their first house, Felmersham, Chalfont St Giles, in 1943.

Ursula's first letter to John from Lido was dated 26 July 1941. The house and garden, having been unoccupied since February, were in need of a lot of work. Ursula referred to two gardeners John had found. They brought their scythe this morning, and disposed of the hayfield satisfactorily! *Ursula was still hoping that Mrs Stenzel might be able to come and live with her. She had now been moved to an internment camp in the Isle of Man and John anticipated being able to visit her. Air raid warnings still occurred, of which Ursula wrote:* We had an air-raid warning last night, much to our disgust. At first I thought I wouldn't bother about it, but

then we heard gun-fire, so I took Frances downstairs and put her in
the corner of the drawing room with the desk stool over her to protect
her a bit and I slept on the divan. Barbara didn't come down as she
hasn't had a good night's sleep for some days and was determined to
get one last night. There was a little local gun-fire, but I didn't hear
any bombs, nor the all-clear. Frances wasn't at all put out, and I took
her upstairs at 6 am for her feed as usual. She is still being as good
as gold. *As always, Ursula was looking for something she could do to
contribute to the war effort.* I have also got down to the question of a
Savings Group, got particulars from the Town Hall and have been
going round this evening roping people in. They have all contributed
except Mr Moss who is apparently more or less on the rocks and living
on his capital anyway, his business having been so badly hit. When
everybody is roped in I have to write up and get the Group affiliated
and they advance me stamps and books and stationery and all the rest
and then off we go. I'm so glad that I shall be able to do at least this
little something to help the war effort. ... Mrs Stenzel writes that she
has been reclassified as Friendly Alien and will therefore be released
when she has somewhere to go, so I am writing to the authorities
today to say she can come here. I hope you can visit her before she
leaves, there's sure to be some delay. It will be nice to have her here.

*Letters are full of details of running the house, a major task with no
electrical equipment. Washing machines, vacuum cleaners, refrigerators
etc. are all things for the future. Washing was by hand and with a 'dolly
tub'. In spite of hand washing, John continued to send dirty laundry to
Ursula, as did her brother Peter. There was no central heating either;
heating was by coal fires – in as many rooms as one could afford and was
prepared to carry coal to, and they created a great deal of dust. Ursula
also put in a tremendous amount of time in the garden growing fruit
and vegetables, so help in the house was essential. A constant theme in
the letters is the search for a 'char' – someone 'to do the heavy'. Ursula
was always advertising for someone; the 'ideal' woman would turn up
but after a week or two disappear. By now Ursula had got the Tenterden
Grove Group affiliated to the National Savings Group, with nineteen
or twenty members all promising to contribute, bringing the total to 37/6*

per week. With a shortage of almost everything, and coupons needed for purchasing many items, a great deal of innovation was needed. Ursula wrote: I have tackled the question of the bathroom blackout and solved it, by buying 1 ½ yards of table oilcloth from Woolworths in a green and white pattern similar to the one on the kitchen table and cut this in half to make two blinds to roll up like those nasty bits of corrugated cardboard did. They really cover the windows and I think they would be light-proof alone, but anyway with the black curtains they are absolutely OK and they will be more permanent and tidier than the cardboard. … I wonder if you listened to the 9 pm news tonight (*3 August*). I didn't like the way they presented the news from Russia, it left a nasty taste in one's mouth, it had such a patronising tone. They describe one RAF raid at great length and then add 'The Russians aren't doing too badly either', when millions of men are probably deciding our fate for us there. I've got an unpleasant feeling that they are preparing us for bad news. You will be sorry to hear that your wireless set blew up today. There was a blinding flash and a loud pop, and then silence and an awful smell. I suppose it was the valve that blew, and that costs about 7/6 to renew doesn't it? I propose to leave it and listen on the radiogram, unless you definitely want me to get it seen to. *On 12 August:* The news from Russia about Germany's successes in the Ukraine isn't so bright today, but we must hope it won't turn out to be really serious. I do wish we were attacking more vigorously on this side by sea and land as well as in the air.

The Isle of Man apparently didn't suffer from shortages in the way the mainland did and Ursula was delighted to receive a jar of honey, some chocolate and some sweets – all wrapped up in a parcel of dirty socks. It arrived intact and had only leaked a wee bit on to one sock, and I've washed the socks now so there's no damage done at all. Thank you ever so much, darling. *Compulsory billeting was the next thing facing Ursula – due to a shortage of accommodation for war workers of one sort or another.* This morning I received a form from the billeting officer requiring particulars of the people living in the house. I counted Mrs Stenzel one because she's sure to arrive soon now that she's started sending her luggage here, and I put down you and Peter

as those for whom accommodation is reserved. The house will be just
pleasantly occupied when Mrs Stenzel comes and if I do have to have
a war-worker and someone billeted on me I suppose I shall have to
give up the nursery. The worst of it will be I shall feel bound to remain
here later when I might perhaps be able to go to you, unless Mrs S.
would run the house for Ba and the billetees. However, I needn't
worry about that yet.

*Ursula went to visit an old school friend, Jean Serpell (married to The
Times correspondent Christopher Serpell), who had also recently had
a baby, and heard a terrible story of her sister Felicity's journey over
to America.* Jean told me a little about Felicity who apparently had a
ghastly voyage over to America crammed with 50 other mothers and
their children into the hold of the boat (so she said) and when they
were 4 days out there was a terrific bang in the middle of the night
whereupon the 1st class passengers rushed to the life boats, filled them
and left the boat, while Felicity and some of the others down 3 flights
of steep ladders in the hold knew they couldn't get out with their
children so prepared to meet their maker where they were. However,
the boat didn't sink, and after a lot of bother picking up the lifeboats
they proceeded to America. They thought it must have been a small
iceberg not a torpedo. Rather unpleasant anyway with a small boy and
a baby only a few weeks old. Now of course she's as sick as mud that
she's left Kenneth and wishes she could come back, but apparently she
isn't allowed to till after the war. I'm glad I didn't go to India. Johnny
my dear, I love you so much whether you're good at bomb aiming or
not. Perhaps they'll put you on some super-bomber where you have
an underling to drop bombs and you only do navigation. Anyway,
I love you and always will.

*Ursula's letters continued, filled with the minutiae of daily life, battling
with cleaning and gardening interspersed with little snippets.* Did you
hear Attlee's speech yesterday at 3 pm? Probably not, I suppose. It was
certainly pretty dramatic on Churchill's part to go sailing about on
the Atlantic like that chatting to Roosevelt – characteristic of him. I'm
very glad they've issued some sort of peace aims, even if they're not as

specific as one would have wished. At least they are the rock bottom
fundamentals on which everyone agrees. Your letter this morning
contained solemn warnings about invasion and advice on how to sink
a submarine which I think is very good. Personally I don't see that the
Nazis can attempt invasion now that we are so much stronger until
the Russians are well and truly beaten, which they are not yet, and
even then I should have thought the Germans needed a little time to
get their breath back. However, I suppose we mustn't put anything
past them. Today a note has come from the Town Hall to say that an
indoor shelter is now available and will I kindly send £7 within a week
or else. … I suppose I'd better stump up. If I can't manage to put it
together myself, Peter will be down at the beginning of September and
can do it for me. I sigh to think of spoiling the sitting room's beauty,
but it will be nice to have somewhere to put Frances with complete
confidence.

On the strength of your warning and also because I've been
meaning to do it for ages, I popped her in her gas mask this morning
before the bath. She was quite unperturbed and I kept her there for
5 minutes while I pumped. She seemed to enjoy it, so that's a blessing.
Next time I'll put on my mask at the same time so that she gets used
to seeing me in it, beastly tho' it is. *On 18 August Ursula wrote:* Today,
at long last I had a letter from Mrs S.; she is hoping to arrive on Friday
of this week, and will send me a wire if all goes well. As regards her
history it is as follows:

She is a Jewess, wife of Dr Julius Stenzel, rather famous professor
of Kiel, Halle and sundry other universities in classics, and author of
various erudite books chiefly on Plato which Mrs S. helped to write.
She is a Dr. in her own right too (also classics) and is the sister of
Dr Mugden, now deceased (1919) the father of the Mugden family
with whom I had an exchange after I left school. The second son Klaus
Mugden came here for 3 months and then I went there in the summer
of 1934 before proceeding to India. Otto Stenzel, Mrs S's eldest son,
used to visit the Mugdens and the two daughters Anna and Maria
were in London at that time and I got to know them too. They are
now in the USA and so is Jochen, the younger son, whom I first got
to know in Italy. It was actually through Otto that I went to Italy.

I was wanting to learn another language and was thinking of a
Scandinavian one for a change but had no connection or means of
getting there, when Otto suggested Italian and said his brother was
there and would doubtless help me to get a job. So I went and he did.
That Christmas (1937) I went from Italy to Berlin to stay with the
Stenzels (the father by the way died some years ago) for a fortnight, a
nasty drear city it is too, good job if the RAF does knock it down, tho'
the lakes and woods round about are lovely. Mrs Stenzel also came to
stay with us here once when Mother was here and when she (Mrs S)
was on her way over to America to visit her children, or at least Anna;
I believe Maria was still in England then. Now she is once again on her
way to America, but it is taking a jolly long time to get there. She came
over, leaving Germany for the last and final time, shortly before the
war, 1939 I believe – you remember I had some bother with my MP
to get her application attended to. Her name is on the list for a visa
to USA but I'm not sure how soon she's likely to get it, or whether she
can get a passage if she does. When she can, she'll go of course. Her
other guarantor over here is Dr Harold Balme of Harley Street, who
knows her because his son David Balme went over to stay with the
Stenzels while Dr Julius S was still alive for coaching in Classics, and
Maria also stayed with them when she was over here. David Balme is
a classics don at Cambridge and now in RAF as pilot.

When you write to your people you might as well harp on her
children in USA, specially Jochen who has volunteered for USA army.
Otto is presumably still in Germany, but of course she has no news
of him. It was on his account that she was interned, because I suppose
the authorities thought that with one son in neutral America and the
other in the enemy's camp she might be a potential danger. However,
she is heart and soul with us, in spite of her treatment over here. Her
stay with me may quite well be short, all too short for my liking, if
there is any chance for her to get over to USA and now that she is free
naturally her children over there will do everything they can to get
her over. Since Mrs S has been over here her story is as follows. She
went to live with David Balme and his wife who had a small baby and
stayed till David joined up when they couldn't afford her, so she went
to Mrs Balme senior, and while there had to fill up some forms about

her antecedents and on the advice of Mrs Balme and against her own judgement she didn't mention Otto. Later in conversation with some friend of Mrs B she mentioned Otto, and this woman asked if the police knew she had a son in Germany and she said 'no' and explained why; this woman informed the police and she was clapped into Holloway forthwith. After a time she went to the Isle of Man and was eventually released without explanation. She then applied for and got a job in some family but when she went to the police for the necessary permit to work, they looked up her records, found she had been interned, and promptly arrested her again, once more with no explanation. She was again in Holloway for a time, then Isle of Man, and has at last been before a tribunal again and definitely reclassified as 'Friendly Alien', so that she should be alright this time. Never once has she been charged with any crime or infringement of rules and regulations; in fact she has never been able to get out of the authorities exactly what she is detained for. It is the usual muddle and prejudice. However, we hope it's over now. At Port Erin she has been giving classes in classics and philosophy and generally making herself useful.

At the end of August Ursula commented again on the war: What did you think of the news of our marching into Iran with the Russians? Best thing I've heard for a long time. I've been pining for them to pinch it before the Germans have it entirely under their thumb. When I mentioned it to Roy he rather took the wind out of my sails by saying he'd been tipped off about it a month ago and had only been hoping they'd do it soon enough. Well, let's hope it isn't as hard and costly as the Syrian Campaign. Perhaps that was why they sent Wavell out to India knowing that that is going to be of primary importance now that he has cleared up the Near East, for the time being at least. It makes me feel much more cheerful. If only the campaign may come to a swift and successful conclusion.

Did I tell you that Auntie Con has invited herself here on Wednesday? She is staying with friends at Reading and so is taking the chance of seeing Frances while she is comparatively near. You may remember her at the wedding, a queer old stick with white hair and vague flowing clothes. She is the red-headed member of our family, with her twin brother Uncle Tom, of South Africa, and as such should take a special interest in our infant prodigy. She is one of these spinster aunts who generally contrive to get offended or hurt whenever they come to visit, for which reason they are held at arm's length as far as courtesy will allow, which makes them more spinsterish than ever.

I wonder what all this business is about in Australia where the Labour party seem to be making things difficult for Mr Menzies. Of course we know so little about their internal politics that it is impossible to judge; still on the face of it, it looks as tho' they are playing at party politics while the Far East is about to flare up, which would be in the worst possible taste. I have heard that the airmail to India via USA arrives punctually and regularly in about 3 weeks, so altho' it costs 5/- ½ oz. I have sent Mother one letter that way enclosing the photo of you and Frances, as I should so like her to have that one and the Japanese may start a war anytime now and spoil that air route as well. It seems that things are going alright in Iran, which is a blessing. It will be a great relief when that is secured.

At the end of August the Morrison shelter arrived and was stored pending Peter's arrival to put it up. Ursula mentioned visiting Westminster Abbey and being shown the bomb damage in the cloister and deanery by a verger. She thanked John for another jar of honey and asked for some soapflakes 'preferably Lux or Sylvan', now unobtainable in local shops but freely available on the Isle of Man. Ursula finally learned that she would have a 'billettee'. On 29 August Ursula heard that John had not got a commission, which was obviously a great blow to them both. Altogether this is a bad day. Mrs S heard yesterday that Otto has been killed, on July 18, presumably on the Russian front, tho' she has no details. It's pretty awful for her, tho' she seems to be calmer about it than I am over your commission! My WAAF arrived last night, a nice girl, Dorothy Smith by name. She's older than me I should think, and a quiet homely type, intelligent and very grateful for a home atmosphere. She's only been in the WAAFs for 2 weeks (at Bridgnorth!) so is rather strange and homesick still. I've got to go and

register for National Service this pm. It's a nuisance. I get 4/2 a week
for the WAAF. She's sleeping downstairs at the moment as we are full
up. I don't have to provide any food, only 2 baths per week. *(Dorothy
quickly fitted into the household routine and became a welcome member.)*

In early September Ursula mentioned a few more war titbits: In case you
haven't heard the news I may mention that the Allies have occupied
Spitzbergen [sic]. We apparently sent a mixed British Canadian and
Norwegian force and quietly took the place some little time ago. It
looks jolly important for us on the map, but I don't know how ice-
bound it is right up there. It seems there are large coal mines which
may be useful – anyway it's better the Germans don't have them.
Altogether it appears to be a good show, incredible isn't it? Peter told
us two rather nice stories. One is from Lilliput, I don't know whether
you've seen it. There was a picture of an irate Kangaroo holding her
trembling offspring out by the scruff of its neck and saying 'How
often have I told you not to eat biscuits in bed?' The other was a true
one from Rugby where they have a rag week in aid of the local
hospital and all go a bit mad. Apparently some apprentices from the
works strolling thro' the town saw a chemist's shop window displaying
toilet rolls built up into a large V. So they wrote out a notice & stuck
it up on the window saying 'Buy a Victory Roll & help to wipe out Jerry.'
    That must have been a terrific raid on Berlin two nights ago,
I expected a reprisal last night but all was quiet. A few nights ago there
was gunfire and a few bombs were dropped but there was no warning
and so we did nothing about it. The air-raid shelter is a terrifically
heavy thing and once we've got it up we shan't be able to move it
about. Apparently it can't stand right in the corner because you have
to be able to get all round it to tighten up the springs on the floor.
However, unless peace breaks out quickly we shall be very thankful
to have it, however bulky it is. What do you think of your chances
of leave? Do most people get it? You really are due for it by right
aren't you? *Ursula was now planning Frances's christening, hoping that
Bish would be Godfather and she wondered whether he could take the
service.* Suppose, if he accepts, that we have the ceremony here in the
house, since you surely can't borrow a church from under another

parson's nose? In which case I shall have to rig up an altar. The air raid shelter would make a topical one. However, I am asking Roy for hints in that direction in case he will undertake the job. We have been having a gloriously mucky time putting it up. It is perfectly simple to do, though the parts are heavy to lift, and Peter and I did it in an hour or so. It doesn't look as bad as I'd feared. The Persian rug conveniently covers it, and when the divan is moved out (ie when Mrs S goes, I suppose) the room will be quite respectable, though of course you can't disguise the fact that there's an air-raid shelter there.

However, in the event Frances was christened in St Mary's church, Hendon (where her parents had been married), on 4 October, with Roy Cowdry as godfather and Barbara as godmother. John had completed the ab initio gunnery course on 29 September 1941 and then had around seventeen days' leave before being posted to Upper Heyford in Oxfordshire. Neither John nor Ursula had been brought up as Anglicans and Ursula was very keen to be confirmed, John less enthusiastic. Attending classes had proved difficult for both of them and finally Ursula decided that it might have to be put off until the spring or summer, with the comment, 'Ba says she will come too, so Frances can consider she has saved three souls with one baptism!' Meanwhile, life continued as busy as ever with Mrs Stenzel as an enthusiastic helper, in gardening or sewing or cooking. Ursula described a typical day: Ba came home to a late, large breakfast, after which there was Frances's bath and feed (we took her photo swimming in the big bath today), then the washing, your socks and pyjamas etc as well as the usual baby wash, interspersed with hurried expedition to town to get the materials for lunch, all this while Mrs S was making jam and the whole kitchen was littered with elderberries and marrow and preserving pans and all the rest of the paraphernalia. Anyway it's nearly finished now, and she's made about 6 lbs of elderberry and apple; 4lbs of elderberry and marrow; 4 lbs of elderberry jelly; 4 lbs of elderberry syrup; and 4 lbs of marrow and ginger. I went round the neighbours last night distributing their Savings Certificates; Mr Greenish had only contributed for 5 weeks and when I told him all the others had got certs. this week he was so jealous he produced £1, which brought him up to date with the other

2/6 subscribers and bought him a whole extra certificate as well. I have discovered that a heavy armour-piercing bomb costs £100, which is about what we raise in a year between us, so I tell them they must hustle and buy one and then you'll go and drop it on the *Scharnhorst* or *Gneisenau* for them.

The Morrison air-raid shelter had its first use on 2 November: At about 10 pm we had an air-raid warning, which came as quite a shock after all these weeks of immunity. There was a certain amount of gunfire and droning of planes, and as I had got Frances down to feed her I thought I had better put her in the shelter, as it would be foolish to take any risks with her altho' the raid wasn't at all heavy. So I popped her in there, and bedded down there myself. Ba was still writing letters when the 'all clear' went at about 11.30. Frances wasn't asleep, so I took her upstairs again and we all slept peaceably in our beds after all. But the shelter is perfectly pleasant and comfortable and it's awfully nice to have somewhere to put her where I really feel she's as safe as may be. She, needless to say, was not at all astonished, tho' she looked at me in mild surprise when I got in beside her. It wasn't a raid on London at all, but only a few stray raiders on their way to the North West.

With John based in Upper Heyford, with its proximity to London, various ideas for being together more were discussed, including buying a motor bike or finding rooms somewhere near the airfield. In the end they decided that the latter was the best idea and John found rooms in a house with the wonderful name of 'Rain Bozend' in Stoke Lyne. This was the cause of much amusement to my parents as Mrs Donovan, their landlady, appeared unaware of the joke, 'Rainbow's End' spelt 'Rain Bozend', and she persisted in pronouncing it as written. Meanwhile, the Tenterden Grove fire-watching continued. Poor Mr Greenish is having a spot of bother over the Fireguards. We have apparently had a new Head Fireguard appointed over the whole area, and he is determined to make a clean sweep of everything and 'organise' everybody. The decree has gone forth that watch must be kept every night, alert or no, from blackout to un-blackout, but that you needn't actually stand out of doors unless there is an alert. Mr Greenish is furious about it and is working himself up into a sufficient lather to make a hell of a row. As he points out, nobody in our party can be compelled. Old Pope is over 70, Mr Moss is a Warden, he himself can do his Firewatching duty at his place of work, about one night a week, and the rest of us, being women, cannot yet be compelled. So he feels in a strong position to make a row, and I shall be interested to see what happens. The idea of sitting up one night in three from now till the end of the war, raid or no, is certainly a bleak and infuriating prospect, and a quite unnecessary waste of time.

John's spell in Upper Heyford began with a stay in Halton RAF Hospital near Wendover. The ENT problems were increasing and there was some talk of an operation, but this did not occur, although it meant that he had fallen behind others in completing his training. Norman Bowack finished his by the beginning of 1942. Life in Lido continued as usual, albeit with a change of WAAF. On 9 December Ursula wrote: What ho for the Japs, the dirty little skunks! I wonder if it will make a lot of difficulties for our supplies now that USA is in it. *And on 11th December:* It certainly is a terrible blow, this loss in the Pacific. It would be awful enough to be defeated by the Germans, but if the Japs should beat us, that would be absolutely unbearable. I hope they don't get into India.

Having had seventeen days' leave in the autumn, the prospect for Christmas time off looked bleak but Ursula came up with a plan. I have been brooding on the subject of your Christmas leave, and the results I have hatched are these: I presume that HM Forces in uniform will not be issued with rail tickets and so will not be able to travel. But suppose one of HM Forces was in civvies, wouldn't he be able to travel as well as any wretched civilian? I don't see why not. I therefore intend to send you your plus fours and if you consider the whole idea useless and a washout, as I am rather afraid you will, there is nothing lost because you'll want your plus fours down there anyway when I come. I realise that there will be the question of getting out of the camp, but perhaps the station master at Heyford would co-operate or at least look the other way if you changed there and left your uniform to change back into when you return. But that's your wrinkle. It certainly would be marvellous to have you home for Christmas and I'm going to do all I can this end. *(And it worked – there are photos to prove it!)*

Subsequently, Ursula moved to Rain Bozend to join John on 31 December 1941. He remained at Upper Heyford until he had completed his training on 15 March 1942. He then had some leave after which Ursula returned to Lido and John was stationed at Scampton in Lincolnshire with No. 49 Squadron to begin operational flying on 6 April 1942.

During her time staying in Stoke Lyne, John and Ursula were confirmed and on her first letter to John after her return to Lido (29 March 1942) she wrote: I went to Communion this morning at 7.15 am – actually got up at 6.30 when the alarm went off!! I was much impressed with the service, it is far more satisfying in every way than Matins, or the average non-conformist service; dignified and beautiful, and a far more real act of worship than any other I have experienced. How I wish we could have gone together – if only the telegram had arrived a bit sooner. Could you point out to the Adjutant that his telegram arrived too late for you to enjoy the extra 24 hours leave and so you'll take it next weekend and make it 48 hours? I'm sure he'd understand. It's good to hear about this raid on St Nazaire, but it doesn't seem very clear yet how successful it was. Mrs Hazard popped in this evening, as friendly as ever. Doug, Olivia's husband, was last heard of in Java, and they've had no news for some weeks. They're still hoping he's got to Australia, but a pal of his has wired from Ceylon and there's no word from him there. It is wretched for poor Olivia. Did you hear Group Captain Helmore last evening? He does speak nicely, and reassuringly too. As for the Indian pickle, I'm glad I'm not Sir S.C., those Congress Wallahs really give one a headache, but personally I have a lot of faith in Nehru, and feel that they'll come to an arrangement yet.

Otherwise life continued as usual. I have had another very busy day. Florence has been spring-cleaning the back-bedroom, & in the intervals of helping her I have washed, dried & ironed the curtains from our bedroom, together with the usual baby-wash, and been to

town with Frances, and this afternoon I cleaned up the front garden a
bit and burned the dry rubbish from there, and then did quite a lot of
ironing. And after tea (at 7 pm) I've been round to the neighbours
collecting cash. So I'm fairly weary, but feel that we are getting things
done gradually. *And a couple of days later:* You will be glad to hear that
I have made the new bathroom curtains. It is surprising how much
bigger the room seems with those awful black things down. I have got
enough material left over to make a pair of dungarees for Frances to
crawl in, to save her white woollies. I have been ever so wicked again
today, and have been to a lunch-time concert in the Nat. Gallery.
It was the RAF orchestra playing Mozart – a delightful programme.
I had a letter from Vera Bowack, mostly on the subject of baby's
layettes. She is coming to London on Friday and I am writing to invite
her to stay here. I'm going to lend her Frances's thick nappies too, she
has just about finished with them. (I won't give them away as I hope
we shall need them again.)

On 6 April John flew his first combat mission. It was lovely to hear your
voice this evening, sounding so cheerful and so confident, and to
know that the ice is broken, the plunge taken and your first ops trip
safely over. May all the others be as trouble-free! The next few months
are likely to be the worst for both of us – but of course not so bad for
me as for you (unless London gets gas or invasion or both!) but the
thought came to me persistently in church yesterday, Easter Sunday,
that because of that first Easter we have now, you and I, the sure
promise of eternal life together if only we fight a good fight and cling
to our faith. For me that makes things so much simpler, by taking the
sting of fear out. The worst that can happen is that one of us dies and
leaves the other to struggle on alone. Admittedly it would be dreary,
but even 40 or 50 years here is not much compared to eternity, and it
is a glorious thought to me that we are bound to win through to each
other in the end if we 'do our duty to God and the King'. Let's hope
that we have the next 40 or 50 years here together, and then eternity
on top of that. You say your approach to Christianity would be
facilitated if you could overcome temptation first. Surely that's the
wrong way round. Christ said he didn't come to call the righteous, but

sinners to repentance and that's one of the most fundamental things
about Christianity. It is just in things like that that Christ can help if
you'll let him. Darling it rather spoils my expectation of eternal life
if you are not to be there, so please please don't give up so easily!

Frances's first birthday was approaching. I couldn't find a thing for
Frances's birthday present, so I am going to make a concoction from
cotton reels and an empty toilet roll, and put the difference into
savings! I did buy one thing for her today, a pair of gum-boots, size 8,
I thought it a wise investment, they were only 5/11, and will soon be
unobtainable. Of course she won't use them probably till the winter
after next, when we hope that peace will have broken out, but rubber
will be hard to come by long after that. I have spent this evening
making her a pair of dungarees out of the remains of the bathroom
curtain material – they look quite jolly and will save her white woolly
ones from too much crawling. Vera Bowack has written accepting my
invitation for tomorrow night – Norman has not got any leave, and
she couldn't find a room in a hotel. It will be nice to have her here.
Still no letter but a parcel of dirty socks arrived, with no note
enclosed. *Two days later:* I was so thankful to get your letter No. 6 of
the 9th, as there had been none for 2 days. I had invented all sorts of
reasons and explanations for myself, but none that quite put my mind
at rest. Thank goodness that the second trip is safely done, now there
are only 28 more! Vera has just left, after lunch. She is looking very
well and cheerful – she says it is a bit inconvenient having a baby now,
but she and Norman are very pleased about it. Incidentally she said
Norman remarked that he'd rather sleep with you than any other man
as you don't snore or come in late or show any other unpleasant habits!

*On 12 April Ursula sympathised with John on two friends of his
being missing.* We can only hope that they have been taken prisoner.
I like the sound of your escape kit – what about a couple of clean
collars and a shirt as well? And what on earth is the whistle for? Here
are your pyjamas, I meant to send them off yesterday but was in rather
a rush – as usual! I was rather worried to hear of another heavy attack
on the Ruhr and ten bombers missing, and shall be glad to have word

from you. Fancy those old Whitleys staggering all the way to Italy and
returning intact! *And two days later:* Your letter of 13th arrived this
afternoon. I was terribly glad to have it. They certainly do seem to be
working you hard, and if you keep this up you will be half through by
the time you come on leave! I was ever so glad to hear you had been to
see the padre and that he was helpful. I do hope that you will enjoy
your first communion as I did. Don't expect any 'experiences', but
it is a beautiful and dignified service and a real act of worship. Pity
about your 15 mile error – do the authorities take a poor view of that
sort of thing? Still I expect it did some damage somewhere and if you
mistook it for your target it must be pretty industrial. It is good to
know that Floyd is proving himself a good pilot in emergences – I bet
he's satisfied with your navigating. *Three days afterwards:* It made my
hair stand on end to hear of your forced landing with a land mine on
board – that must have been good work on Floyd's part. They certainly
do work you hard, making you go over every other night! They're
making the best of the weather. Vera writes that Tim Collins was over
Essen on Friday and had a sticky passage, 2 of the crew were wounded.
Also Jack Connolly is missing – do you know him? If you want to
make me happy, Johnnie, ring me up as often as you can. Ba is on duty
tonight and alternate nights and you seem to be off on those nights,
so it would be specially lovely if you could ring up when I'm alone.

*On 21 April Ursula thanked John for sending ten shillings and a soap
coupon, but replied:* The trouble now is not coupons, but to find
anything to spend them on! I can't get Persil anywhere, and even
Rinso and Oxydol are rare. Do they have Persil at your Naafi? If so I
could send some coupons and should be most obliged if you'd buy me
as much as poss. In view of the fact that fuel rationing is due to start
in about 6 weeks, I have just ordered 6 cwt of coal, which will top up
the cellar a bit. That is the maximum amount they will deliver just
now. The coke is still almost full so I haven't ordered that. I am
sending some envelope stickers, and positively the last seven drawing
pins in Hendon, so don't lose them quicker than necessary. Could you
perhaps do better with adhesive tape? I'm not quite sure what type of
things you want to peg down, whether you detach them often during

the trip or not. If they are maps and things which you want stuck to your table for the whole trip, you might find adhesive tape across one or two corners more satisfactory. All my love to you my darling. I do think it's mean that they didn't give you leave when Floyd went for his course.

Now that John was on combat operations, Ursula was on tenterhooks every day until he contacted her. There was another raid by our bombers last night so I suppose you also were present and am rather hoping you may ring up this evening altho' of course I make a point of not expecting anything. I haven't had a letter for 2 days but I'm hoping you may ring up tonight. It is a pity that operations are held up for a bit, but maybe you went on the raid to Rostock last night. If so, I hope you didn't have any trouble. *And the next day:* I am sitting out in the garden writing this, with Frances crawling round her play-pen in front of me. It's beautifully warm and sunny and I'm feeling as happy as is possible without you, knowing you to be safe after your telephone call last night. It's great to hear about your new crewing-up – or I wonder if you will decide you like the old arrangement better? I should think the new is safer, anyway. There's a dear old Whitley stooging round overhead just now, I've seen several of them on the aerodrome. I suppose they are veterans who have been pensioned off. It's really good to be alive, when I know you are safe! Here comes the old Whitley again – it's almost parking, it's so slow! Frances is performing the strangest contortions, balancing on hands and toes and gazing upside down through her legs. Now she keeps playing Peep-o behind her pink woolly rabbit (a birthday present from Mrs Lowe) and I have to keep on saying 'Where's Frances?' etc.; she's a jolly chubby wee thing, my mainstay in life while you're away.

On 28 April Ursula heard that John was being transferred from Hampden aircraft to Manchesters. So it's Manchesters! I did hope it would be a 4 engined plane, and I'm sorry you're not keen on these. George flew them, didn't he? And liked them! It's grand about Pt/Co Marshall and his crew if they are all safely taken prisoner. I hope the rest of your friends are too – those that are missing I mean. I can't say

I'm sorry that you are off ops for a bit. 17 bombers lost last night was a bit thick. I enclose a letter received today from Vera. We are thinking of going down to stay with her for a weekend on May 30th – when Ba has a long weekend. We shall have to take plenty of rations with us, of course. Naturally it is subject to either or both husbands getting leave – tho' I hope to goodness I see you before then! I doubt if I could survive without!

However, on 5 May: It was certainly a bit of a shock to read from your letter of 3rd that you are starting ops again so soon, perhaps last night. I was so hoping they'd give you leave at the end of your conversion; still if you can knock back a few more hours I suppose it is all to the good. I shall be interested – to say the least of it – to hear how you got on with the augmented crew. Grand show about Madagascar isn't it? I had a letter from Vera today saying that Norman had been home on 48 hours' leave, with a bad cold. After all, you've had a cold too. He has been on the two trips to Trondheim but on the first their engine caught fire over the North Sea and they had to come back. *And on 10 May:* You can't think how happy and cheerful it makes me that night and all next day to know you are safe. Now it looks as tho' the weather has broke so perhaps you won't be so busy. What did you think of Churchill's speech last night? Considerably more cheerful than usual, but I didn't like his warning about our using gas against Germans if they do against Russia. It's only wise of course, and just as well to warn the Huns, but still it sends rather a cold shiver down the spine. I suppose we're bound to have to face it sometime. I have been trying Frances in her gas mask again, and she simply hates it now. So I've just rung up the Warden to see if I could get a Mickie Mouse gas mask for her, I really must get her used to it somehow. She's not a bit frightened to see us in our masks, but she was a bit sick after she'd been in hers – probably the smell. *(I came to love my Mickie Mouse gas mask and was very sorry when it had to be handed back at the end of the war.)* Incidentally I do hope you do not have to carry the beastly stuff over to the Huns. I suppose there's really no great difference between that and bombs, or only a sentimental one, but still I should hate the thought of your having to do the dirty work.

On 13 May Ursula reverted to their religious discussions: When I read
the part about your being afraid you may make a fool of yourself if
you get to the next world and find its all poppycock – I just roared
with laughter! You'd feel a worse fool if you got there and found that
it all wasn't! Still it's not much use writing and arguing about the
matter, it depends upon the gift of the Holy Spirit and no amount of
human nagging will help. The Spirit will come how and when it chooses,
but it is certain that if we keep on seeking, it will eventually come.

Later that day Ursula received a telegram: 7 DAYS LEAVE STARTING
THURSDAY WORKING TONIGHT LOVE – JOHN. *After a happy seven days
she wrote about the plans for the visit to Vera:* We are going down to
Gloucestershire on Friday 29th by the 1.50 pm and returning probably
Tuesday getting home at 3.30 or 4 pm. We are hoping for a really lazy
time. You've no idea of the work that is entailed in a weekend visit to
the country! Naturally we have to take all our rations with us, and I've
bought and boiled a piece of bacon and am taking a tin of butter, and
our meat ration for Vera to cook down there. It's going to be a
problem to get all the stuff, food, nappies etc. for Frances and our own
clothes into a manageable space (we don't want to have to have a taxi)
and rucksacks seem the only solution. I'm sorry the leave situation is
so poor. I have heard various stories recently of all RAF leave being
cancelled and chaps being recalled, so I think we were pretty lucky
that you got yours when you did. I have been thinking a lot recently
about Algy (the bulge, don't you know) and I feel more and more that
we ought to inaugurate him, on your next leave. It seems of primary
importance to me that Frances shouldn't be an only child, even if it
means a harder struggle financially. If all goes well with you, it would
be grand to double our family soon; if you are taken prisoner, then all
the more reason for getting Algy on the stocks pretty soon, and if the
very worst happened, then as I said it seems to me more important
that Frances should have a companion than that we should be better
off financially by that small margin. Let me know what you feel about
it. And then apply for leave!!

Charges to pay

s. d.

RECEI+ NW 4 1251404 30/31 ST 49 + + **OFFICE** STAMP

No.

OFFICE STAMP

TELEGRAM

Prefix. Time handed in. Office of Origin and Service Instructions. Words.

m

73 1712.46 LILT OHMS PTY 49

From

To

'PRIORITY MRS J BALANTINE LIDO TENTERDEN GROVE HENDON LDN
NW 4 =

REGRET TO INFORM YOU YOUR HUSBAND 1251404 SGT BALANTINE
J R M IS MISSING AS A RESULT OF AIR OPERATIONS ON NIGHT OF
30/31 ST MAY LTTER FOLLOWS ANY FURTHER INFORMATION RECEIVED
WILL BE COMMUNIATED TO YOU IMMEDIATELY = 49 SQUADRON +

For free repetition of doubtful words telephone " TELEGRAMS ENQUIRY " or call, with this form
at office of delivery. Other enquiries should be accompanied by this form and, if possible, the envelope.

B or C

'Regret to Inform You' telegram.

Chapter Four

Regret to Inform You

On 30 May 1942 John was shot down on the 1,000-bomber raid over Cologne. Telegrams followed shortly after:

31 May 1942
PRIORITY MRS J BALANTINE [SIC] TENTERDEN GROVE HENDON LDN NW4 REGRET TO INFORM YOU YOUR HUSBAND 1251404 SGT BALANTINE [SIC] JRM IS MISSING AS A RESULT OF AIR OPERATIONS ON NIGHT OF 30/31 MAY LTTR FOLLOWS ANY FURTHER INFORMATION RECEIVED WILL BE COMMUNICATED TO YOU IMMEDIATELY – 49 SQUADRON.

20 June 1942
Important Mrs Valentine, Lido, Tenterden Rd, Hendon N7
According to telegram from International Red Cross quoting German information your husband 1251484 [sic] Sgt Valentine reported missing is now a prisoner of war at Dulag Luft Germany. Report states capture card received from him. Letter follow I.V.O. 1600. Record Glaus Telex.

John's first letter as a prisoner of war was dated 2 June 1942: Address for reply – STAMMERLAGER LUFT 3. My darling Ursula, I am afraid that your weekend with Vera must have been sadly spoilt by the news that I was missing. I sincerely hope that you were not kept too long in suspense. Please tell me how soon you were told of our failure to return, how you took it when they let you know that I was a prisoner. Luckily I am safe and very well – absolutely intact and unshaken. You needn't worry about me in the slightest – food is ample and good and to date the accommodation satisfactory. I am afraid that our skipper was not so fortunate. Before being forced to bale out we had 30 minutes of hell during which he behaved magnificently, coolly and resourcefully. Thanks to him most of the crew are alive today with me. Would you ask the camp padre to send you the address of his parents for I want to write to them. I shall be able to write to you once a week but you can write to me as often as you like and send photos etc. At (Scampton) camp I had quite a store of tobacco, cigs, pipe pouch, socks and toothbrushes. I want the underlined badly. Could you ask the padre if he could have all my personal stuff sent to you. Although we shall be apart until the war ends the chances of our living out our natural span of life together are considerably greater than a few days ago – it is a great load off my mind – we now have something concrete to look forward to – instead of hoping and fearing simultaneously. Look after little Frances. Tell her, her father still has his thumbs up. Please number your letters (correctly!!) All my fondest love, dearest, yours always, John.

It was not until August that John received Philip Floyd's parents address and wrote to them on an official POW post card. Kriegsfangenenlager, Datum 13-8-42. I had the honour to be navigator on your sons machine I flew with him for many months and had a great admiration for his skill as a pilot and character as a man. It is with deepest sorrow that I have to inform you of his probable death. On our last fatal trip he had tremendous difficulties to face and six other lives depended on his handling of the plane. During the period of acute danger he acted with amazing coolness and skill enabling five of us to bale out intact. The machine was then too low for him to follow us and it crashed with our gallant skipper still inside. The five survivors and their families owe him a tremendous debt of gratitude and will ever honour and respect his memory. Yours very sincerely, JRM Valentine Sgt RAF.

Ursula wrote her first letter to John from Lido on 19 June 1942: Gepruft 32.

My Darling Johnnie, I received the news this morning that you
are alive and safe and my heart is almost too full for me to write
coherently, and yet you feel so close to me somehow that I simply
must talk to you. As a matter of fact, you have felt incredibly real
and near me often during these weeks of anxiety, specially at night
just before I went to sleep, and I suppose you haven't been out of my
thoughts for more than two minutes together for the whole of the
time. But just to know that you are alive is the most wonderful relief,
and I have been in a sort of maze all day long. It is now 10 p.m., and
I don't suppose I shall be able to post this letter for weeks as I have
no proper address yet, still I wanted to write. We are awfully lucky to
have got the news through so quickly. Your father speeded things up
through an MP friend, and telephoned me this morning.

But I had better tell my side of the story from the beginning. As
you doubtless remember, I spent the fatal weekend with Vera. The first
blow was when Norman was reported missing from the raid the night
before you – Vera heard on Saturday evening, and when we heard on
Sunday night about Saturday's raid, my heart sank like lead. But there
was no means [of getting] news, and I didn't want to make a fuss
since poor Vera has [... *(illegible owing to damage)*] of trouble while
mine was still only fear. She wanted […] a bit with her, so Barbara
went home on Tuesday, found the wire and […] that evening. After
that we decided that I might as well stay […] week or two, and
somehow it was much easier for us both, knowing that the other had
the same sorrow to bear, than it is to be surrounded with people who
are sorry for you but don't know what it feels like for themselves. You
will be amazed to hear that I hardly cried at all after the first evening; I
thought and thought about you the whole time and remembered and
lived over again all the things we have done together, and they were all
such joyful memories, and every thought I had about you was a happy
one, so that I had a sort of peaceful gladness that at least nobody
could take all that away. Then your letter came, the one you had left
with Harvey to be sent on if the occasion should arise. I must admit
I cried a bit when I read that, it seemed so final as though you were
quite beyond my reach, and yet it made me so proud and happy to
think that we had meant so much to each other. Bless her wee heart,

Frances makes all the difference to life just now.

I only came back to Lido two days ago, and found the garden in a fearfully overgrown state. Last night I had to go round collecting the Savings money and face an absolute barrage of sympathy. All the neighbours have been terribly upset, as though you had been their own son, and now today when they have the good news, several of them nearly burst into tears with joy! They are all most kind, and send you all kinds of good wishes. About ten minutes after your father rang up this morning, Mrs Hazard came round to rejoice with me. She had heard through her husband, and while she was here Freeman rang, he had heard at the office [*G.A.Touche*]. Bish is coming to supper tomorrow, he is overjoyed too. We have been putting up an absolute barrage of prayer, as you can imagine. I have had awfully nice letters from Cairns, Slee, Harvey and the Padre, so I suppose I must write to them now and give them all the good news. I haven't seen any of your people yet, as I only got back two days ago and they are all down at P.M. this weekend. I think I must pack up for tonight, it is nearly 11 pm. Goodnight, my dearest one, all my love and thoughts and good wishes are with you now and always.

Tuesday 23.6.42. Your father has sug[…] may as well try writing to as much address as we already […] will finish this and post it tonight. Shall we start a game of chess? As you can't argue, I'll be White and move P-04. I'll keep the game played out on my small board. Would you like me to send you yours? If it has already occurred to you to suggest playing and you have started a game too, let's carry them both on. I'm afraid they will take long enough anyway! I don't know all the regulations yet about sending you parcels, but do let me know anyway what things you would like. I expect you will want some warmer clothing for the winter – would you like your warm dressing gown, and slippers? I had a letter from Olga today. Jack seems to be alright so far. I have heard nothing further of Norman yet. Kennedy is training overseas. John Wilford (subs.) is missing. No more news of Olivia's husband. I send you all my love, my darling. We will keep the flag flying this end and just long for the glorious day when you come back to us and we can start our life together properly, at last. I shall love you for always and always. Yours for ever, Ursula.

P.S. This letter seems to be all about me, when after all you are the chief actor in this drama. But you know I long to hear everything you can tell me, and must fill up my letters with odd and unimportant news from home. You can imagine how I'm longing for your first letter, to know whether you are wounded, how you are treated and as much about the raid as you may tell me. How I long to look after you and see you are alright – thank goodness for the Red Cross anyway! I hope you are with nice chaps.

John always understated situations – witness his first letter to Ursula after being shot down. When he was first captured he was taken to Dulag Luft reception camp, where conditions were good because it was well established. It was when he was moved to his first permanent camp that the situation deteriorated. It was a new camp, regular supplies of food were not yet organised and Red Cross parcels were not yet delivered. Here the conditions were of near starvation. A frank description of this would have been censored (censoring was common anyway and is marked in his letters with 'xxxxx') so they are only hinted at. In his first postcard of 15 June 1942 John says he is not yet used to new standard of living. Feeling weak physically, depressed mentally but that will pass. Wish you could send food but that's impossible.

In letter 4, dated 22 June, He added that he was ... still hungry. If you or my parents know of anyone living outside the British Empire, would you ask them to send food parcels as often as possible. *And later in the same letter:* I am still too weak to take much exercise but hope soon to be more used to less food and thus feel stronger. Jock Wight says that if he were to meet the most beautiful girl in the world all he would say is 'Sister you would look much nicer roasted.' *On 25 June, in letter 5:* Not feeling too fit yet but time passes quickly. My senses have completely returned but alas I can put them to little use here since I don't eat half as much.

In letter 8 of 3 July: My dearest Ursula, Am glad to say that I am at last feeling much more like myself since my constitution is slowly adjusting itself to the new conditions xxxxxxxx. This can only be done from outside the Empire since all Empire food parcels are pooled and communally distributed. Would you ask Grunfeld if his connections in Sweden, Turkey etc and my parents if friends in Argentina or America could help us – and anyone else you know. We want regular parcels – not merely one. Please also arrange for a regular flow of tobacco and cigarettes, which, duty free, are not costly. Get all the support you can for the Red Cross for their magnificent work xxxxx xxx. Sorry always to be asking for things. I'm deeply ashamed of my personal appearance. Having no razor or shaving brush I now possess a five weeks beard. When our plane was hit I was drenched TO THE SKIN in oil and I had to wash every article of clothing. My uniform shrank several sizes and was still very discoloured and being my only costume I look like a scarecrow. Everyone is the same, the camp population closely resembling a crowd of beggars clothed in every conceivable type of tattered garment. What an age it seems since I last saw, phoned or had a letter from you. You are always in my thoughts, my darling. Ever yours, John. *And at last a more positive note on 7 July, in letter 9:* What about your settling down somewhere in the country for the duration or better still acquiring a rural residence for ourselves near London and making a start with our OWN home. *However, even as late as 26 July, in letter 11:* Am slowly getting stronger but haven't tried any violent exercise. At one time I could barely walk round the camp.

John was allowed to send two letters (written in pencil only and on official, rather small, forms) plus three postcards per month and one postcard to his parents. Ursula was permitted to send as many letters as she liked, plus photographs. The speed with which letters arrived varied enormously, and withholding letters from prisoners was regularly used by the Germans as a form of punishment and releasing them again as a bribe. Letters to John from friends and family were allowed, but as they could impinge on those from Ursula he was not keen on having too many, and equally he begrudged using one of his quota to Ursula to reply to them. A parcel was allowed every three months. It was forbidden to weigh more than 10lb, and if it was under that weight the Red Cross made it up in chocolate. Tobacco and cigarettes were accepted duty free from the manufacturers. A great deal of letter space, therefore, was taken

up with Ursula making suggestions and John stating his requirements.
Quite often his list of essentials arrived <u>after</u> Ursula had sent off the parcel!
John's first request, in letter 2, was: I am badly in need of clothing and
would greatly appreciate the following: Pyjamas, <u>socks</u>, underclothes,
<u>hankies</u>, shorts, <u>scarf</u>, sweater, bathing pants, slippers and sports shoes.
I know you won't be able to manage all in one parcel but those
underlined I need most, also my pipe, pouch, tobacco and cigarettes.

Ursula sent the first parcel on 19 July. Last Tuesday I sent off your first
next-of-kin parcel too. It contained the following: 2 pairs pyjamas, 2
vests, 2 pants, 1 pair sandals, 10 hankies, RAF long sleeved pullover,
scarf, bathing costume, 3 pairs socks, 2 reels cotton, mending wool,
needles, toothbrush and powder, shaving stick, buttons, Kiwi, an
indelible pencil and a small penknife. I hope this last is allowed
through, as it has a wee pair of scissors incorporated, which would
doubtless be useful, and the whole thing is so small that it could
hardly be called a dangerous weapon. The pyjamas are new ones,
because I am not allowed to send anything but striped ones and your
winter ones haven't yet been returned from the RAF. The Red Cross
allow me 40 coupons for your first parcel and 20 for each other one,
so we don't have to go short of anything in making up your parcel.
The vests and pants are your own old stock, so are the other clothes.
I thought the sandals might serve the double purpose of slippers and
sport shoes until I can send the proper things – here again the things
I should have liked to have sent haven't yet been returned to me *(from
Scampton).* You will see that I have sent a collection of haberdashery,
but since you will only have limited clothes and have to look after
them yourself, I thought it would be useful for you to be able to mend
them. I had to send Eucryl tooth-powder as I may not send anything
in tubes – hence the shaving stick instead of cream. When I had
collected all this stuff, filled out numerous forms and labels for the
Red Cross, tied the whole thing up and taken it down to the Post
Office I found, of course, that it was too heavy, 9 ¾ lbs in fact, so I
took it back, undid it, removed a few things and got it down to 9 lbs,
so that the Red Cross will be able to enclose some chocolate for you.
If the parcel only weighs 9 ½ lbs they put in ½ lb of chocolate as a gift,

and if you can make your parcel lighter still, you can put more chocolate from the Red Cross to be enclosed, so you ought to get 1 lb of plain chocolate if and when you receive your parcel. I do hope that the fact that it doesn't bear your P.O.W. number will not prejudice its arrival. I had first of all intended to wait for it before sending off the parcel but your letter sounded so urgent, and I thought that since your camp is a new one there may be some delay in issuing numbers, so that I decided to risk it.

Ursula's long chatty letters began as soon as she had the correct address: 1251404 Sgt. J.R.M. Valentine, Stammlager Luft 3. In No. 2: All the neighbours have been so kind; they were all very cut up when they heard you were missing, and several of them nearly burst into tears when I told them the good news! Even Freda the tobacconist, sends you all good wishes – pity she can't send something more smokeable! You will be glad to hear that I have taken over the Red Cross Penny-a-week Fund for the road, and of course when I ask for 'a penny for a food parcel for John' they all just have to fork out! I work it in at the same time as the Savings Group, so that it isn't much extra work.
On the family front she announced that Frances had just started to walk, and that John's sister Irene had become engaged, although two months later: Your Mother will doubtless have told you the news that Irene's engagement is off, much to their relief I gathered. Considering that they were to be married the next time they got a week's leave at the same time, sometime before Christmas, it all seems rather sudden. The reason seems to be that the Australian whom Irene met earlier on in the battle and who is now back in his own country proposed to her by cable and so she is engaged to him instead. So it looks as though we shan't have to worry about wedding presents until after the war!
She added that his brother Leslie, who was in the Army, is being put through a toughening course, and even he seems to find it tough!
Life in the local community, visits to and from friends, gardening, concerts at the National Gallery, often with Myra Hess as soloist, give a vivid picture of Ursula's daily life. Once again she and John start to play a game of chess, but this had very little success mainly because of the erratic arrival of mail and later because it was blacked out by German

censors, convinced it was some sort of code.

Wartime losses also appear frequently. In letter 10 John wrote: I'm afraid that Norman's chances of survival are poor. I believe all those alive from his raid are here and they give no hope of others. It is almost certain that he is dead. Please give Vera my sincere condolences, her circumstances are tragic. Only a small minority of our losses survive and I count myself as extremely lucky, especially having you to return to and to think of and love all the time. *And from Ursula in letter 5:* I was terribly sorry to hear about your skipper, but of course I am glad and proud that he acted so well in the emergency, as you describe. Today Eileen Johnson came to tea, Frank's fiancée, you remember. Poor girl, she had heard only at lunch-time today that Frank is missing from last night's raid – a daylight raid. I thought it awfully plucky of her to come out to tea after that, and she bore it very well. I do hope she will hear as quickly as I did that he is safe and perhaps in the same camp as you. *Ursula's fund-raising activities continued.* On Monday, in the evening I went to the A.G.M. of the Savings Group Secretaries at Golders Green. It was quite amusing, the Mayor presided, and we passed quantities of resolutions and amendments, amid much argument. The whole business is going to be organised into innumerable committees and subcommittees, and there was endless discussion as to the composition of these various committees, but nobody made it very clear what all the committees were going to do. Perhaps that isn't important!

In John's letter 15 a major event was announced: Started violin lessons 10 days ago and would like the following urgently: Tutor: Books of Elementary Exercises & Pieces: Rudiments of Music; 2 Manuscript note books, Elementary Solos & anything else you think of. …

On arrival at Stalag Luft III the men were put into huts holding 164 men. John was appointed leader of his hut, which meant that he had a small room that he shared with three Dutchmen. Being hut leader entailed a fair amount of work each day. In letter 16 John wrote: We live in huts of 164 men, 80 being in each of 2 rooms while the block leader and 3 others share a small room. My three colleagues are all Dutch. Every morning of the week is taken up with block duties, e.g. dealing with queries, seeing that rooms are cleaned and keeping the peace generally. Monday morning is particularly busy for we get our towels changed then, coal for cooking and most of the Red Cross food (if available). German rations are dished out at midday and have to be divided and then the fellows take turns on the stove to cook concoctions from Red Cross and German sources. Our turn is at 12.30 & after lunch (!!) I usually put in some time on the fiddle. A cup of tea at 4 pm is followed by more fiddle work, a wash and then evening parade after which we have a bit of supper and then are locked in. I usually have several hut duties to attend to then (e.g. Announcements, preparation of sick list) followed by reading or bridge with lights out at 11 pm. I attend a bible class on Wed. (studying St John's Gospel); Debating Society on Sat, violin lessons Tues & Fri. Church on Sun morning and evening with gram. recital in afternoon. Owing to lack of accommodation the school hasn't started yet but I am to study German & English literature when it gets going. There is plenty of reading here so don't worry unduly about book parcels.

Almost all the POWs had volunteered for aircrew duties and were not regular RAF personnel. So once they were shot down their interests returned to their peacetime occupations and the numerous activities that started up reflect that. Often there were opportunities to study things that had never been possible in peacetime. For John the activities he mentioned were either dropped or failed to materialise, but learning the violin was his main source of activity throughout his imprisonment, and his struggles to find somewhere to practise are extraordinary! Regular references to it occur, such as in letter 17: Struggling very hard & painfully on the violin. Hope to get one of my own soon. *In Letter 18:* Have managed to get a fiddle of my own and am grinding away patiently. *Letter 19:* You will be amused to know that I have to retire to the lavatories to practise my violin. There is a little cubicle there intended for showers which have not materialised & I grind away to the accompaniment of cat calls from irate washers & the smells of stagnant sewage. (There is no main drainage here.) *And in letter 20:*

I am doing 2 hours daily on the fiddle but progress is slow especially for a musical dunce like myself.

When a neighbour of Ursula's heard of the 'practise room' he said he would compose a 'Sewage Symphony' for John. In letter 26, dated 11 November 1942 John acknowledged: I don't hope to do any good at all but shall try really hard. My chief difficulty is an efficient instructor –a fellow POW is doing his best for me but doesn't know how to teach. Second difficulty is a space to practice. It is too cold now to go where I first started and I am now forced to play in the lavatory of our own barrack being the only (more or less) unoccupied room. It's like practising in a public WC with people attending to nature on all sides of one.

Because of the delay in the arrival of letters, Ursula did not hear about the food shortages until August and in letter 12 she wrote: This latter missive, appealing for food parcels, perturbed me very much, and I at once got to work in a big way on the problem. I wrote long and touching letters to my boss in Wimbledon, our mutual friend at Tooley Street, and Jimmy Tait; also to Felicity, and Aunt Bertha to pass on to her children. Barbara took your letter to the station where they were all very upset on your account and several wrote by the same post far and wide to friends and relations. That letter of yours is a masterpiece of appeal through understatement; Barbara and I nearly choked over our own good breakfasts when I read it. I have now sent it on to your Father, suggesting he get in touch with Ian and Uncle Stanley's family, and he probably has many other contacts of his own. I did my group collection this afternoon, and Mrs Noyelle and Mr Turner promised to get in touch with friends of theirs. Freeman rang up, since apparently my letter to Jimmy had had effect and said that he too would get hold of some friend of his. I have 1 or 2 rather more forlorn hopes living near Uncle Sam, and also Mr Wilford when I can get hold of him, and after that I must sit back and await developments. If even half of them respond, and the parcels reach you, it ought to relieve the pangs of hunger a bit. *At the end of September:* We have had good news from the influential friend of Saz *(Saz Gunn, pianist Myra*

Hess's secretary and manager; she and Barbara met driving ambulances during the blitz and became firm friends) in America. She enquired about sending you a parcel through the ordinary channels and was told it was impossible; so she wrote to the President (of the USA) who is a personal friend of hers and has got some sort of special permit for sending what she wants, so I am fairly hopeful of your receiving something from that source. *When John received that letter he replied on 11 November 1942:* Shall I write to Roosevelt himself if anything comes from the USA?!

Another regular activity for Ursula was helping Barbara take photographs, many of course of Frances. Since she was a professional photographer the standard was very high. These photos went with John from camp to camp. The large photos of you and Frances are prominently displayed on the walls of my room and much admired by all including a German officer who inspected the barrack once. I get a tremendous amount of pleasure from gazing at them but often they fill me with agonising longing. *Most of them returned home with John at the end of the war. Frances's progress was also described in great detail; in letter 15 Ursula wrote:* Frances has been showing marked signs of musical appreciation lately. Whenever she hears music she listens attentively, and now she very frequently picks out the rhythm correctly and claps it or sways to it – all without the slightest help or encouragement from others – music simply takes her that way. She tries repeatedly to sing notes too, but if the music goes too fast or is too complicated she can't manage it; but if it is slow and sustained she often sings quite a true note in imitation and she invariably sings the 'All clear' because that goes on long enough to give her a real chance. *To which John's comment when he read that was* I hope Frances isn't getting too much practise at joining in with the 'All Clear'!!

Vera Bowack's baby Michael was born at the end of July, and the two mothers kept regularly in touch, but because of wartime restrictions on travel they did not meet up for some time. On 31 August Ursula noted: Vera wrote to say that the Red Cross now presumes Norman to have been killed, so I am afraid it really is hopeless. I'm so sorry for her, but

I hope she will marry again some day, she is young and attractive. She has gone back to Lady Cottage now, and is coping with her small son Michael on her own. *Ursula's other activities continued unabated:* The Firefighting group continues ... I have this evening been appointed Fire Fighting Group Leader's Secretary, an honorary and not very arduous post. Mr Greenish came in to say that as things are getting more and more organised and involved in the customary forms and red tape, he would be grateful if I would occasionally take down his letters from dictation and type them for him, which of course I am glad to do – it will help to keep me in practice, for one thing. He has managed to get unofficial permission for us not to have to sit up actually dressed and awake all night when fire watching now; we must be dressed but can sleep so long as we can turn out at a moment's notice, which is much more reasonable. I am supposed to be on until 2 a.m. tonight. ... These last few days I have been busy bottling fruit and making jam. I made a strange concoction yesterday out of orange and apple peels, cooked together, strained and made into jelly with strips of orange peel added to make it look like golden shred and it tastes good!

The other main concern for Ursula now followed on from John's early suggestion that she might start looking for a house. With her parents due back from India early in 1943 and their future plans uncertain, this was something she had to face and she was filled with misgivings about the whole thing. I am rather doubtful about the wisdom of my going house hunting on my own. Just supposing I should come across a suitable house, I couldn't move in till my parents are home, and supposing I were able to find tenants for it in the meantime it would probably involve us in a good bit of money for repairs and maintenance, because their rent would presumably go towards paying off the building society, or whoever puts up the cash. Shall I really plunge into the whole business and put it into the hands of a house agent, or do you think it will involve us in unreasonable risks? Please think the matter over in detail and tell me what you think.

The local Red Cross held a meeting for next of kin of POWs in the area,

which Ursula attended. I believe the next-of-kin wear labels bearing
the name of their prisoner's camp, so that they can get together. I have
put my name down for street collecting when the special POW week
takes place sometime in December and offered to help with other
activities too so far as I can fit it in and also offered to type for them at
home in my own time, if they ever need that. It is really decent of the
local Red X to have got up this meeting. They answered questions and
pointed out a few new regulations with regard to parcels etc. We all
wore labels with the name of our POW camp, and went round peering
at each other. I peered in vain at countless Stalags and Camps, for the
one woman whose husband is at your camp but she came in late and
hadn't a label! I should think there were at least 100 people there –
just from Hendon!

In letter 24, dated 20 September 1942, Ursula wrote: On Thursday
Frances and I went to tea with the vicar's wife. She is a very vigorous
and capable woman; she has to be since she runs that large house, big
garden, quantities of hens, ducks and rabbits, a big bounding sheep-
dog and her 3 sons aged 9 and twins of 8, not to mention the vicar,
all single-handed. I like her very well, and she is proposing to have
these informal tea-parties every Wednesday for wives of men in the
forces. One woman's husband is still missing from Dieppe. When Mrs
Boyd let the ducks out to go for a swim in the pond, Frances chased
them all back into their house again and proceeded to dabble in the
pond herself! When Frances has done something she knows she
shouldn't – which is quite often – she generally comes to me very
solemn and round-eyed, saying 'Ooh' in an accusing tone of voice and
shows me what she has done or leads me to the scene of the crime.
It doesn't occur to her not to do the naughty thing; in fact sometimes
she even starts saying 'Ooh' while she is contemplating on committing
the crime. *But sometimes she was helpful.* Frances has now been
harnessed to the war-effort in the capacity of picker-up of acorns
which are useful for supplementing pig and hen diet. She certainly
doesn't stick at the job for very long, but on the other hand she
doesn't pick up anything but acorns, which is rather intelligent of her.
John's letters telling Ursula that he had started to play the violin reached

her on 4 October. Now as to your violin lessons, you can probably imagine how <u>thrilled</u> I was to hear about your learning. I read in 'The Prisoner of War' this month that your camp runs a 12-piece dance band & a symphony orchestra so that I hope in due course you will be able to play in the latter, which must be the greatest fun in the world and a grand way to get to know the great music. I shall have to start practising again in real earnest, and then Frances shall learn the cello, and we shall be all complete. *With every mention of the violin in later letters, Ursula replied full of encouragement and requests of music, strings, rosin etc. were all promptly complied with.*

Another POW made a camera in the camp and in letter 21 (12 October 1942) John wrote: I'm sending a putrid snap of myself with this letter and hope it reaches you. My fellow 'kriegy' (our name for ourselves) is Frank Pepper, but neither of us feels flattered. ... My record of chess moves has disappeared, probably during a search. Would you let me know them once again, please. Also tell me how to wash socks without them shrinking (incidentally soap is plentiful here). I'm very fit now (played soccer twice last week) and getting plenty to eat although diet is monotonous (swedes ad nauseam). I feel rather ashamed of the earlier letter written when we were so hungry although we may well be in the same state again and any food gifts arriving might then be worth their weight in gold. I hope you were able to send off the violin music – I'm hopeless of course but mean to have a real try. The mail ban still prevails and I haven't heard from you for some weeks now – I miss your letters sadly. We are locked in very early nowadays (4.30 pm) but the evenings pass amazingly quickly. (Just remembered – 2 or 3 sets of violin strings wanted urgently.)

In Ursula's letter 28 of 10 October, she described a near disaster: Last Wednesday was about the most awful day I have spent since I knew you were safe. Frances ran away from home! Choosing a moment when I thought she was with Florence upstairs and Florence thought she was with me in the garden, and when the front door had somehow been left ajar, she calmly took her yellow beret and walked out. She must have been gone a few minutes before I came in and missed her;

then of course I dashed out in search of her, which was made the more difficult by a swirling mist; I went down to Finchley Lane first but she was nowhere in sight so then I went back up the Grove and met Mr Moss who joined in the chase; then back up to the Quadrant and to the police station to see if she had been found and taken there, but no, and then a Bobby on a bike joined in; I met Mrs Greenish and Helen and Mrs Regan and they all started searching. I was getting really desperate by this time, not knowing who could have taken her in, when Mrs Greenish ran her to earth in Hill's Garage, sitting up on a stool in the office drinking cups of milk! She was perfectly good humoured and thoroughly enjoying herself. It took me nearly an hour to pull myself together enough to get on with my washing! But imagine it, at the ripe age of 17 months! The thought of her crossing Finchley Lane on her own still sends cold shivers down my spine. *And a few days later:* When I came to cook the supper after Frances was in bed, using the little tin oven I told you of before, I was nearly overpowered by a terrible stench of burning rubber, and found Frances had thoughtfully put a squash-ball in the bottom of the oven, and of course it had melted!

In letter 30 Ursula described two events: On Saturday afternoon we went to a Red Cross meeting; Frances dozed through most of the speeches, which was perhaps wise of her. This meeting was called to present mementos from the Duke of Gloucester to those who collect regularly for the Penny-a-week fund, which I have been doing since June. It is not much extra bother for me because I work it in with the savings group. The memento consists of a rather pop-eyed photo of the duke with the inscription: 'H.R.H. The Duke of Gloucester wishes to record his grateful thanks to Mrs U.Valentine for help so generously being given to the Penny-a-Week Fund for the Red Cross and St.John' – the name being typed in, of course. We each had to go up separately to receive our memento, and Frances came with me and the County Organiser for the Red Cross said a few kind words about your being a prisoner. Afterwards tea was served and while I was trying to have mine Frances escaped, disappeared for a time and was then perceived making a flank attack on the platform, with the Red Cross big-shots

waving her on. She was pretty good on the whole, as it was hardly
the sort of entertainment to appeal to her. *And two days later:* I was
present at a big meeting and church service specially arranged for
next-of-kin of prisoners of war. It was held at St Martin's in the
Fields, and the church was absolutely packed out. The Bishop of
Southampton conducted the service and gave the address; he was a
prisoner in the last war so he knows something about it. Afterwards
we all went over to the Coliseum, where we were seated according to
the camps of our prisoners, so that I was surrounded by mothers and
an aunt of chaps you probably know. The meeting was addressed by
Christine Knowles, founder of the Books & Games Fund, and by Lord
Elton, a prisoner of the last war, Dame Sybil Thorndike, The Bishop
of Southampton and an R.C. prelate. A lot of it was interesting, and
somehow it does one good to get together with others who are going
through the same troubles. Apparently an enormous number of
people applied for tickets and had to be refused, so I was lucky to
get one. I felt a bit chewed up afterwards. Some film company was
constantly taking photos, so maybe I shall appear on the screen! The
whole thing was broadcast to the Empire too, so it was quite an affair.
Ursula added to this: You may sometime receive cigarettes from a Miss
A. Hoare – don't be alarmed, she is a friend of my Aunt Con who
contributes to the Books & Games Fund and has adopted you as her
special prisoner.

*In letter 29 (20 November 1942)) John gave an interesting (and
uncensored) account of daily life in Stalag Luft III:* The various barracks
of this camp take turns in acting as 'Duty Block' for 1 week when they
do all the jobs of work necessary for the maintenance of the camp and
we are in the middle of our turn now. It is a wretched week for me
because I have to supply the men as/when called for by our hosts.
A POW loses all incentive to work even for his own benefit and I have
no real authority over my men being of the same rank as most and
junior to some (F/Sgts & W.O.S). Consequently I have to exercise the
maximum of tact and curb my temper for often they adopt a most
offensive attitude to my call for labourers. It's most trying and uphill
work for which no bouquets are awarded. I shall soon have completed

my 1st 6 months as a POW and I can honestly say I hate the life – hate
every single minute of it. Of course most of the fellows here have been
prisoners for much longer and I admire immensely their fortitude.
You might imagine it to be a pleasant indolent existence with nothing
to do all day long but be on a bed and read a book or sleep. But it's
quite different from that. The sense of confinement, lack of comfort,
loss of freedom, separation from kith and kin and ignorance as to day
of liberation are ever in one's thoughts. This seems to be a gloomy
letter which is not what I intended for I feel no worse than usual or
anyone else. *And then he indulged in some happy daydreaming:* I think
you might well start looking around for a house, well in the country
but within easy reach of a good train source to London. The best idea
would be to get one with say 50 acres and sublet the land until we
want it. Don't buy the house, rent it. I would suggest taking say 5/10
acres with the house to play about with, to gain experience e.g. cows,
pigs, hay, grain. As to rent, I'm rather ignorant but £100 p.a. for rent,
rates and taxes as the absolute maximum. I would like you to get a
house and move into it as soon as possible. I don't suppose for a
minute that you will succeed in doing anything in this line but it's
food for pleasant contemplation on my part. I think a reliable agent
is your best method of setting about it.

In letter 35 Ursula wrote: You will be amused to hear that I have got a
job! I have been looking about for one vaguely for ages, because I am
so anxious to do something directly to help the war, but with Frances
and Barbara to fit in it wasn't too easy. However, the right thing has
come along at last. xxxxxxxx *(censored)* really useful work, where I can
do xxxxx. It is doubtless dull work in itself still it will be great to feel
I am really in the war effort at last. I am starting tomorrow night, so
I shall be able to tell you how I like it next time. Of course I shall go
on the nights when Ba is off duty, which means that she will be stuck
in the house. *And in her next letter:* My factory job is going ahead
satisfactorily. I have been 3 times now and go again tomorrow
evening. I have been promoted (at least I consider it promotion) to
the workshops where I manipulate an electric lathe – last night I had
one with 4 different tools on it, so that it was quite fun to work. I have

also received my first pay packet, containing 6/10½ – not much perhaps
but still I earned it. That is the rate for one evening, and I am hoping
to save a good bit out of my wages. But more important than the
money is the job itself and the satisfaction that I get out of it. *And a
few days later:* I have been to my factory on 4 nights doing various
jobs, some quite interesting. *A week later:* The work at the factory has
been proceeding according to plan, except that last night the wireless
had been removed, nobody knows quite why, and we all missed it
tremendously. It makes the time and the work go far more quickly
if there is music or something interesting on to keep your mind off
fatigue and the clock, specially when it gets towards 10.30 pm and
later. I was able to buy 2 certificates out of my pay last week, which
made me very proud.

In late November Ursula received a big surprise. The main item of news
this week is of Irene's wedding. Writing about something else, your
Father mentioned that they were busy over preparations for the
wedding, and I was surprised because I had understood that the
wedding was off and that she had got engaged by cable to the Australian
whom she met at the beginning of the war, and would have to wait till
after the war to get married. But next day an official invitation came,
and lo and behold, the lucky bridegroom is yet a third candidate, a
quite new one on me, one F/O William Birnie, M.B., B.Ch., an M.O.,
presumably at her station. Anyway he is not letting grass grow under
his feet, and the wedding is fixed for December 12th, at Crown
Court, luncheon afterwards at the Waldorf, However, I am taking the
precaution of not sending our gift until a little nearer the day, in case
the whole thing is cancelled again. *(John replied to this in letter 32.
Irene's romances leave me gasping. To whom is she really finally
engaged? Tell her if she wants to explore any fresh avenues I could put
her in touch with some nice 'Kriegys' as we call ourselves.) Ursula
continued:* I have made myself a new hat for the occasion. I chose
some rather snappy feathers to trim the hat I have made and when it
was finished it was greeted with howls of derision from Ba! However,
I think it is a nice hat and propose to wear it tomorrow to go to the
bazaar at her ambulance station which is being opened by Dame Myra

Hess and at which Frances is apparently to be one of the main side-shows. *Ursula sent a photograph of her wearing this hat and months later when John had received it, and made a rather scathing comment on it, Ursula replied (letter 55, dated 4 April 1943):* You remark that in a snap of me in a black dress I seem to have some 'flowering shrubbery' over my hair; I don't know what this can be unless – oh unkind thought – you are referring to the photo of my new brown dress in which I am wearing MY NEW HOME-MADE HAT. If so, the above mentioned phenomenon would be the snappy blue feathers which adorn the said hat.

On 2 December Ursula wrote: Last Friday Frances made her first appearance in the world of celebrities. The bazaar on Ba's ambulance station was formally opened by Dame Myra Hess, and Frances was asked to present the bouquet afterwards! We arrived a few minutes early, so that Frances and Dame Myra could get acquainted, and they made friends quickly. When Dame Myra had finished her short speech opening the bazaar, Frances tottered forward from the wings under a large bouquet of carnations – luckily she only had a few steps to go – dropped the flowers, recovered them and staggered on, whereupon Myra came to the rescue, relieved her of the carnations and presented her in exchange with a pink pig. Frances was thrilled with the pig, and hugged it to her for the rest of the afternoon. *(John heard of this on 8 February and replied:* I was delighted to hear how Dame Myra was honoured to receive a bouquet from her.*) Ursula continued about books, which were beginning to be of interest to Frances.* Lately she has been marauding a great deal in the bookcase in the dining room, taking for choice either Liam O'Flaherty's 'Black Soul', or a commentary on Nietschze's 'Zarathustra', so I decided it was time she had a book of her own, in the hope she might leave ours alone. So I got a book of nursery rhymes, illustrated, and a dog story called 'Ginger's Adventures'. I meant to give them to her for Christmas, but when I got home I couldn't resist showing her Ginger, since she is so passionately interested in all and sundry dogs, though I hardly thought she would recognise the drawings as representing the 'Wow-wows' which interest her so much when we meet them in the street.

However, after a moment or two's investigation, she gave a shout of joy and came running to me to show me the 'wow-wow'; she was thrilled to death – & so was I. This afternoon I was working in the garden and she went indoors and after some time emerged with the brush belonging to the crumb tray, and started sweeping up leaves with it. I removed it, and after another pause she came staggering out again, this time with the ceiling brush, a large brush on the end of a 7ft bamboo. ... You will be sorry to hear that your daughter has started making up already! The other day I found her in front of my dressing-table, powdering her face with a very professional air with the puff from my empty powder bowl, and then to my amazement she took the little red shovel which I use for filling powder compacts and proceeded to rub it over her lips like a lipstick!

On a more serious note: On Sunday I went up to the Coliseum to a meeting got up by the Red Cross about Prisoners of War, at which Sir Walter Monkton, of the M.O.I. was the chief speaker. He gave a very lucid factual review of the status and rights of prisoners, mentioning some infringements, and afterwards the lady in charge of the correspondence department of the Red Cross gave some idea of the work they do there. It was an interesting meeting – and naturally we were urged to do our best to raise funds for the special Prisoners of War Week which is on now. The flag day for London was yesterday, and Frances and I were out bright and early, at 9 am with our tin and our tray of emblems. Trade was quite brisk; I continued selling flags till 11 am. I haven't heard yet how much cash I got in my tin, but when I handed it in I was able to present my cheque for £8, being the proceeds of the raffle of the two Christmas cakes and the Christmas pudding which I made. Several people had told me gloomily that the cakes wouldn't keep, being made of national flour and dried eggs, but they were perfectly alright when I handed them over. I am really rather pleased to have made as much as £8, I shouldn't have thought it possible.

On 12 December Irene was married and Ursula described the day in detail. The reception was at the Waldorf. We had a pretty good lunch,

limited as to courses naturally, but not as to wines, since there was
sherry, white wine, champagne, brandy constantly flowing. The first
toast after the loyal toast was to 'Absent Friends', rightly enough
considering that besides you and Leslie several other prisoners and
men overseas were being drunk to.

Now to our Christmas festivities, last Friday, 18.12., Frances and
I dutifully went over to Barnet to tea with Grandma and Ann; we took
over the Christmas cake which I had made and iced for their family
present and it was very well received, as they hadn't another one.
We had quite a pleasant afternoon and Frances was on best Barnet
behaviour. On Saturday took place the Christmas party given by
the local Red Cross for children of prisoners of war. It was a terrific
success, Frances thoroughly enjoyed herself. There was a big Christmas
Tree, a conjuror, music and dancing and games, an excellent tea and
presents for all, a whole bag of toys for each child. There must have
been at least 50 children there just from this borough. I think the
Red Cross put up a marvellous show and all the children thoroughly
enjoyed it.

You asked for violin strings to be sent, 2–3 sets you hopefully said.
I have arranged for 1 set to be sent off by Chappells but they cost 9/-
a time, so I thought I would send another lot later on. As regards
washing socks, the rules are warm water, good lather, plenty of rinsing
in same temperature, and pull the feet to stretch them a bit while still
wet. Try to avoid rubbing soap straight on to the sock, just squeeze the
lather through them – but as you doubtless won't have soapflakes but
only cakes of rather hard harsh soap, just do the best you can, pull
them out well, dry as quickly as possible, then pass them on to a chap
with smaller feet and I'll send you some more!

John's letters during December 1942 were descriptions of his routine
existence. Trouble with his nose persisted. When I get back, I'm going to
have my nose attended to if I do nothing else – of that I'm certain.
Having struggled unsuccessfully with Argotone for a few weeks I went
to the camp doctor about my nose, but he said that only an operation
would cure it but as it was not an 'essential one' it would not be
sanctioned by the Germans. *The violin was also mentioned again:* Wish

I could feel more hopeful with my fiddle. I'm really keen on it but get very little help from my master. I've been going 4 months now but I have made astonishingly little progress. Both my wrists and the fingers of my left hand are confoundedly stiff – getting them supple is going to be a life's work. *All Ursula's efforts over parcels had proved successful.* All your splendid efforts for me are bearing fruit at the right time. I can't say how much I'd like to thank you for all you've done. Their arrival just before Xmas is providential. We look like having some good Xmas fare from the Red X as well – unfortunately I'm still tasteless. Our Camp Choir and orchestra rendered excerpts from the Messiah tonight, which I loved.

And on New Year's Eve John wrote: Xmas here was fairly dull despite efforts to enliven proceedings. We were allowed a little watery beer which failed to produce the slightest semblance of intoxication. Last night we had a show at our theatre – a revue of sorts which was quite bright in spirit. I think that exhausts all my news. I thought of you often and I shall again do so specially tonight when we sit up to greet 1943. We are being allowed lights in our rooms till 2 am. The privilege of ushering in a New Year in your company has been denied me so far; perhaps next year I shall be luckier, but more likely the following year I fear. I still keep very busy and never, never find time hanging heavily on my hands. The reverse is quite the case. Despite the rapid passing of days and weeks, the months seem to mount very slowly and I have just completed my seventh. It seems a much longer time since I saw you last while for those unfortunate colleagues of mine who have now spent their 4th Xmas in captivity, home and freedom must seem like another life. Grim monotony just about describes the life perfectly but I really don't grumble – I'm very lucky to be alive and am as well treated as is possible in this Country. We just about cope on the food but wouldn't mind a spot of variety.

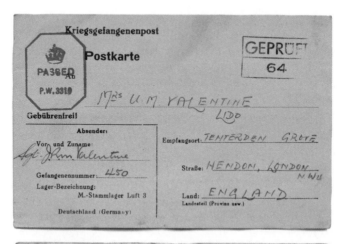

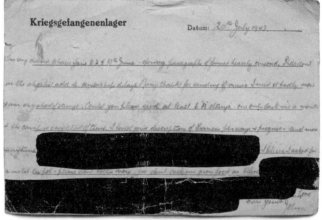

Postcard from John to Ursula from Stalag Luft III in July 1943.

Chapter Five

1943

*John's first letter in the New Year commented on Ursula's 'factory
work', of which he had only just heard and was worried about; and also
the violin.* I still do 2–3 hrs daily on the fiddle but tuition is at a
discount. I haven't had a lesson from my master for 6 weeks. He tired
of it sooner than I! Violin practice in the outhouse adjoining the
latrine is impossible now but I still put in 2 hours daily in the latrine
belonging to our block. It is as cold as charity there, but not so
intensely frigid as the other spot. If only I could send you a photo of
my practice room you'd howl with delight. My music stand is fixed
to the wall while the trough which conveys the urine to the drain runs
between me and the music, at the same time I have a portable closet
at each side of me. I won't describe the atmosphere. However, I'm
thankful to have a place to practise and only wish I could produce
results commensurate with the time devoted. Tuition is still lacking
and that is a great drawback.

I want to persist with Dutch for I'm really keen to master at least
one language and that might be useful in the office after the war. The
Theory of Music classes are still going and we hope to sit some exams
from the London Schools of Music, and to get some certificates thereby.
German I'll have to let slide for the time being. If we are to spend
another winter here I might be able to tackle agriculture. One of my
gravest wants is a watch. My own being the property of the RAF was
confiscated when I was captured. Do you think Mr G. or anyone else

could get one sent from Switzerland. It really is a confounded
nuisance being without one. My 3 Dutch friends came down 'in the
drink' and all their timepieces were ruined. *(Lack of a watch was often
mentioned and at some point John swapped seventy-five cigarettes for a
Zenith wrist watch, now in the possession of his son, Ross.) In letter 43,
dated 16 January 1943, he wrote:* I was privileged to go to a show in the
officers' compound today. They are housed in a camp separate from
ours and no intermingling or fraternising is allowed, but as a
concession a number of us were allowed to go over to see their show
(Treasure Island) on condition that we did not speak to any officers.
It was a good show, lively and with plenty of laughs. We have had
some really cold weather recently; one night there were nearly 40(F)
of frost. The next night a mere 20 degrees were recorded and it felt
quite balmy by comparison. Today it has been thawing slightly and we
positively sweltered. The cold is not nearly such a trial as I imagined
thanks chiefly to being an inhabitant of a small room. The coal ration
is meagre but we manage to get enough to produce sufficient heat
from our small stove whereas those fellows in the large rooms are not
nearly so lucky. Skating has started and I have had about 30 mins on
the ice. 8 pairs of skates (clip on variety) are available for our hut (144
men) and we have a roster which gives each man a short session every
other day. Should I be here next winter skates would be a most useful
gift for I believe we are in for a long spell of suitable weather. A few of
us have been trying to construct an ice rink for our own barrack and
as all water has to be carried by hand, we've undertaken a tough job.
To crown it all, it thawed today and several days' labour disappeared
in little streams of water going in every direction away from the rink.
We have made a communal ice hockey rink here (of sorts) but it
seems to be monopolised by Canadians and Poles.

*All through January very little mail arrived and on the 31st John
commented:* Still anxiously awaiting mail from you, practically a
month having elapsed since your last arrived. I believe your 2nd parcel
is in the camp but, if so, it won't reach me for a day or two. Just now
I'm often thinking back a year when we last lived together, those days
are grand to look back upon although they had their uncomfortable

moments didn't they? I often think of Norman, too, and the time I
spent with him at I.O.M. How much luckier am I than he, still to be
alive and able to look forward to reunion with my beloved wife! *And
two days later:* I am still awaiting mail from you, but I have at last seen
your precious handwriting today – on the list of contents of my 2nd
personal parcel. Thank you very much for everything you sent dearest.
The most important item in that delivery was Ba's knitted rug. It is a
grand article, beautifully warm and yet so light. *He had also received a
letter from Ursula's mother in Delhi.* I actually had a letter today too
(my 1st for a month) from your Mother – together with a snap of
herself and in the background a most opulent looking edifice which
she termed a 'bungalow'. As a result of my period of tastelessness
(which is much better now) I still have quite a lot of tobacco left and
am enjoying it in my new pipe. Probably as a result of the drier
climate here my tastelessness has been much better than in Britain
and apart from the blank months of Nov & Dec I have tasted most
of the time here.

Ursula wrote her first letter of 1943: I dashed back from the factory last
night just in time to tune in to Big Ben and drink a glass of ginger
wine to you and me and the future. Ba was asleep in bed, but I roused
her out to drink to the New Year too – she dropped off to sleep again
at once. Your double letter 26 and 27 of 11.11.42 arrived last Sunday,
thank you so much for this lovely long and newsy epistle. I have duly
acknowledged all the letters you mentioned. Lucky you did not write
to Irene direct about her Australian fiancé since she is now safely
married to a Scotsman! When Mother comes, in the warmer weather,
I am really going to try to practise the piano regularly. I am so proud
of you for your energy and determination in taking up the violin; we
will have some fun together when you come home with the Haydn
and Mozart sonatas for violin and piano, even if we are not up to
concert standard. So stick to it, in spite of the really formidable
difficulties that you have to overcome as regards tuition and practice.
    Today your letter 29 of 20.11.42 arrived, in which you were feeling
rotten with tummy trouble. I do so hope this has cleared up, I'm
afraid it may be caused by the unsavoury localities where you practise

the fiddle! *There was more news on the domestic front:* Last Saturday
Frances and I went down to the allotments and had a chat with old
Thompson. He always enquires kindly after you and is very friendly.
I bought some shallots, which I haven't had time to plant yet, and also
56 lbs of that favourite fertiliser of his, N.O.M.; we staggered home
under this considerable load, Frances had to walk as the pram was too
heavy. So I hope we get a better vegetable crop next year. Thompson
has now started a pig club, and built the styes himself, next to the
greenhouse. It is a flourishing concern and the pigs all look very happy.
*Ursula was also always on the lookout for possible items of furniture for
their future home. She went to a National Gallery concert with Roy
(Bish) and afterwards* We mooched along Piccadilly looking at the
shops – Roy is real fun to shop with. We called in at Heal's and I saw
to my amazement that the antique walnut cabinet which I fell in love
with when I was there before Christmas was still apparently unsold.
We looked it over again and Roy admired it as much as I did, and
encouraged me in a most irresponsible way to buy it there and then.
He is really largely to blame for the fact that I have <u>bought</u> it – I only
needed someone to agree with me how very nice it was. Anyway I left
it then and all that evening while I was working at the factory I kept
thinking about it. I was quite convinced that it was good value for
money, a beautiful and useful thing in itself and a sound acquisition,
but I was worried lest £45 was too large a proportion of the money
we have for furnishing to spend on one item. However, in the end
I decided it was worth risking it. *The next day she returned to the shop*
... and asked one of the extremely refined salesmen about it. He
remarked what a fine thing it is, I asked him about what date it would
be and he said 1730, in any case not later than 1750. *(The cabinet
is still in the family and much loved.)* I was going to have them keep
it there and store it for us, but on second thoughts I want to have
it home as soon as possible. How I wish you were here to choose and
decide with me, but as you can't be, I think I have been wise to buy
these few things; now we have the nucleus of a home (though perhaps
this cabinet wasn't strictly a necessity!). Work at the factory goes on as
usual. If I keep it up long enough I shall have paid for the cabinet out
of my earnings!

In letter 48 at the beginning of February, John wrote: To my exceeding joy 2 letters arrived today. Nos 35 and 39. I now have all yours up to 39 except 36 and 38 and as more mail seems to be coming in just now I may be lucky enough to get those soon. Your factory job is still a mystery to me because the censor obliterated all remarks about it. All I can hope is that you don't overdo things and I applaud your determination to aid the war effort to such an extent. I was very glad to hear of your investments for our future home. Make as many of them as you can for opportunities of so doing will become progressively rarer. Sorry to hear that there is no news of Frank Routledge. I'm afraid that we here represent only a small section of those reported 'Missing'. I do love your letters, my dear. After writing my last letter to you and feeling most despondent because I hadn't heard from you for a month, I spent 2 very happy hours reading through everything you had written to me up to that time. It made me long for you more than ever – sometimes the longing gets almost intolerable. Of course I hate this place and the life, as do all of us, but there is nothing to be done but to grin and bear it, knowing that every other prison camp is more unpleasant than this.

A second American food parcel for me is in the camp, but I don't know the donor yet as I haven't received it. The two packets of music have also arrived for which many sincere thanks. I now have something to get my teeth into and lack only the skill. It is an incredibly difficult process, violin playing, and I require fully 10 years to reach any sort of reasonable standard. However, I'll plug away because 1) I enjoy it 2) If I can ever be good enough to play with you, it will be worth any amount of effort. Thanks for tips on sock washing. I cannot comply with them all. Hot water isn't easy to come by and I could never get enough to rinse them in warmer water. However, my technique is greatly improved and I won't have to give away any more pairs to fellows with smaller feet. Delighted to hear of your investments in our future home, although £45 for a cabinet does seem a bit steep considering that neither our bedroom nor our dining room suite cost that complete. However, I would urge you to go ahead and get all you can, now that I am apparently going to live (which I very much doubted a year ago). I have implicit trust in your discretion as to the disposal of our fortune and if you think anything necessary and the cost reasonable (in present day circumstances) by all means get it. Getting a house would be the best idea of all and I am very much in favour of renting one for the time being. Neither of us has the slightest idea of post war conditions and I would rather not commit myself to the purchase of a house. However, if you see your dream house and it is only for sale buy it. I should suggest a £1,000 limit. You have probably guessed that we are extremely well treated here. The German officers who run this camp without exception treat us very properly and with a great deal of sympathy. The same applies to NCOs and men with whom we get on very well. Admittedly supplies of many things are not abundant but that is not the fault of those who run the camp – who give us quite a few concessions in one way and another.

Towards the end of January, in letter 45, Ursula wrote: I went up to Red X headquarters last Wednesday and while I was there I asked if they would send more sets of violin strings to the camp, since I suppose if the camp leader has a stock you can get replacements as necessary. I will send off another set to you soon. I am afraid that there are not going to be many more private food parcels, export from USA is now forbidden and from most other countries too and I don't think there is anything I can do about it. However, as long as the official Red X parcels get through regularly I suppose you will all manage to keep going, but things are bound to get worse as the end approaches, so cheer up! Last Thursday was quite memorable in a minor way – I played squash with Mary Simmonds. We both very much enjoyed our freedom and hope to play regularly. *To which letter John replied six weeks later:* Wish I could have a game of squash with you – both sorts of squash! *Ursula's correspondence returned to the subject of household chores.* When I read in your letter 32 the section bewailing the amount of time taken up by 'dull domestic chores e.g. Cooking, keeping the room clean, washing clothes (how I loathe it) washing up, darning and mending etc.' in your day, I uttered a dry sardonic laugh. Well, now you know what it is like, now you know what I am up against, except that I have ten times as much to do and then Frances on top of that. I hope your experiences of the daily round, the common task, may inspire you to buy me an electric washing machine, when such things become available at last! *(John replied to this when he got her letter at the end of February:* After my experience of agonising washing in ice cold water, I'll willingly buy an electric machine after the war. Let's hope we get the refrigerator too.*) Ursula continued:* Talking of that, Frances and I went over to Church End to meet Grandma and Ann at the end of last week, and among other things your Mother mentioned that their old refrigerator (they have recently bought a new one) is still at Moffats and she said she would ask Mr Moffat if he could repair it and keep it for us. I wasn't at all clear on what terms we should get it, by instalments presumably, or what it would be likely to cost, still it would be marvellous to have a refrigerator, and I suppose they won't come back on to the market immediately after the war. So I said enthusiastically that we certainly would be interested in the proposition, and it now remains to be seen whether anything comes of it or not. *But a week later she wrote:* There has been no more mention of the refrigerator which I mentioned in my last letter, so I suppose it won't come to anything. Your father terrified me as much as ever when we spoke over the phone – he always gives me the impression that he is displeased with me or you or both; I hope he doesn't feel as cross as he sounds.

Smoking was an almost universal habit during the war years and so the supply of cigarettes to the POWs was very important to them. In the POW camp they were also used as currency. Letters frequently mention the need for supplies, receipt of them, or some being sent. John's father mostly sent cigarettes on a regular basis, but, as John remarked in one letter, 'My folks do like to be thanked', and on another occasion that My parents seem to be worrying about my not acknowledging their parcels – would you assure them that I always make a point of doing so and have done so without exception. Possibly some letters have been delayed – or lost. *As a young man and a teenager John had been an enthusiastic member of the Scouts. His local troop was attached to the Whetstone Congregational Church. Once John became a prisoner they became regular supporters. Ursula heard from her father-in-law, and wrote to John:* The Whetstone Congregational Church, who have apparently sent you two consignments of 500 cigarettes, were asking him if you wanted any special books, and he complained that you had never answered his queries on this subject, so I told him that the library was adequate at the camp and you had told me not to send books. I must ring up the Whetstone people and explain to them too – much better if they continue to send cigarettes, though your father doesn't wish them to send too much since you are no longer a member there. You did enough work while you were there and they doubtless enjoy sending them, so I don't see why they shouldn't continue if they want to. Anyway I shan't discourage them!

Ursula went to tea with Mrs Boyd, the vicar's wife. We ladies had terrific discussions about how best to overcome the paralysing inertia of the majority of stay-at-home women in all matters of public and municipal interest. Mrs Boyd has been contacting the Mayor and various other dignitaries with a view to getting up some sort of discussion and lecture group for housewives, and of course she has my enthusiastic support in this. Her idea was to get women to know more about their own local municipal affairs, which is very sound, but personally I wouldn't stop at local affairs but bring to their notice too some of the gigantic and pressing national problems, mostly connected with post-war reconstruction, which make life so very exciting and challenging these days. If women had some idea of what the problem consists of, they would be more competent to vote when the time comes. I do hope something comes of all our plotting, it is often very difficult to get a thing like this going, people are so puddingish.

John remained concerned about Ursula's factory job in his letter 52 of 8 February 1943: I continue to ponder on your factory work and am tremendously impressed by it. Please tell me 1) How often you work per week; 2) What are your hours; 3) The mortality and accident rate among workers; 4) How far away is the factory and how do you travel. I love you all the more for your splendid spirit but am worried about the possibility of your over working yourself. *Ursula replied to his concerns in her letter 55 of 4 April 1943:* You needn't worry one bit about my job. There are very few accidents and anyway I never work on the machines now but at the bench. I go 3 times a week, xxxxx and it is within walking distance. I really enjoy it and am thankful to have found some war work to fit in with my timetable. *John continued on the subject of the violin.* Your set of fiddle strings arrived and will make me independent in that respect for some little time. It has been a nuisance hitherto, to have to beg a new string whenever one broke, which isn't very often though. I've broken 4 in 6 months. Progress, by the way is negligible. My 'Prof' is a lovely player but a poor instructor and is not the slightest bit interested in me as a pupil. I haven't had a lesson for 10 weeks although I practise diligently. All the same I feel sadly in need of a helping hand, for the photographs in the books you sent showed me that I wasn't even holding the bow or the fiddle correctly. By the way would you make an appeal to anyone likely to respond, for gifts of music manuscript paper for the camp. There is a great deal of musical activity here – many tunes are composed here while others are arranged for the available instrument, so that the demand is large and the supply hopelessly inadequate. Any gift need not be of such fine quality as those you sent me and would be tremendously appreciated. I asked you to send me some just in case the music was withheld but as all yours came and gave me plenty of work I shall present one M/S book to the musicians, and possibly the other later.

Although John tried to remain positive he admitted to periods of depression, as all the POWs felt at some time or other. But notwithstanding this, his letter 55, dated 18 February 1943, was one of the most exciting to reach Ursula. It has just occurred to me that although I have been here all these months I have never given you any details of my entry into Germany. I can't tell you where we were shot down nor what got us but we had a pretty hot time almost from the time we crossed into Germany. Eventually we were flying at about 1,500 ft with one engine ablaze when Floyd gave the order to bale out. I then had a miraculous escape for just prior to jumping I grasped the handle to the rip cord so that I shouldn't have to fumble for it during my fall, which looked like being of short duration for we were losing height very rapidly. A second later I found to my horror that I had pulled the wretched thing in my excitement and that the chute was opening in the plane under the draught from the open escape hatch. I made a hurried grab at all the silk flying around and caught as much as possible with both arms and just fell through the hatch. Mercifully none of the trailing chute caught in any part of the plane, it just filled out automatically and I was floating gently down. A few seconds later I saw the plane hit a house below and burst into smithereens and flames instantly. Floyd was on it and just before leaving the kite I shook hands with him. When I felt the chute opening my first thought was – 'Damn it, I'm going to live after all', although I hadn't had the slightest thought of doing so even in the height of the excitement. Actually I suppose I had been subconsciously thinking of death for months before. I landed in a few seconds, just missing a house, but I fell into a ring of people and didn't get a chance to get away. I spent what was left of the night in a civilian gaol and went on to Dulag in the morning. The whole episode still seems very vivid to me and I am lucky to be alive. *In letter 68 (20 March 1943) John wrote:* When we arrived here, one of the crew sent our names and home addresses to the Caterpillar Club, a body formed by the makers of Irvin parachutes and open to all those who save their lives with their 'chutes' by baling out from a plane which subsequently crashes. We have heard from the club that we have been admitted and that badges are being sent to our homes. *(These are safely preserved!)*

Towards the end of February John described entertainment in the camp: Tomorrow the so-called symphony orchestra here gives its first performance and despite its appalling reputation I am looking forward to the concert. *And then in the next letter:* A word about entertainment in this camp. The standard of production as far as scenery and effects are concerned is excellent especially considering the very very limited facilities xxxxx number of competent musicians and a few excellent ones, but we do not seem to have many good actors – the officers present much better plays. Since the theatre was finished last autumn, we have had 2 formal shows i.e. dance band numbers interspersed with comic acts: 1 Revue; 1 Pantomine with chorus of dancing girls (male); 1 orchestral concert (quite good); 3 Plays – 2 of which were presented by the Officers' compound.

Exerpts from the 'Messiah' were given at Xmas and we had 3 German films at different times. We have therefore been getting one show of some sort per fortnight. Costumes and paint for scenery are great drawbacks. The POW Magazine is most unpopular here. While the fellows do not wish those at home to pity them in any way, they do strongly resent the hints appearing in the mag. which give the impression that this or any prison camp is a heaven on earth. Actually I feel as if I were buried alive – I'm given enough to eat to keep going and all the activities in which I indulge are just drugs to dull the brain and to prevent one from thinking. Cases of mental derangement are not unknown here but so far these are confined to fellows who have been in captivity for some time. *This POW magazine had been mentioned several times and apparently mostly gave a false impression of how good everything was. 'Unmitigated tripe' was one comment of John's when Ursula mentioned an article she had read.*

Meanwhile, Ursula had been finding out more about possible houses, with John being in favour of renting rather than buying and with a view to farming eventually. I have been up to the West End to see some estate agents. It seems it is very hard to get the sort of thing we want to rent and even if we could rent, we shouldn't get anything like the property you mention for £100 pa. More likely £170–£200 if it is within daily reach of London.I must say I am in favour of buying if we can afford it. It would at least give us some capital when we move out and buy a real farm, and anyway is more satisfactory, to my mind. One agent produced particulars of what seems the very thing, in Sussex, 8 miles from Lewes. I rang up a Building Society which would advance ¾ of price at 5% repayable not less than 20 years. This was the most advantageous offer I had and I am getting in touch with owner and shall try to go and see it, and meanwhile keep on looking for rented farms. In view of above prices, what can we undertake? Daren't leave it till you come, conditions will be far worse. How can I finance it? Will write at greater length. Reply quickly won't you! *And in her next letter:* I wrote you an airmail letter card xxxxx all about my housing enquiries last week; renting a house and 50 acres of land within daily reach of London is going to be pretty well impossible. There is more hope of

buying such a property, but it would cost about £4,000. It looks to me
as though we shall definitely have to confine ourselves to something
nearer 10 acres for a start, and even that would cost, to buy, about
£2,500, or more. None of the agents seems to hold out much hope of
renting and I have written to 3 local agents in Herts. Even suppose
I got hold of a suitable house with 10 acres or so to rent for, say £150
pa., ought I to take it at once and if so, where on earth am I going to
get the £150 pa. from to pay for it? Also I am not very keen on the idea
of living by myself in a strange neighbourhood in the country – it is
quite bad enough living alone here for half the time, you know what
a goose I am for that.

Please when you write your reply, consider the question xxxxx
of how to finance it. Sometimes I feel I would like to leave the whole
business till you get back, yet I feel things will be very much worse
then and I would like to have a home ready for you. I got in touch
with the owner of the 18 acres farm near Lewes which I told you of
before. I had told him we were interested but I must have your verdict
before deciding and that would take 2–3 months, and he rightly
pointed out that it was most unlikely that the farm would still be on
the market then. I have been reading a few odd books on farming and
they all take great pains to point out that it takes years and years of
experience to make a farmer and nothing but experience on the job
will ever do it. This makes me wonder what age you and I are likely
to be when we eventually reach that exalted estate and whether maybe
we wouldn't be wiser to confine our activities somewhat. The thing
we want above all, I take it, is to live in and of the country, not the
town, and to make sufficient money out of it to bring up our children
decently and educate them well. I'm wondering if maybe we wouldn't
be wiser if we utilised your already specialised knowledge,
accountancy, and turned it in the desired direction by your becoming
a farm accountant. Then we could live in the country, in much the
sort of house we are considering now, keep animals and poultry,
have a nice garden and orchard and altogether be thoroughly happy.
What do you think or do you take a dim view of accountancy in any
shape or form? One point that has worried me is this: suppose we get
even as little as 10 acres, who is going to do the work while you are

away at the office all day? I can't do a great deal more than house, garden and children, since there doubtless won't be any domestic help. If it means a farm labourer, can we possibly afford that? We can't leave all the work till the weekends.

Ursula heard of another property in Hertfordshire that sounded a possibility. The train service was bad, though in the old days it took not much more than an hour; then there was a long 5 miles walk, and at the end of that I was informed that the house had been sold last Sunday! I'm furious with the estate agents; they knew I was going to see it and ought to have let me know. *And then came a trip to the dentist:* I got rather a shock for the dentist says I have 8 stoppings, some quite big and he insists that I must use dental floss *(apparently the first course in the country in dental hygiene was opened during the war in Hendon by the RAF; Ursula's dentist must have been affiliated to it)* to clean between the teeth, for that is where all the decay starts. I am going to send you some in your next parcel and advise you to use it too. I am also sending in your parcel a new type of cigarette lighter, the only one permissible (we call it a Gow Lighter), and only hope it works. You have to singe the end of the wick first and afterwards light it by striking the flint and blowing on the wick to make it glow. It may keep you amused for a while, anyway.

John had managed to bribe one of the camp guards (with cigarettes presumably) to allow more letters to Ursula than the prescribed amount. I hope you are getting all my letters. Don't be surprised if the number I send to you drops off at anytime since I might have to use my very limited ration by writing to others!!?? Sorry I can't be more explicit. In one of my letters, which might have gone astray I asked you not to mention to Barnet how many letters you had from me, nor to comment on the number when writing yourself. I should be grateful if you would comply with these requests and be the soul of discretion on the subject. Things aren't easy here in that respect and I don't want to spoil a certain arrangement. You see, mail is so strictly rationed that I am not keen that others should know the high proportion of my monthly allowance which goes to you. You probably don't quite

understand but please do as I ask otherwise I might have to write even
fewer letters to you. *Initially the number of letters from the UK were not
restricted, but on 12 February 1943 Ursula wrote:* I'm afraid most of my
correspondence in future is going to have to be on these forms. We
have to cut down the amount of mail and only these letter cards will
go airmail all the way. So I have arranged with your father that he and
I will send one in alternate weeks, and on my off week I will write an
ordinary letter, with photos when possible, which will have to go
overland from Lisbon and will doubtless take ages. However, I hope
you will get them eventually. *But a week later she reported:* We have
now been told that after all we may write letters, not only letter-cards,
to be carried air-mail all the way, but are still encouraged to keep the
quantity down to one a week. I'm so glad, for it means that you
should receive the photos I send within a reasonable time.

*Meanwhile, John continued writing mainly to Ursula plus the weekly
card to his parents and only occasionally to other people. So when he
learned of the death of Mr Pope, one of their neighbours in Tenterden
Grove he asked her to convey his condolences, but when he also heard
of the death of Mr Tait, his boss in G.A. Touche he asked her:* Please
convey my condolences to the Popes. I share your feelings about the
old lady. I had an awful shock when I read of Mr Tait. I had a very
great liking (almost affection) for him. He was the kindest of bosses
that any man could have. I shall send a card to Mrs Tait but can't spare
one to Touche – would you tell George T. of my very real sorrow.
And later: It's a pity that the sender's name does not accompany books
and cigarettes always, but I'll let you know of all I get and perhaps you
will do the needful. I'm afraid that I must impose a lot of extra
writing on you, but I really can't spare any more letters for outsiders
than I do – after all you are the only person to whom I wish to write –
just for the pleasure of writing and without ulterior motive such as
thanks. *In his next postcard he informed Ursula it was* A big day for me
today – as far as tobacco parcels are concerned. I received 4 of them:
200 Churchmen; 1/2lb Cut Golden Bar – senders unknown; 200
Weights from a Miss A. Hoare whom I believe to be a friend of your
Aunt Con; also a large one containing 1 lb tobacco + 200 Cigs from

'The Wardens' whoever they might be. *(They turned out to be the Wardens of Whetstone Congregational Church.)* It is annoying that these parcels are so anonymous. If you can trace the senders well do send my very grateful thanks – I now have a full stock against cessation of supply. Unfortunately I'm still tasteless and unable to enjoy these gifts.

In John's letter 65, dated 13 March 1943, the uncertainty of mail was apparent. Incoming mail has diminished sadly during the past week. I hope we're not in for another period of 'belting'. The local term for any type of shortage – although it originated of course in times of lack of food. There are quite a few odd terms in use here, the word 'gash' for instance is used as a noun and adjective to describe anything surplus, or inessential, e.g. a 'spare man' is a 'gash goon'. *And a few days later:* Still no mail to answer. I hope I'm not in for another long wait, for your letters are the chief joy of life here. Rumour has it that we are likely to be moved in the not too distant future. For my part, I shall be sorry, for we are well treated here, the climate is good and the accommodation quite reasonable even if crude. In addition, a lot of work has gone into organising the camp into its present state of smooth running. *John often commented on how lucky he was to receive long and regular letters from Ursula. Fellow campmate Frank Pepper, in contrast, rarely heard from his wife, and then only on the lettercards. Then, also, men quite often found out that their wives or girlfriends had met someone else. In letter 64 (9 March 1943) he wrote of one of the Dutchmen in his room.* Hans Lensing heard from his fiancée in Holland yesterday that she had fallen in love with another man and so it's all off. If I were to get similar news I think I would try to climb over the barbed wire – thus inviting a merciful end from the sentries' machine guns. It would mean the end of everything worth living for if I were to lose you – at times this separation alone is almost intolerable. *John often asked for news of other people, his brother Leslie in particular, but also* Any news of the following – Frank Routledge (Eileen Johnson's BF), Olivia Hazard's husband? We are to have a show next week – a revue with a chorus of 'girls'. I'm not looking forward to it and in any case I think male legs etc are ugly. *(Many of the photos taken in the camp are of the various shows and include two magnificent ones of male legs!)*

In letter 70 (24 March 1943) John had some good news on the violin front. My main item of news is that I think I have secured a violin instructor. I haven't met him yet and know him only by sight. He probably isn't quite such a good performer as my first tutor but I think he is [a] more reliable type of fellow and I hope he won't lose interest in me after a few weeks as did the last one. In addition the star violinist in the camp has promised to keep a fatherly eye on me! The latter is a New Zealander named Frank Hunt, not a professional musician but a very excellent amateur with a profound knowledge of music. He rarely entertains us on the fiddle but he conducts our orchestra, being easily the best man for the job, but we are to hear him playing at a light classical concert next week when he and our concert pianist will render solos and concertos – without orchestra. *The concert pianist was an American, Herzstam; there are photographs of both of these men and of the orchestra. Two weeks later John wrote:* The concert which I told you about earlier was marvellous, I went 3 times! Each show is given 5 times to enable the whole camp to attend and I scrounged the extra tickets. I had more pleasure from each performance than any other show or concert to date. I had a game of rugger today and scored an absolutely wizard try! (although I shouldn't say so). I'll be 31 tomorrow – what an age!

In letter 53 (20 March 1943) Ursula talked again about Mrs Boyd and the plan for a discussion group. Last Wednesday our first tentative meeting took place, at Mrs Boyd's house. Of course she is an invaluable person, because she knows almost everybody in the borough, and she invited a most able woman, a JP, councillor etc. etc., to talk to us and start us off. There were about a dozen women there and we got up a really lively discussion on various aspects of women's social work in the borough. On Wednesday fortnight we are having the ex-mayor along to talk to us about education and the work of the local council. We are rather hoping to find a suitable name for ourselves, as a body, and then gradually work for some particular agreed object, bring pressure to bear and work up a real demand and interest. A maternity hospital is a crying need which we all approve of – however we must wait and see how things develop. If it only starts a few more people thinking & arguing about public affairs, it will have done some good. *Ursula also mentioned:* Olivia's husband is reported alive and a prisoner, after well over a year of silence. I'm so glad and know just how she must be feeling now. *But there was no news of Frank Routledge, Eileen Johnson's fiancé. On 27 March (letter 54) the fourth parcel is described, including* The largest item is the kitbag, made up partly by the Red X locally and when the working party there had broken a number of their sewing machine needles on it they gave it up in disgust and I got the local cobbler, whose wife works in the factory with me, to finish it off on his tougher machine. Anyway I hope it will be useful and will come in handy when you start travelling again. We are starting work on another patchwork rug, for your June parcel, which should arrive before Christmas, and I am going to see if I can get any skates for you too, clip-on ones I should think, for I don't suppose you want me to send your proper skating boots, do you? After all, you might have started for home before they got to you.

After three weeks of no mail, John received her letters with all the queries about housing and replied in letter 71 (26 March 1943): I'm sorry to say that I think the properties you describe are quite beyond us. *There followed a detailed discussion of, as he saw it, insuperable problems in buying a farm – John suggested approaching a County Agricultural Adviser for help.* In any case, before taking on a property I should consult the County bloke for his OK. It is his job to help people like us. I'm afraid you've got a rotten job to do and if I were doing it I should be more than loath to commit an indigent couple like ourselves to [a] contract involving £2,000–£3,000. I have since been speaking to some agricultural experts here and they confirmed my ideas. They strongly advise approaching a County Agricultural Adviser as a first step towards securing a small holding. I am told that the Adviser is a purely impartial man and should be very helpful – especially to us considering our present state of helplessness. You might therefore contact the advisers in Herts, Essex, Bucks, Surrey,

Sussex or Kent (even Beds) but from my limited knowledge I would suggest Herts first and Bucks 2nd. Another idea has struck me several times lately, assuming I get some months leave when the bloody battle is over – we could do a lot worse than spend much of it at an agricultural college on an intensive course or living at a farm and working with the occupiers.

At last, letter 74, dated 30 March 1943, offered some positive news on the violin front: My greatest joy today, apart from your letter, is that I have a new violin instructor. A charming fellow named Harry Friend is taking me over and I've had my first lesson. He said I'd done quite well on my own and was quite encouraging altogether, although I've a hell of a long way to go yet. Could you send me the following music please: 'KAYSERS Studies for the violin' Op 20. *(This book duly arrived and came back with John after the war. My eldest daughter used it in the 1970s and the pencilled dates on various studies such as 6 October 1972 and 5 February 1944 show their users! As it was quite battered and marked 'GEPRUFT' inside, her teacher covered it with Christmas paper –'We want to forget the war,' she said.)*

My new instructor seems to be taking me quite seriously, but I have really progressed very little so far. However, I am as keen as ever and if I still feel the same when I get back to you I shall endeavour to carry on with it. I'd love to be able to play with you eventually. I aim now at doing 3 hours practise daily; sometimes I manage a little more and sometimes less, but rarely less than 2 hrs. *John also commented on activities in the camp:* The Merchant of Venice is being presented tomorrow night – it will be the last show for which we shall be allowed to hire costumes – the Germans having banned such procedure for future productions. However, I've no doubt that the fellows will contrive to make excellent costumes out of almost nothing. The incredible ingenuity of the fellows here thrills me. They have made several excellent timekeeping clocks, one out of scraps of wood and the others from old tins. Model steam engines and a steam driven model boat (which actually goes) have been made from empty tin cans – and a host of other really wonderful models or bits of machinery have been made. *(It is extraordinary to think of the*

Germans hiring costumes to the prisoners! There are good photos of this production, and also of the Bosendorfer grand piano, which they also loaned to the POWs.)

Once again John asked Ursula about her factory job. BUT what about this factory work of yours?? I am still absolutely in the dark about it. Could you possibly tell me (in such a way that the censor won't object) the following: (1) How far away from Lido you have to travel; (2) How often you go; (3) The time you start and stop work; (4) Whether you use machines likely to remove limbs if carelessly worked. Do please, please realise that I have an interest in your well being – it matters to me more than anything else in the world and I am not a little disturbed by my ignorance of the truth. But I want truth – not flannel! … *(and)* … Now about the factory work of yours I gather only that you go thrice per week and that it is within walking distance. So is John O'Groats, if you like long walks. At least you can tell me how long it takes you to walk and the time you start and stop on each of the 3 weekly occasions. If you could tactfully enlighten me any further I would be most grateful. (*Ursula replied on 16 May:* By the way you needn't worry about Mary Griffin's work in the slightest, it is only one minute from her home and involves nothing more lethal than a screwdriver. She works 3 evenings a week, and looks well on it.) Thanks for your information (in last) re M. Griffin's work. You might tell me now the times she clocks on and off on each of the 3 weekly occasions. Does she go to the little place at the end of Tenterden Grove? *So John finally stopped worrying. He also suggested that when her parents came home* What about your taking Frances to live on a farm till I get back and am demobbed. It would be grand for her and you could help with the farm work learning a lot and also helping the War effort just as much as you do now, if not more. You could plough and sow, reap and mow, drive tractors, milk cows and become quite a 'land girl' or 'land mother'. You would also find out if you really liked the life too, which would be a good thing. Let me know what you think. *And to reinforce the idea, in letter 79, dated 10 April 1943:* I wonder if you have had my last card with its suggestion that after your people come home you should go to live on a farm, giving Frances the benefit

of a rural life, both of you immunity from air raids and yourself a
chance to learn some of the tricks of the trade. Quite frankly I don't
expect you to be able to secure a house for us and you could very
usefully help the nation by working on or near the land. It would be a
better life for you after your years of undiluted housekeeping and
factory work.

*In general, apart from the chronic ENT problems, John remained
healthy, but occasionally there were problems.* I've had a series of minor
misfortunes recently. First of all we had a mild outburst of fleas in
which I was one of the affected. The Germans insisted in taking
prompt measures but by that time I developed a plague of spots from
some minor blood disorder so that I couldn't be sure if the fleas had
gone. Then I spilt boiling water on my foot which despite immediate
attention blistered. Two or three days later the whole turned septic but
is now responding to treatment. Then I caught a lousy cold which
was followed by a fresh disappearance of my senses. From everything
except the last I have more or less recovered. I have had a couple
of games of soccer now and am hoping to play regularly. I have to
confess that I'm putting on a lot of weight nowadays – possibly the
large quantity of spuds consumed is the cause – but whatever it is I am
certainly much heavier than in the autumn and my face is getting
very fat. Will you still love me if I come home 'completely circular'!
The next difficulty John had was coping with an influx of new prisoners.
A rare event in the form of an influx of new prisoners has kept me
fully occupied. How I loathe my job – trying to keep the peace between
a lot of argumentative and rather selfish POWs calls for endless
patience and tact. Also, being of the same rank or in some cases lower
rank than them I have no authority to give orders. *And in letter 80
dated 12 April 1943:* We had some more new arrivals today and the
blocks in the camp are well over strength now – terribly over-crowded
in fact. We are indeed lucky in the small room. One of my room mates,
Louis Den Boer, had a visit from his 19-year-old brother who is doing
a spot of work in Germany (not of his own free will of course). It was
a great moment for him because he hasn't seen any relations for
3 years now. I wonder when I shall be visited by my brother?

Ursula and John Valentine, taken while John was training in Scotland.
(Unless stated all the photos and images are from Frances Zagni's collection)

John and his siblings, Bunty, Leslie and Irene, approx. 1919/1920.

John and Ursula's daughter Frances.

Ursula Valentine.

No. 29 Course Pilots and Observers. John on the back row fourth from the right.

Bomber Command Observer John Valentine.

RAF Aberystwyth, No. 1 Squadron 'D' Flight, March 1941. LAC Valentine on the back row eighth from the left.

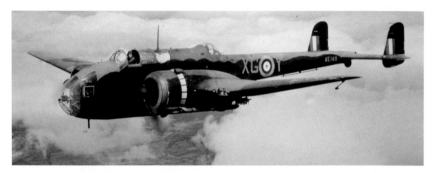

Handley Page Hampden.

Avro Manchester.

John's pilot Philip Floyd.

Telephone No. : SPRINGWELL (GLOUCESTER)............2407

Telegraphic Address :
    RECORDS TELEX, GLOUCESTER.

Any communications on the
subject of this letter should
be addressed to :
AIR OFFICER i/c RECORDS,
        Address as opposite,
and the following number
quoted :—   C7/1251404
    Your Ref. :................

RECORD OFFICE,

ROYAL AIR FORCE,

GLOUCESTER.

1st June 1942
Date...

Dear Madam,

      I regret to confirm that your husband, No.
1251404 Sergeant John Ross MacKenzie VALENTINE of No.49
Squadron, Royal Air Force, is missing, the aircraft of
which he was the navigator having failed to return to
its base on the 30th May 1942 after an operational flight.

      This does not necessarily mean that he is
killed or wounded. I will communicate with you again
immediately I have any further news and would be obliged
if you, on your part, would write to me should you hear
anything of your husband from unofficial sources.

      May I assure you of the sympathy of the Royal
Air Force with you in your anxiety.

        I am,
          Dear Madam,
            Your obedient Servant.

            Air Commodore,
            Air Officer i/c Records,
            ROYAL   AIR   FORCE.

Mrs.J.R.M.Valentine.
"Rain Boyend",
Banbury,
Bicester,
Oxfordshire.

Letter to Ursula on 1 June 1942 reporting that John was missing.

Charges to pay
s. ___ d.

RECEIVED

Prefix. **25** Time handed in. Office of Origin and Service Instructions. Words.

No. ___ 1 0

OFFICE STAM

returned for Butter

from ___ 5.52 Gloucester Teles O.H.115 49 To

Important Mrs Valentine, Lido Tenterden Rd. Hendon N.7

According to telegram from International Red Cross quoting German information your husband 1251484 Sgt Valentine previously reported

Charges to pay
s. ___ d.

RECEIVED

Prefix. **26** Time handed in. Office of Origin and Service Instructions. Words.

No. ___ 16

OFFICE STAMP

from ___ m To

missing is now a prisoner of war at Dulag Luft Germany. Reports states capture card received from him. Letter follows T.V.O. 1600. Records Glous Teles.

20 June 1942 telegram reporting that John was a prisoner-of-war.

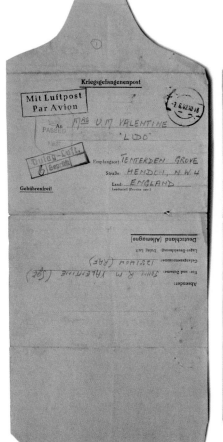

Telephone No. : SPRINGWELL (GLOUCESTER) 2042
Telegraphic Address :
RECORDS TELEX, GLOUCESTER.
Any communications on the
subject of this letter should
be addressed to :
AIR OFFICER i/c RECORDS,
Address as opposite,
and the following number
quoted :—
C7/1251404
Your Ref. :................

RECORD OFFICE,

ROYAL AIR FORCE,

GLOUCESTER.

Date.... 20th June 1942 ....

Dear Madam,

In confirmation of my telegram dated the 19th June 1942, according to a telegram from the International Red Cross Committee quoting German information your husband No. 1251404 Sergeant John Ross Mackenzie VALENTINE of No. 49 Squadron, Royal Air Force, previously reported as 'missing' is now a 'prisoner of war' at Dulag Luft in Germany. The report states a capture card has been received from him.

Instructions for communicating with prisoners of war are enclosed herewith.

I am,
Dear Madam,
Your obedient Servant,

Air Commodore,
Air Officer i/c Records,
ROYAL   AIR   FORCE.

Mrs. J.R.M. Valentine,
"Rain Boyend",
Banbury,
Bicester,
Oxfordshire.

Official confirmation that John was a prisoner-of-war, 20 June 1942.

(Left) Red Cross list of parcel contents sent to John 17 July 1942.
(Below) An example of how thoughtful the censor was, taking the trouble to write out again any information that was lost on the reverse of this letter (19 March 1944) from Ursula following blacking out.

17 JUL 1942   RAF/M/2444   P/4

BRITISH RED CROSS SOCIETY AND ORDER OF ST. JOHN

PERSONAL PARCELS CENTRE.

Sent to :

Service No. 1251404

Name VALENTINE, John R.M.   Rank Sergeant.

Prisoner of War No.

Camp Address Stalag Luft III

CONTENTS   Gft Choc.

No.	Item	No.	Item
2 pr	Pyjamas	1	Shaving Stick
1	Pullover		
1	Bathing costume		
2	Vests		Reel cotton
2	Pants		
1	Scarf	1	Tin Shoe polish
	Pair Sandals	1	
10	Handkerchiefs		Pencil
3	Pairs Socks	1	
1	Toothbrush	2	
1	Tin Tooth powder		

86. 1c. 7

On Friday Frances and I went to look at another dancing class which seems to be more fashionable and to which several from Mrs. Mawer's class are deserting next term. It was a much bigger class, not really as advanced as ours, it seemed to me, more romping and not so much real ballet. I think I will leave Frances where she is for the time being, unless Mrs. Mawer's class becomes so small that it ceases to be fun.
I had a letter from Bish today ████████ but he sounded as cheerful as ever. I hope he will come over and see us soon. Bunty has invited us to go and stay there for a few days, and I am proposing to do next week, she says there is some furniture which your Mother days we can have if we want it, some odd chairs I gather - I shall look it over but it is really no good cluttering the house up with things we don't need. However, she also says she can let me have some cooking apples so that is worth going for at any rate! Also I want to make the acquaintance of my new niece Margaret Jean, now about 9 months old. Frances is thrilled at the idea of seeing Muriel and Robert again, they ought to play together better now that she is older and has more sense.
All my love, darling

We have had quite a busy week socially altogether. On Monday we invited Gwen Milliner to tea with her two children Pemma (aged 4) and Robert (1) and an expectant mother she has staying with her called Denise X? I don't know her surname. Actually only Denise and Pemma came, as Robert had a cold and Gwen lumbago. This girl Denise X as Cicely Donovan (do you remember her?) for spinning romantic yarns about herself which bear no relation to fact with the same inability to stick to one yarn, however fancy, with the result that although I have only had two or three chats with her (she often takes Pemma to the dancing class) she has already contradicted her previous stories in many particulars. Not that I care two hoots about her past, murky or gay, but people of this kind are rather interesting psychologically, and I should think that this weakness for romantics is connected with an unhappy or insecure childhood and that the person tries to make up for the lack of a safe family anchorage by making out that her childhood and youth have been so exciting and glamorous. Denise, in any case, seems to be a rather unstable

X staying with her called Denise.   X ONLY DENISE AND PEMMA CAME, AS ROBERT HAD A COLD AND GWEN LUMBAGO
X This girl Denise is a queer cuss, she seems to have the same twist X

(Left) John's Royal School of Music certificate, 1943.
(Below) NCOs Arts and Crafts exhibition at Stalag Luft III, August 1942.
(Bottom) Girls, Girls, Girls, Stalag Luft III March 1943.

(Top)Frank Hunt's
Orchestral Concert, Stalag
Luft III, February 1943.
(Centre) Merchant of Venice,
staged at Stalag Luft III.
(Right) Sports day at Stalag
Luft III in August 1942.

'The man next door' – the problem of getting peace and quiet.

'Please don't speak to me now – I feel a little depressed'.

LESLIE L. IRVIN
F.R.A.E.S., F.R.S.A.
HONORARY SEC.
EUROPEAN BRANCH

c/o IRVING AIR CHUTE
OF GREAT BRITAIN LTD.
ICKNIELD WAY
LETCHWORTH, HERTS

CATERPILLAR CLUB

March 16, 1944.

Mrs. Valentine,
"Lido",
Tenterden Grove,
LONDON......N.W.4.

Dear Mrs. Valentine,

I was very glad to hear from Sgt. J. R.
M. Valentine, in August 1942, that he had
saved his life with one of our chutes.

I apologise for not having written
before, but due to supply restrictions we have
been unable to obtain the small gold Caterpillar
Pin to which Sgt. Valentine is entitled, and
which he requested us to send to the above
address.

As I regret it now seems unlikely that
this Pin will be available until after the War,
I am sending a membership certificate for Sgt.
Valentine, with our best wishes for his early
return home, and the assurance that his Pin
will follow at the first opportunity.

Yours sincerely,

Sec. to L. Irvin.

MBL.
Encl. Card.

(Above) John and Frank Pepper.
Sent to Ursula on 12 October 1942.
(Right) 16 March 1943, letter
to Ursula informing her that
John was a member of the
Caterpillar Club.
(Below) POWs celebrating their
liberation at Stalag 357,
Fallingbostel, 16 April 1945.

19 April 1945

My Dearest Ursula,

The camp was liberated by a unit of the British Army on the 16th April, unfortunately only one third of the fellows were still there The germans having evacuated the rest a few days earlier, I managed to stay behind because I was in the sick bay recovering from diphthria, I was moved from the camp today to an Army hospital where this letter is being written, I have got over the illness with the exception of the usual after effects, The worse of which is a temporary but more or less complete (paralisis) of my limbs, I dont know when I shall be bought back to Britain nor when

(Above and opposite) On 19 April 1945 Ursula received a letter from John, but in another hand, as John had been too ill to write it.

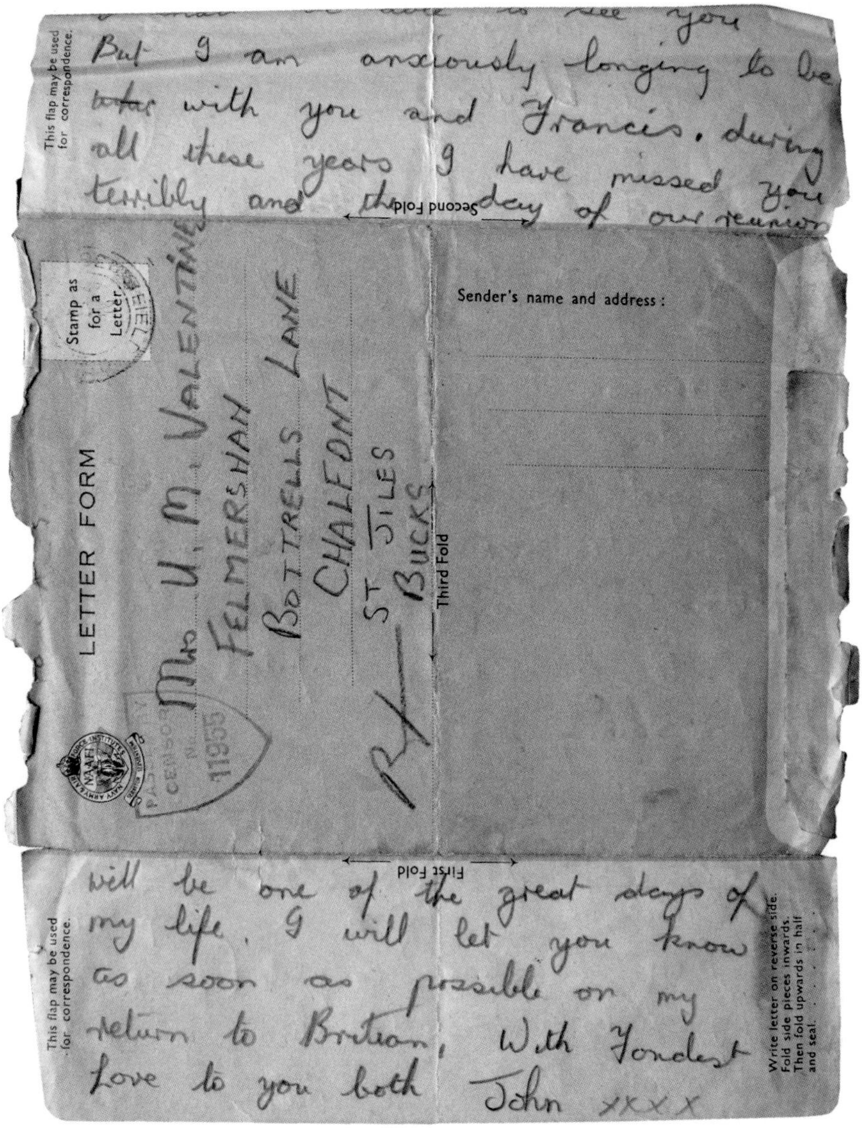

This flap may be used for correspondence.
... to see you
But I am anxiously longing to be with you and Francis. during
all these years I have missed you
terribly and the day of our reunion
Second Fold
Stamp as for a Letter.
LETTER FORM
Mrs U. M. VALENTINE
FELMERSHAM
BOTTRELLS LANE
CHALFONT
ST GILES
BUCKS
PASSED BY CENSOR No. 11955
NAAFI
Third Fold
Sender's name and address :
First Fold
This flap may be used for correspondence.
will be one of the great days of
my life. I will let you know
as soon as possible on my
return to Britain, With Fondest
Love to you both John xxxx
Write letter on reverse side. Fold side pieces inwards. Then fold upwards in half and seal.

Ursula, Sark, circa 1985. John Valentine, Channel Islands 50th Anniversary of Liberation Day, 9 May 1995.

*John foresaw more and more problems if they went ahead with their
farming ideas.* I frankly admit that I find the study of agriculture very
dull in parts and I'm not really doing it very seriously. It is so divorced
from reality here. In addition I become daily more certain that Touche
is the only workable proposition for us after the war. I don't want you
and Frances to have to endure penury on the top of all the other
tribulations of recent years. The most I hope for is a home in the
country and a few acres to dabble with. The end of the war still seems
remote and I am firmly convinced that I shan't see you this year – and
what is to happen to me assuming the German conflict finishes first?
Shall I then be sent out against the Japs? I certainly don't lack smoking
material now. For months we smoked anything obtainable, dog ends,
re-rolled were favourites, but we drew the line at dog ends of dog
ends. *There were obviously some complications in the camp and reprisals
were enforced, the postcard describing those (no. 25 for 1943) must have
been censored for it never arrived. On 22 April John wrote:* Reprisals
which I described in my last card are being partly relaxed during
the Easter week end but we do not know if they will be resumed
afterwards. *But on 2 May John wrote:* The reprisals for alleged minor
offences have been increased by our captors. Yesterday all Soccer and
Rugger balls were taken out of the camp and hand written news sheet
were banned. They seem to think we are getting out of hand somehow
and impose all these little petty punishments but as far as we are
concerned they can go on doing so. Our theatre has been shut for
some weeks now and we have also been parading (are also being
paraded?) thrice daily for counting instead of the usual twice.
It is a pity, really, that our relations with the Germans have worsened
of late for we have lived quite harmoniously for some months (accent
on the word 'quite') and I had developed a certain respect for their
tolerant attitude towards us – but things have changed slightly during
the last few weeks. However, our spell here is part of the privilege of
being alive and things aren't too bad when everything is considered.
I have now entered my 12th month of captivity, while on 12th May
Frank Pepper completed his 3rd year. He hasn't gone utterly to seed as
I may have given you to understand but he has a very gloomy outlook
on life. Actually I think he is a very intelligent fellow but his mind is

limited to one thing only – the Air Force and things relating to it. He is rough and uncouth in many ways and shows it particularly in his choice of words and way of uttering them. However, he is good hearted and did all he could for me when I was a new arrival.

At long last my spots seem to have disappeared, but I am still having trouble with my nasal organ, blast it! The camp leader received a letter from Jean Potelle today – it was merely a request for some of his clothes and he said nothing about his state of health nor the treatment he's received. However, it was good to hear from him and to know that, at least, he is still alive. *This POW had been taken away from the camp in spite of all representations and great fears were held for his future.* This is a terrible place for moods and I am in the depths of depression just now – for no real reason, of course. I feel most gloomy over my fiddle prospects at the moment and am absolutely convinced of my inability to be anything but a very poor performer. The work that lies ahead of me is nothing but colossal – you can have very little conception of it – and I tremble when I think of it. However, I try to adopt an ostrich like attitude (not of course when actually playing the bloody thing) and to plug away as if the end were actually within sight. In our study of elementary harmony we are now delving into minor scales and the whole subject is about as clear as mud. These two subjects (fiddle and harmony) are about all I manage in that line although I do dabble occasionally in Dutch and Agriculture – but conditions are very definitely against study here. One can never get two minutes away from anyone else or free from interruptions of one sort or another. Queries are constantly arising in the block and I am often called in as arbiter in some petty dispute. Incidentally we have more men in the hut now. We started with 164 packed like sardines and after complaining to the Red X the number was reduced by 20. Recently there have been fresh arrivals. Although we remained up to strength and we now have 152 men – and the huts aren't enormous either. However, we are better here than in Japan, I guess. *And then a week later he wrote:* Some more new arrivals are expected tomorrow and we shall be back to our original sardine strength of 164 per barrack.

As ever, Ursula comforted and encouraged John. You have mentioned

on various occasions that your studies in which you rely on other
people's teaching, violin, Dutch, theory of music for instance, do not
get on as fast as you would wish, and I can well imagine that under
those conditions you cannot get all types of men to stick to a routine
of teaching or anything else; and how the sense of frustration, which
must be bad enough in any case, is increased when your timetable is
upset because others do not carry out their teaching programme as
arranged. I certainly hope you won't give up your violin at any rate
but that you will be able to get some help from a more interested
fellow. You mention that you notice a change in your own outlook
on life due to the monotony and sense of frustration – what sort of
a change? Do not get cynical, will you, Johnnie, remember your ideal
of service. I've got the most tremendous faith in you, in your steadfast
spirit and in your sense of humour – I often wish I had got some of
your courage to prop myself up on. *Otherwise her letters are full of her
everyday affairs: Ba going on holiday to Wales for a week, Vera Bowack
and her little son Michael coming to stay, and news of Frances.* In the
last week Frances has begun to talk a lot more and to copy quite
accurately whatever she hears us say. Her passion for cheese continues
unabated and whenever she happens to think of it she will demand
some. 'More cheese', she says, 'more cheese, MORE CHEESE', getting
more and more insistent, but if I refuse she gives up after a bit and
accepts it quite philosophically. She plays with her dolls like a real
little girl now – the other day I found her putting Doggy on the potty
and encouraging him with the most realistic noises! Today she has
been giving Teddy a 4 course breakfast out of fish paste jars!

*In letter 89 John rejoiced in the arrival of Ursula's letter 56 after a month
of silence and then continued:* Relations with our captors are better
now and all reprisals for alleged offences have been lifted, so we
should have a show at the theatre soon. We have a private jail here to
which fellows are sent by the Germans for any sort of misbehaviour,
e.g. attempts to escape, smoking on parade. Nobody minds a spell in
the 'cooler' as it is called, and there is a steady stream of temporary
tenants. Last week a fellow was sentenced to 3 weeks' confinement on
bread and water for shouting 'Huns Up' when a German entered a

barrack. We always give a warning in that or a similar fashion in case any of us are busy at things we ought not to be doing but the word 'Hun' isn't appreciated by the Germans. Bread and water confinement includes sleeping on wooden boards. *(This letter had a label attached saying 'the British Censorship is not responsible for the mutilation of this letter', but the only apparent damage was the removal of 'No. 31'.)*

Ursula replied to John's reference to possibly being sent to Japan if Germany was defeated first. It is strange that you should mention the question of what will happen if this war ends before the Far East war, as it is fairly sure to do. It has been my private nightmare for some time now. I just couldn't bear it if you had to go out east. Anyway you will <u>have</u> to get your nose attended to first, I shall really insist on that this time. It ought to have been done that time in Oxfordshire. *On a more cheerful note she enclosed some photos, and news of Frances.* These photos of Frances 'cooking' are very good of her and taken together should give you a pretty clear idea of what she is like just now. It is quite impossible to scold her for her misdeeds because she immediately agrees with me and deflects the scolding from herself on to the object of her misdeed. The other day she got into the bathroom, turned the taps on and started flooding the place. I caught her in time and gave her a very serious talking to about how naughty it is to turn on the taps on her own, and now whenever we go near the bath or she sees the picture of the bath in her picture book she harangues me on the subject of the naughty taps, carrying on at great length and with the utmost seriousness, often mimicking me until I really can't keep my face straight. Last week she got hold of a pencil and scribbled all over the tray of her high chair. As a result Ba and I had a long lecture on the naughty pencil and the naughty tray – never naughty Frances, mind you!

The date of 30 May was the first anniversary of John being shot down. It is just a year ago tonight – what an anniversary! I expect you will be remembering it too, but let's hope that we may spend the next one together. It seems a terribly long and dreary year to me, but not half as long and dreary as it does to you, I expect. I should like to tell you how much I admire the way you have faced up to your captivity and the grand spirit and the cheerfulness you have shown. It is the sort of experience that shows up a man for what he is worth, and it has always been a real comfort to me to think that you, with your depth of character and general stamina, will come through this nightmare as well as anyone can. I do love you so much, my darling, and I love you more and more as time goes on so that if you don't come home soon I shall simply burst with unexpended affection! So hurry!! *This letter also came with the news that Ursula's parents had returned home from India. Her father was hoping to get a job.* Anyway it was grand to see them both looking so very well. In due course, when we have had a bit of time to settle down and get straight I shall have to start in again on our housing problem, but now that at last this long dreary period of living alone (for most of the time anyway) has come to an end, I am really not eager to get a house in the country and condemn myself to solitude again while waiting for your return. I was sorry to hear about your Belgian friend *(Jean Potelle)* too, poor boy, and I pray that he may be alright. My father is naturally anxious to get a job over here. I hope he will get a job for he is full of life and ideas – he has hardly changed at all in the 7 years since I saw him. Mother is just the same too except that her hair is greyer.

In John's letter 94 he mentioned a parcel: I had 150 cigarettes from Rothmans in which was note saying that the cigs were a gift from the company and that my name had been supplied by a customer named Miss Frances Valentine. Whilst I deeply appreciate the kindness of this lady in proffering my name I am surprised that a daughter of mine should become a customer of a tobacconist at such a tender age – they say that smoking hinders growth too! Somehow I suspect the heavily disguised handwriting to be the penmanship of Aunty Ba – anyway I'm grateful for the gift. I wonder if I'll get a similar sort of gift from a firm of gin manufacturers, thus proving how you have let Frances go to the dogs so soon. *The violin was going well.* Harry Friend is quite pleased with me. It may sound insignificant to you but I am starting on the 2nd position next week. I hardly think I am good enough on the 1st position yet but Friend seems to think so and I consider it a definite step forward for me. ... If I am to keep up the fiddle after my return, time for regular practise will have to be worked into our scheme of things. I reckon I shall require at least 5 years before I can dream of being able to play with you. Practise is necessary to maintain proficiency so you must get used to my habit of retiring to the lavatory for a long period daily. That is what I do here and the habit might be difficult to shake off. *And on the subject of food:* With the coming of warmer days we shall have to scrutinize Red X food tins more carefully. All tins are punctured by the Germans before they are given to us (to prevent the amassing of stores for escaping purposes) and for lack of anything else the food has to stay in the opened tins until it is eaten which may be as much as a week later.

With the return of her parents Ursula was (for the time being) less keen on buying a property, but John was more enthusiastic. I was very much annoyed to hear how the estate agents had let you down by not informing you of the sale of the house before you undertook that wretched journey. As I've told you I prefer the idea of renting but am not entirely 'agin' buying if you see something you really fancy and should put the absolute maximum price at £1,300 (£1,000 much better). I must say I'm greatly taken with the thought of the possibility of your acquiring a home.

For some time John had been mentioning the possibility of their being moved to another camp, but the rumours were very vague. In his postcard No. 102, written in June, he told his wife: We are definitely moving shortly but much further than we had anticipated – East Prussia is the latest tip (and, I think, a reliable one). *On 2 June John wrote:* I have bad news for you – in a few weeks we are to be moved not just a short distance as we once thought – but to a place in East Prussia called Heydekrug, about as far East as one can go and still be in Germany. It will mean, alas, less correspondence for my arrangement will fall through and I will not be able to renew it on account of different circumstances. As you told me that you enjoyed hearing from me, it has been one of my greatest pleasures recently to be able to devote most of my 'limited ration' to you. *Meanwhile, Ursula had written:*

Last week I only wrote you an airmail letter card, or rather two, one
to this address and one to Oflag 21b, where your father had heard that
you had been moved, but since then I have been up to Red X H.Q. and
they seemed to think that it was unlikely that you had gone there, so
I am continuing to write to Stalag Luft III as before until I hear
something definite from you. I am risking the first of the colour
photos this time and I do hope it gets through to you safely, because
it does show up Frances's hair well. You should look through the
transparencies in strong daylight to get the best effect. There are 6
altogether, taken in the garden, and I will send one per letter. Look
after them won't you, because of course these can't be replaced like
ordinary prints. *(These survived and caused great excitement when
I took them into a photographic shop in Bath a few years ago.)*

First home, Felmersham, Bottrells Lane, Chalfont St. Giles, with Frances in the garden.
Moved in on 28 November 1943.

Chapter Six

Buying a House!

The possible purchase of a house came to the fore when Ursula's parents announced that they were going to sell Lido and move to the country. My parents are actively looking round for a place in the country to retire to, and they want me to go with them, but I think I must try to find our future home and move into that instead. It seems highly unlikely to me that they will find a house and I shall find our house and they find a purchaser for Lido all at about the same time, still that is what we have got to try to do. *The fifth parcel was also being prepared, to include a second rug of knitted squares especially requested by John and a pair of skates.* I have also been trying by every means to get you some skates and have advertised locally at last in despair. But last Sunday I had a reply to my advertisement, a girl rang up and said she had a pair of skates, not clip-ons but complete with boots which she thought would fit; they had belonged to her husband who had been killed in the RAF and she would like you to have them. She wouldn't consider letting me buy them, said they were not for sale but only to give to an RAF prisoner so I accepted them gratefully. This girl has now joined the ATS, she seemed an awfully nice sort and I felt so sorry for her and realised more strongly than ever how very lucky I am that you are still alive and will some day come back to me. *Mrs Boyd and Ursula's Current Affairs Club had another meeting with* the chairman of the Married Women's Association, a sort of housewives trades union, formed largely to fight for a better legal position for

married women, who have practically no status before the law at
present and to change the all too widespread tradition whereby the
husband doles out the weekly housekeeping money and the wife has
no money she can really call her own for all her work.

Meanwhile, on the housing front: We have all been in a state of uproar
this week over the housing question. Mother is anxious to sell this
house and move out into the country without delay, probably Devon
or Cornwall. A local estate agent has been to look over the house and
seems confident of getting well over £2,000 for it – so you can judge
how prices have gone up and what we are faced with. Meantime I am
faced with a horrid problem. What I should like to do, of course, is to
find our future home and move into it with Frances and the furniture
we already possess and set about gradually acquiring the other things
we need. But first I have to find the house and then I have to find the
means to rent or buy it. Everybody I apply to tells me it is almost
impossible to rent unfurnished nowadays and that I shall be darned
lucky if I come across anything to buy. The whole problem looks so
thorny that I should give it up entirely, go and live with my people and
wait till you come home, if it weren't for the fact that I know it will be
far worse then, when the real scramble for housing begins – reaches its
climax, at least. So I keep on trying. I wrote to the Executive Officers
of War Agricultural Committees in Herts, Bucks and Essex. They all
said NO, with varying degrees of politeness, but the Essex man was
the clearest of all. He said 'I do not think that it would be very
advisable for you to take over a smallholding at the present time, as
it is essential to obtain maximum production from all the land and
unless you have had any experience in the working of a farm, my
Committee would not approve of your obtaining possession of a
holding such as you mention unless you were prepared to install a
competent worker and the area you mention would be insufficient to
warrant this.' So there you are. I really think we shall have to give up
any idea of getting a smallholding until after you get back. After all,
you may not be demobilised for ages and the main thing is to have a
roof over our heads at all. So I have now taken to pursuing a country
cottage, so far with no results. The whole thing is getting so urgent,

for when once my parents have found a house I shall have to decide whether I am going with them and putting our furniture in store, or not, and if not, what the devil I am going to do. Once I go with them down to Devon or somewhere, I feel I shall be too far away to do anything much about getting a cottage near London, and you will come back with no home to go to.

In letter 104 (4 June 1943) John wrote: Stories of the new camp indicate that it won't be up to the standard of this and that we shall be massed together in buildings holding 450. I don't expect to be Block Leader there, the older prisoners will naturally take all the reduced number of jobs and privileges. I bitterly regret that after our move I shall be unable to devote such a large share of my monthly ration to you and you must be prepared for a slump in receipts from me. My new address is Stalag Luft VI (Six). The date of our departure is not yet known but the 1st party leaves on 10th June – there will be 5 parties altogether but we don't know who is in which. We are all busy speculating as to the means whereby we shall be transported to the new place (cattle truck is the usual conveyance for a POW here) and what conditions will be like there. *Later he added:* We shall be travelling in ordinary coaches and not cattle trucks as once feared. I ask one thing in particular, a place to practise my fiddle on which I am as keen as ever. We anticipate that it won't be exactly balmy in the winter time. Mail and parcels will take even longer to arrive but we will have to put up with that. At first I didn't want to leave this place but I am now eagerly looking forward to the change. I have been outside the barbed wire only once in 12 months (once more than most of the camp 'tis true) and a spot of variety will be refreshing. The train journey will be most exciting although we shall probably travel 'bare foot' to prevent us escaping. Frank Pepper, I believe, is quite happy because we are to be shifted in decent carriages. In his previous moves he has always had the most uncomfortable conditions – cattle trucks with a tin in the centre of the floor as the only sanitary convenience. He thinks we ought to experience the same thing to be able to know what it can be like.

In the midst of getting ready for departure to the new camp, John sat his Royal Schools of Music examinations. I have sat the first part of my music exams. Harmony Grade 2 – set by Royal Schools of Music. Conditions for writing exam papers were not good and I made the usual mess of the paper. I'm sitting 2 more – Harmony Grade 3 & Grammar Grade 3. I don't intend carrying on with Harmony – it is entirely theoretical, we never hear any of the stuff we write and it's getting a bit boring. *And the next day:* I have sat the 2nd music exam but it was a fairly easy one, although it was a wretched day for it. I was frantically busy getting rid of the Yanks & Poles, I had to play a final game of football – to prepare lists of the chaps travelling under my wing next week and answering innumerable queries. I was late for the exam and had to leave early to get on with my work – but I think I passed (Grammar of Music). The final paper is tomorrow and I expect the same frantic conditions. *And finally:* I have sat the 3rd music Exam but fared poorly. I expect to pass 1 of them (Grammar) – 1 of the Harmony papers a doubtful pass and one a certain failure. I don't intend carrying on with the study of Harmony, but there is a possibility that our Harmony Instructor will branch out into musical history at the next place and I'll follow that for amusement only for it fascinates me.

Letter 107 (15 June 1943) was John's first letter from the new camp. It was sent to Lido but took so long to arrive that it had to be forwarded to the Griffins' new home, Little Close, in Salcombe, Devon. This is my first letter from the new camp. We had a very crowded but otherwise tolerable journey, 2 nights and 1 day with little sleep en route, but soon made up for that. This camp is brand new, unfinished and in a very raw state generally. No longer do I enjoy the sheltered privacy of a small room but am in one holding xxxxx men of which I have been elected the Fuhrer. It is certainly a better room to live in than the barrack rooms at Luft III but we fear that it won't be too warm in winter. My greatest disappointment is that there is positively nowhere suitable for fiddle practise. Just now it looks as if I'll have to give up the instrument and I'm terribly depressed at the thought. It was my main interest in life, I was extremely keen and thoroughly enjoyed even the most monotonous of exercises. I was looking forward to being able to produce something of value at the conclusion of this otherwise completely wasted chunk of my life. Study too, especially organised study, will be at a dead loss on account of lack of accommodation. As a result of these setbacks I have been very gloomy since my arrival here 3 days ago and consequently have longed for you even more.

In his next letter he expanded his view of the new location: The surroundings of this camp are better than before and the potential accommodation is enormous so that there are possibilities of great improvements in the course of time. All I can do is hope for the best and take the rough with the smooth to which I am fairly reconciled anyway. We are slowly settling down here but a lot has to be done before the camp reaches the standard of the last. As yet we have no sports field, theatre, or facilities for organised education or library. These things normally fill in the time for most of the fellows who at present are mooning about like lost souls. In addition, we don't cook our own food as we did before so the days are long almost to the point of distraction. However, we hope in time to get some of the things we need to help the time along. Deprived of facilities for playing my fiddle I spent a miserable and inactive week until yesterday, when in desperation I went into the tiny little box like chamber leading off the barrack room which serves as xxxxx. I fitted a mute to my violin and struck up. There is only a flimsy door to keep the sound out of the barrack where the fellows live but with the aid of the mute I have been able so to muffle the hideous strains as to excite only good natured leg pulling from the unwilling listeners. It isn't good for a learner to play with a mute and the room is so small that xxxxx subject to the continued tolerance of the audience, I intend struggling on. I like the barrack rooms and surroundings of the camp much better than the last, while the train journey and change has acted as a real mental tonic to me and everyone else. The sight of women on roads and stations caused the greatest excitement for they are phenomena quite unknown to prison life. Despite many caustic comments from the fellows, my fiddle practice in the block latrine continues – I muffle the instrument as much as possible and produce the most awful squeaks but they are not loud ones. I went to a German doctor today about my nose and am going again tomorrow for a more thorough examination. Equipment is very limited here but the doctor is most sympathetic and anxious to be of real assistance. I have been tasteless off and on for nearly 7 months now. Don't forget your holiday.

Meanwhile, back in England Ursula had her own issues: This week has been another of alarms and excursions about houses. I meet with nothing but blank refusals wherever I turn. One agent in the Epping Forest area sent me particulars of a house in Buckhurst Hill for £550, which seemed too cheap to be true. So I wrote to enquire further and found it was in the middle of the town, thoroughly dilapidated, lavatory at the end of the garden and altogether hopeless. But my parents had various offers of houses down in Devon and decided to go down and see them, but then Daddy had a letter offering him a job in Edinburgh and he decided to apply for it and so the whole business of the houses was dropped. Everything seems to be topsy-turvy, everybody's plans are in a state of flux and no-one can get anywhere. Even Ba may be leaving her job and going into another which would take her away from home; if I can't find the house we want and shall probably have to put our own furniture into store and go with the parents, if I can't find a cottage before they leave here – if they leave here; Daddy wants to get a job but hasn't yet found the right one; Mummy wants them to retire quietly to the country and give up trying to find jobs and just live happily ever after. In fact Frances is the only one who has no problems and she sails through life as blissfully as ever. I suppose things will sort themselves out in time but the interval is rather unsettling and trying.

On 4 July the Current Affairs Club had another meeting: This time I had to be in the chair because nobody else had been appointed in time, though that must be out of order since I am secretary. However, it doesn't amount to much, merely a couple of polite speeches introducing and afterwards thanking the speaker. This time we had a local doctor to tell us about the proposed state medical service. Unfortunately the man has a kink on the subject and made some

pretty slanderous remarks of an ultra-Tory kind in the course of his talk. I being chairman had to preserve a semblance of impartiality!'
But after that it was back to housing: There have been terrific comings and goings again this week on the housing question. On Tuesday Mother said she would look after Frances, so I jumped on my pushbike, cycled over to Barnet and caught a train out to Hatfield. There I made enquiries at the local estate agent but drew an absolute blank. So I cycled across to Hertford where the agents again gave me no hope at all. A certain estate agent at Royston seemed to have things to offer, so I decided to go over and see him. He was more hopeful than any of the others and gave me 4 or 5 addresses in Essex, which made me feel a lot better. However, it was then 3 pm and a terrific rain storm had started, so I decided I couldn't make Essex that afternoon; instead I hiked into Broxbourne, took the train to Edmonton and cycled home from there. I was soaked to the skin and it is a wonder I didn't catch a cold; however, I am none the worse for it.

I had intended to go and look at the addresses in Essex the next day, but next morning there was an advertisement for a bungalow with ¾ acres of garden in Ashdown Forest, which sounded rather nice for £1,350, so I decided to go for that first. It was Barbara's day off and she said she would come with me. We met at Charing Cross at 10 am and believe it or not but we didn't get to that bungalow till well after 1 pm. When we did find it, it turned out to be a horrid poky little place we couldn't have got our bedroom furniture into! We got home about 5 pm after a totally wasted day. On Thursday I was allowed out again – I hardly seem to have seen Frances this week! This time I went for the Essex houses. I cycled into Liverpool Street, in the rush hour too, and caught a train by the skin of my teeth out to Chelmsford. The first place I went to turned out to be about 6–7 miles from the town; it was described as an attractive well arranged small holding of 8½ acres and turned out to be the most depressing dump I have ever seen. There was no sanitation or bath, an ancient range to cook on, only 2 dark poky bedrooms, just a Victorian villa dumped down among pig-stys [sic]. These stys were extremely up-to-date and roomy – in fact we should have done better to live in them ourselves and let the pigs have the house! So I went off in disgust. On my way back into

Chelmsford I noticed an attractive old black and white house standing empty and I had a bit of a look at it. I then enquired from a local shop and the pub who the owner was, but nobody knew. So I tried an estate agent in the town and eventually ran to earth the agent in charge of it. Of course he was out to lunch, but a dopey-looking girl took down my name and said they would send me full particulars, which they have so far failed to do.

After this, I set out to look for the next two on the list, near Southminster. This turned out to be a long slow train journey down a branch line and long before I got there I saw it was no earthly use for your daily travel. However, I went to look at the better one, a fruit and poultry farm of 5 acres with 3 bedroomed house for £1,250 and when at last I found it, they told me it was sold long ago and the new owners well installed! So I haven't really got any further yet. Tomorrow my parents are going down to Devon again to see a house at Salcombe that Daddy saw before and I rather think they will take it if it appeals to Mother. Then it will be all up with me. Of course it would be lovely to go down to Salcombe with them for a bit, specially for Frances to be by the sea, but oh, how I wish I could get all our belongings into our own home first. I'd give almost anything to have you with me for a week or two now! It seems to be totally impossible to rent unfurnished, and if I buy, the house is sure not to come up to expectation in every way and one of us may be disappointed. However, it does seem to me that the first essential is to have a home of some sort, and I am going to do my damnedest to find a home fit for my hero to live in!

Ursula's letter 69 of 16 July 1943 was still filled with concerns over finding a suitable house: I'm in the throes of an acute crisis – the time has come when I have got to make up my mind, to buy or not to buy. To begin with, my parents went down to Devonshire a week ago yesterday to have another look at the house they are considering at Salcombe, and they have decided in favour of it and bought it! So one thing at least is settled. They are free to move in at the end of this month, but I think they probably won't leave Lido until they have a purchaser in view for otherwise it might easily be requisitioned. While they were away, on the Tuesday, I took Frances with me down to look at a house in Surrey; just to make sure I rang up the agent before I went to ask if it was still on the market and was told it was. However, when I got there I found the new owner proudly strutting round and examining his property, so I snapped the man's head off, rather unjustly I suppose, but I was somewhat mad, hustled Frances back the way we had come and caught the next train home. After that fruitless effort I received, on Thursday morning, the particulars of the house at Broomfield, outside Chelmsford, which I had seen the week before and mentioned to you in my last letter. It looked quite hopeful, so Mother and I went out together to look at it, and this is the house which may turn out to be your future home, for a time at least, or may not. *(Ursula gave a detailed description of a lovely old house)* – it is very attractive. The garden is small, which is the chief snag, but could be made very pleasant. The bus service into Chelmsford takes about 10 minutes and fast trains to Liverpool Street get in in 40 minutes, so that for your travelling to the City it is as good as could be hoped for.

On the Thursday evening I went over to Barnet to tell your people about my housing efforts and they seemed very interested and I think approved of my efforts to find something for when you come home. We went into the financial aspect – I have offered £1,250 and the agent has just rung to say she will take £1,300 but not less. Your father volunteered at once to lend us £200 towards the deposit money and I think my people would be able to lend £100, though till they have sold the Lido they are a bit tied up. Barbara says she would lend up to £100 too, so that is fine. I was very impressed with your father offering to lend me the money, for I should never have dared to ask him for it. Oh how I wish I could ask your advice about it all! I have got an option only till tomorrow. Sometimes I feel it is worth anything to have a home for you to come to and to tide us over the next few years, at other times my heart fails me when I think of all our earthly possessions and a liability for years to come being destroyed by bombing. I really don't think I could ever do better with as little as £1,300, houses are scarce and prices are going up. I don't much look forward to the prospect of living there alone with Frances this coming winter, but I might be able to get someone to share with me.

When next she wrote, Ursula reported (in letter 70): Things are now underway in the matter of buying 'High House' Broomfield. I told Grandpa I had decided it would be wise to buy it if the surveyor's report were OK and he sent me a cheque for £200, being his loan towards the deposit, as well as an introduction to his lawyer, F. Burges, of Walter Burges & Co. Moorgate. I made an appointment on Friday and went to see him, he was exceedingly kind and friendly, I discussed it all with him and he seemed to think that if the surveyor's report is OK the house would be quite a bargain for £1,300. He seems to be an old friend of your father's and in consideration of your present state also he said he would like to handle this purchase for me free of charge, which I think very decent of him indeed. It makes me feel much safer. So I paid a deposit of £130 on the house through him, and we now await the Abbey Road's surveyor's report. My people have fixed Aug. 10th for our zero hour here, and so I have to get on with our packing and get stuff away first. It's pretty ghastly, I loathe packing. *And a week later she told John:* Practically the only thing that has happened since I wrote to you last is – packing. The whole house is a welter of boxes and suitcases and piles of things awaiting packing, and we have been up into the loft heaps of times, bringing down forgotten treasures, many of them moth-eaten but some still worth keeping. I have arranged for our furniture to be collected from here next Friday and taken to Batty's warehouse to be stored until further orders. That will cost only £3.15, which seems to me quite reasonable, since it includes packing up all our china and stuff. It is a really gigantic job sorting and packing all our belongings, specially with Frances 'helping' all the time and taking odd items off up the garden, where I find them some time later! I did my last night's work from 7 till midnight same as ever. I have given my notice there and collected my last pay-packet, so once more I am one of the idle poor. I have also handed in the Penny-a-week Fund, and have wound up the Savings Group as well. Nobody in the Group would volunteer to take it over from me, so tomorrow I must take the whole works up to the local office and hand it back. I have had it almost exactly two years, and in that time we have raised over £800, which seems to me to have been worth while. I shall be so idle after this I may even have time to read!

Unfortunately our affairs as regards the house have not progressed any further, I am still waiting for the report of the Building Society's Surveyor, and the longer I wait, the more despondent I become. This evening I had a chat with Mr Neal on house purchase and building societies in general, and in the end I asked him if he would survey the house at Broomfield for me, and he says that if he can fit it in this week before he goes for his holiday he will do so. You see, even if the building society's surveyor does pass it and they agree to lend us the money on it, that doesn't prove that it is sound structurally, and I shall feel so much happier in my mind if I have an independent opinion on it and I am sure Mr Neal would give me good advice and not let me buy a pup. If I have to turn it down in the end, I just don't know what Frances and I will do. To begin with we are going to stay with Bunty down at Gable End, leaving here on Monday, today week, and I daresay we could stay a couple of weeks, but in any case that is only a holiday. I expect you have heard that Bunty is expecting her third, lucky blighter. What will happen to us after that I just don't know at the moment. My parents will be down in Devon and I suppose we could go to them for a bit, but frankly I don't want to stay for months and months. Frances is sometimes too much for them and it hasn't been all jam these past two months. And besides I do so want to get a home for you to come back to. I suppose this slowing up of mail was to be expected. Still, I don't enjoy it. Just now I am missing you desperately. I do hope you are alright in your new camp and have got somewhere to practise your fiddle.

Meanwhile, in Stalag Luft VI John was pining for news of home and the new camp was not proving as satisfactory as the old, as he informed Ursula in letters 111 to 113: We have been here long enough now to realise that it is far from being as good a camp as the last. It will be a long time before we have enough room for a sports field and the site for a theatre is still under discussion and when that is settled we shall have to build it. A library is promised soon and also a few rooms for education purposes. The big obstacle to all our plans is lack of space. However, given time, we hope to be able to build up something worth while. My fiddle practise is still a dead loss since xxxxx *(three lines of*

censorship) xxxxx in a small wooden barrack housing only 26. Frank
Pepper is the room leader and it was at his invitation that we moved
in. I like him a lot more than I did at first. I have also got rid of all my
surplus clothes to various new POWs but have retained enough of
everything. One big thing that we lack here is news. We used to hear
quite a lot at the last camp but since we moved we have almost
completely lost touch with the outer world – absence of mail also
aggravates that feeling. The climate here is wretched – dull, cold and
windy in marked contrast with that at Luft III. I have been curiously
disturbed by the move. At Luft III I had got into a 'lovely' rut. I was
fully occupied and worked quite hard – but here I have much more
time on my hands but cannot settle down to a regular routine. Once
my fiddle gets going (if ever) I shall be alright for it is more or less the
back bone of my activities and I'll build other things around it. ...

Have only had 1 letter from you in the month since we left Luft III
but that is only to be expected, I fear. However, some parcels came this
week. The local weather is shocking xxxxx I'm still tasteless but have
found a temporary haven for fiddle practice ... I have been doing
a lot of fiddle practice during the past week by dint of being extremely
persistent in my effort to find a suitable sequestered spot. I am getting
quite a reputation in the camp for being discovered playing the thing
in the most unexpected spots. Latrines are my favourite hideouts –
if for any reason they are unserviceable as regards their normal
function. But I don't turn up my nose at a felonious entry into an
untenanted barrack. Unfortunately as the camp is full now and the
latrines recovering from their initial teething troubles my quest for
practice room grows daily more difficult. I think I have played in at
least a dozen different places, some of them quiet and some containing
unwanted spectators busy on other things unconnected with music.
However, I shall persevere since I have much more time on my hands
here than at Luft III where I had a job of work to do. We have had a
tremendous amount of rain since we came xxxxxxxx every drop of
water xxxxxxxx we use has to be pumped – well some wag has adorned
one of the pumps with a placard bearing the words 'Per Ardua ad
Aqua'. Incidentally the pumps are always breaking down since they are
in use from early morn to late evening and cannot stand up to the

strain. We are promised a library very shortly xxxxx. We shall be glad
of fresh veg when their season arrives for we have had none for
months now. For fruit and milk (fresh) we shall have to wait till after
the war alas. Thank goodness for Red X food. … Many thanks for
sending off music. I need it badly now and am very short of strings.
Could you please send at least 6 'A' strings – one only lasts me a month
and the camp is very short of them. I loved your description of
Frances, her ways and progress. Send more anytime. xxxxx

In letter 115 at the end of July: Our mail address is now definitely Stalag
Luft III – no 'vias' or such like while for everything else it is Luft VI.
This is final and I'd be glad if you'd pass it on to anyone likely to write
to me. I am happy to say that my dormant senses are showing signs of
life after all these months of slumber. During the past day or two I
have been able to taste etc most of the time so I have got busy on some
of the chocolate and pipe tobacco I had accumulated. I am enjoying
life a great deal more than before. Just at the moment I am able to find
space for fiddle practice since one of our latrines is u/s and unused
pending repairs. I wish with all my heart that I could get a regular
place for practise. I'm looking forward to those exercises you sent, for
I'm badly in need of material to play and also strings of which there
is a grave shortage here. I've been doing a lot of thinking about our
own post war position (assuming that this war will end) and I grow
daily more certain that farming is not for us for years ahead. As I see
it, my duty (and inclination) is to provide you and ours with the best
standard of living within my powers and Touche undoubtedly offer
the best opportunity. My views on a home must differ from those
of a few months back when I visualised a more or less immediate
attempt at farming. I would definitely like it in the country, but until
I have found my feet once more in the city I would be unwilling to
encumber myself with some acres of land and their attendant worries.
The requested A strings had obviously not yet arrived. Thanks to
another latrine becoming u/s I manage to do quite a lot of practice
but am sadly short of strings. I have no 'A' string at all and am using
an old banjo one for that purpose. I think I progress but wish I could
have a permanent haven for practice.

In letter 72 (8 August 1943) Ursula wrote about the impending move:
This is the last letter you will get from Lido! Tomorrow Frances and
I start on our travels, and at the moment I have no idea where we shall
fetch up. As regards High House, Broomfield, I had gathered from
Mr Neal that the acceptance or refusal of the house as security by
the Society was no proof of its structural soundness and I asked him
to survey it for me. He managed to go and see it on Wednesday and
reported back in the evening that it really wasn't very sound; problems
with the walls and floors and he thought it would be very damp in
wet weather and altogether he advised against it. The same day I had
the reply from the Building Society and they also refused to grant a
loan on the house, so that was obviously that! Mr Burges, the Solicitor
is getting the deposit money back for me and I'm back where I started
from. I suppose I might have known that if the house had been
sound it would have been snapped up right away, but I just hoped I'd
been lucky.

However, I have to clear out of here because my parents are moving
into their new house in Devonshire on Tuesday, although they haven't
yet succeeded in selling Lido. All their furniture and curtains are going
so of course I can't stay on here any longer. On Monday I am going
down to Gable End *(Priors Marston)* with Bunty. Barbara is leaving
about ½ hour later taking up her new job with the YWCA somewhere
in Hunts., and my people go on Tuesday so it is certainly a parting of
the ways. All our furniture has gone to be stored by Batty's. I had an
awful job packing up our clothes because I didn't know until the day
before whether or not they were going into store for a few weeks only,
pending the negotiations of High House, or maybe for months and
months while I search around for another house. Now of course it has
turned out to be the latter, and heaven knows what they'll be like
when I get them out again! I suppose I shall have to start writing
round to agents again though I get very few results from them. I think
we can stay with Bunty for two or three weeks, if the children get on
alright. The thing I hate about it all is that your letters, which seem to
be as scarce as you warned me, will waste precious days or weeks
wandering round the country after me. I haven't heard from the new
camp yet and am anxiously awaiting news. For some time to come –

I hope it won't be very long – you will have to decipher handwritten letters from me, as the faithful typewriter had gone into store. …

Well Lido has gone – actually I believe Mr Neal sold it to a Polish Jew, the deal wasn't concluded when we left on Monday. … Unfortunately our housing problem hasn't begun to solve itself yet, but I feel there is little I can do about it from here *(Gable End)*, so I'm trying to put it out of my mind for the time being and enjoy myself. Frances and I went for a walk today and were watching some cows over a gate when the nearest one did 'potty'. Frances was staggered and accosted the first stranger we met to explain all about it and how the cow had got dirty feet. Luckily she doesn't talk very distinctly yet and I was able to turn it off! As the children *(Muriel, Robert & Frances)* seemed to be settling down well together, I decided to go up on Wednesday to look at a house at Fyfield. This involved getting up at 6 am to cycle in to Woodford to catch the 7.10 up to town. This arrived some time after 10 am, so I had a cup of coffee, proceeded to Liverpool Street caught the next train out to Epping, changed on to a bus to Ongar and from there hitch-hiked out to Fyfield, arriving about 1 pm. After some trouble and asking of strangers and deaf mutes I found the house and was bitterly disappointed. It was far too large and ungainly and very inconvenient – no proper kitchen or decent bathroom. The garden was neglected of course but even without that it wasn't nice. Altogether it was a flop and I was awfully disappointed. It took me till nearly 9 pm to get back to Gable End and so here I am with absolutely nothing in view. However, I suppose something is <u>bound</u> to turn up sometime.

By the end of August, with no immediate prospect of a house, Ursula arranged to go down to Devon to stay with her parents in their new house, Little Close, in Salcombe. But a few days before leaving she wrote to John. The week has flowed past very peacefully except for one terrific day, last Thursday. I have had a few replies from house agents with one or two offers, mostly quite wide of the mark financially, and from these I selected two possibles, neither very hopeful, and decided to go and visit them. The first was a modern 3-bedroomed villa in Chalfont St Giles and the other a large old house at Hatfield Peverel,

near Chelmsford. So I got up on Thursday at 6 am without waking the
others, and left at 7 to cycle the 7 miles into Woodford. Unfortunately
it was raining and when I got there I was pretty well soaked, specially
legs, feet and forearms. However, I partially dried off in the train
which I left at Amersham to cycle 3 miles to Chalfont St Giles. I found
the house, which is called 'Felmersham', Bottrell's Lane. The outside
is definitely dull, the usual semi-detached urban villa. The road is not
yet fully developed and there are lovely views of fields and rolling
woodlands but the houses there are not inspiring. Inside the house
is well planned and in good condition. The garden is not large, but it
has a few fruit trees and quite a lot of vegetables and a very small
lawn. Altogether I wasn't thrilled with it, but on the other hand it is
doubtless a sound, sensible house, convenient and easy to run, easy
to get rid of again. The price asked was £1,650, but I have written the
agent that I couldn't in any case give more than £1,500 and have asked
if the owner would consider that xxxxx I shan't know what to do
about it. It isn't as attractive a house as I had visualised for us, but
I am despairing of ever getting that within our price limits and this
at least is sound and serviceable, in a pretty locality and within easy
reach of town for you. On the other hand the price seems high to me –
all prices are these days! If only I could rent it I wouldn't hesitate for
it would do us quite nicely for a while. But the Rent Restrictions Act
has resulted in an absolute dearth of unfurnished houses to let, so no
agent yet has been able to offer me one.

So I returned to Amersham, proceeded to London, crossed to
Liverpool Street and rang up my next appointment. The agent
arranged to meet me at Chelmsford and take me to see this old Rectory
at Hatfield Peverel which he was offering for £1,050, with its 2 acres
of gardens. The house was very large, in very bad repair and had been
unoccupied for five years. The garden had possibilities though it was
terribly overgrown. But it all needed a mint of money spent on it, and
so no good for us. So I returned to London and got there too late for
the 6.11 pm train home to Woodford. There was nothing else till 10
pm, getting there at midnight with my 7 mile cycle ride still before
me. So I decided to catch an earlier train to Rugby instead, got there
at 9.30 with my bike and set off in the dark on an unknown cross-

country route. The first part of the way lay along 1st class roads but then it went off down a bye-road and got quite exciting. At one stage I rode into a herd of cows grazing at the roadside and they stampeded off in a fright and I drove them before me for a mile or more and had visions of escorting them all the way to Priors Marston, but luckily they shot off down a side turning eventually and I went on alone. My lamp was getting dim xxxxx I got home about 11.50 pm. Just about all in.

Four days later she informed John: In my last letter I told you of the 3-bedroomed house in Chalfont St Giles which I went to see last week. Much to my surprise the agent wired to say that the owner would accept £1,500. I expect even that seems a lot to you for a fairly ordinary 3-bedroomed villa, but considering that Lido went for over £2,100 you can see how things have gone up. I frankly admit that it isn't my ideal house but I don't think we have any chance of getting that within our price limits, specially since renting is out of the question. How I wish it were possible to rent, I'd much rather! This house is in a nice position, easy and convenient for me to run and will be easy to sell when we can fly higher. It is within easy reach of London, and in short I am negotiating to buy it!

John's letters through August were as compassionate and supportive as possible. I sincerely sympathise with you over your housing problems and admire your tremendous energy in tackling it. I wish I could help but I'm so distressingly impotent here. I shall take immediate steps to increase my allotment to you to the maximum possible just in case you need it. I'm somewhat relieved to hear of the negative replies from the Agricultural people and of course am all for your getting a house as soon as poss. since I agree with you that difficult as the matter may be now, it will be more so after the war. At the same time I realise that it would be more pleasant for you to live with your people until I come back and if you decide so to do I won't object. Anything you do has my whole hearted approval. I have signed two forms, one increasing my RAF allotment to you to the maximum possible dating from 31/5/42 and the other requesting that my remaining available credit in my RAF a/c be paid to you. It may be months before you receive anything but you should eventually have our entire fortune in your hands just in case you do manage to get a house or furniture. In case of need ask the P.O. if you may broach our joint a/c – to do which you have my full sanction. I am full of admiration for your tremendous efforts to find a home and deplore my helplessness more than ever. How I wish I could be of some assistance to you. I fully understand all your difficulties and from the bottom of my heart hope that you overcome them. Bless you for all your efforts on my behalf.

The violin, of course, received regular mention, such as in his letter of 20 August 1943: I'm very short of strings, the banjo string I was using has gone and I haven't an 'A' left, and am using an 'E' which is most unsatisfactory, thin and reedy. Please send me a few 'A's if you haven't done so recently. One by one, my havens for fiddle practice have disappeared but I now have a place which I had long born in mind as a last resort. It is awful – but that is why it is available. It's a semi-underground cellar used as a potato store. It is low roofed (sitting down I can't even get in a full stroke of the bow), dark (so that I have to strain my eyes to read the music), draughty, damp and oh! so smelly. Piles of spuds lie around giving off an awful effluvium of dank rotting vegetation. But it has space which is what I want. Considering my extremely slow progress I'm almost ashamed to mention the hours I put in nowadays when I can. 4 or 5 is not uncommon, in fact it is the only form of study at which I find myself able to persevere. Of course the conditions tend to vitiate the value of all this time, but nevertheless I ought to progress more. Am still badly in need of strings and eagerly await the music you sent. xxxxx am having even greater difficulties than ever in endeavouring to learn the fiddle. My own has started to split and while efforts are being made to repair it I have to use a shocking one rejected by everyone. *In John's letter 124, dated 15 September 1943, the situation was no better:* I am having an uphill struggle with the fiddle here. Every conceivable obstacle seems to arise to thwart my efforts. I badly need a proper instructor (though Harry Friend does his best for me) I am flat out of strings – haven't had an 'A' for months, have exhausted all my music and now to crown it have been evicted from the one and only possible practice room xxxxx. The

authorities xxxxx and can't imagine that I retire to the xxxxx merely
to practise a fiddle. They think I'm xxxxxxxx I'm trying to get the
order countermanded. Practice was difficult enough at Luft III but
here it's ten times worse. I hope some strings are on the way. I need
them badly.

*By 5 September 1943 (letter 122) John had learned of High House,
Broomfield.* I don't know yet whether you have bought the house but
I'll assume that you have. The house sounds so attractive from your
description – I hated the thought of acquiring a suburban villa.
I wonder if you are living there now. How I wish I could help you!!
I am very stirred by this news and anxiously await further details.
In letter 123: I wish I could write more about the house, which has
excited me considerably, but I'm just useless here. *And a few days later
in letter 124:* I was bitterly disappointed to learn that the negotiations
for High House had fallen through. Since first hearing of it 3 weeks
ago I had deluded myself that it was already ours and built a lot of
castles in the air based on that assumption. I'm terribly sorry that you
should have all the worry and trouble while I do not also serve but
merely stand and wait. I'm sorry that Lido has gone out of the family.
Some of my most sublimely happy memories are associated with it
(and Ashley Lane!). *And in letter 125:* Still haven't got over the
disappointment re High House. I didn't realise what a kick I got out
of picturing you and ours in a home of our own.

*In Ursula's letter 77 (7 September 1943), which John received on
15 October, Ursula brought John up to date with the house purchase –
and an unexpected blow.* As for our proposed house at Chalfont St
Giles, I have taken the preliminary steps but am not yet sure whether
or not we have secured it. I sent £150 to Mr Burges, our solicitor (!!)
to pay down as deposit. As regards this deposit, your father gave me a
nasty shock. You remember when the other house at Broomfield was
on the cards he had himself offered to lend me £200 towards it and
seemed to approve of the idea of my trying to get a house ready for
you. When that fell through I returned the £200 to him and so had
to ask for it again when this house came into view. This time he wrote

and said he had had other calls on his resources and could only lend me £100, which I take it means he is angry or disapproving of something, I don't know why. That means, now that he has suddenly cut me down by £100 without warning, that I shall have to raise the £75 out of the remaining Nat. Certs. in my name and so be left with absolutely no margin for emergencies. However, it can't be helped and I shall just have to avoid emergencies like the plague. I should also prefer to pay back the £100 to your father as soon as poss, if he is in such straightened circumstances. I will, tomorrow, get a withdrawal form for our joint P/O account and try to send it to you but doubt if it will get to xxxxx I wish you to transfer me £100 out of your RAF account to pay back to your father. He really is a difficult man. At first he seemed to think it was the right thing for me to do my best to get us a home, but now he says he 'has no doubt house property is a good personal investment if one has the means available' – as tho' I'm making speculative investments instead of straining every nerve to get a roof over our heads!

Letter 78 was still showing anxieties over the house at Chalfont St Giles:
I have given up expecting letters from you, looking for the postman and things like that, and when at last a letter does come it is a marvellous surprise. All the same, I wouldn't mind if they came a <u>little</u> more often! The situation re Chalfont is now as follows: Mr Neal has reported favourably on it; he thinks the price is on the high side but that that is inevitable these days; it is in good condition and should be easily resaleable when we want to move on. Mr Burges, the solicitor, has now paid the deposit of £150 on it and we are awaiting the verdict of the building society surveyors to know whether they will advance a loan on it. Mr Neal advised me to go to the Temperance Permanent Building Society, whose Managing Director he knows personally; and as I have no reason for going to any other I have applied there through Mr Neal and hope that his introduction may help to get the full 75% mortgage. I do hope that the fees and stamp duties don't amount to too much. It is all so awkward now that Grandpa has only lent me £100 instead of £200, but still I hope to get through alright if the Building Society is decent.

I'm just longing to settle down somewhere, and get our home ready
for you. It will be thrilling to have our own place at last, won't it
Johnnie? I hope you are not expecting anything too ambitious, it really
isn't possible with present prices. I shall have to buy some things if
I get the house. I have applied ages ago for a permit to buy utility
furniture but haven't received one yet. Thank goodness we bought
some decent stuff when we had the chance! It has occurred to me that
it would be a good thing if you would make available to me as much
money as possible out of your RAF account and also out of our joint
P/O account. I sent you a warrant to withdraw £100 from the latter
with my last letter. It hasn't yet been returned to me so presumably
the censors have kindly allowed it to go through. If this house at
Chalfont should for any reason fall through I should have to return
your father's £100 to him and then if I wanted to borrow from him
again for yet a third attempt he might well refuse or cut it down by
50% again, as he has done over this one, and altogether it would be
much pleasanter if our own money were available for me to use.
Communication is now so desperately slow between us that I've
simply got to be able to act on my own if I'm to act at all. *But in letter
80 (24 September 1943).* I have today heard from the Temperance
Building Society that they will advance £1,025 on 'Felmersham'. This
means that I have to produce £475 on the nail, which is rather a blow,
but I have £100 from ASV, £75 of our own and my people have very
decently consented to lend us £200 altho' the sale of Lido hasn't yet
gone through, tho' it's nearly completed. I do hope that this house
purchase will go through alright now. I have been buying a few tins of
paint, distemper etc to do a spot of decorating more to our taste, and
hope to go up and do that before I get the furniture moved in.

Apart from the housing problem, life in Devon was lovely: Here we are
installed in my parents' new abode, Little Close, a very nice bungalow
with a good big garden and a perfectly lovely view out to sea and up
the estuary. There is everything for a good holiday here, bathing,
sailing, fishing, riding, lovely walks and a garden to sunbathe in.
Frances is absolutely thrilled by the sea and all the xxxxx. We go down
to the beach each day, then xxxxx. Here Frances digs and paddles to

her heart's content. Luckily the weather is fine and warm and I sit on the sands knitting like the old dowager I am fast becoming. Frances and I are still enjoying ourselves very much down here. I have been fishing twice with twin girls of the name of Robinson whom we've met down here. We took a dinghy out, with attendant fisherman, into the bay and fished all afternoon till after 5 pm. The first day was very poor, only a couple of pollock and a mackerel, but yesterday I caught 6 fish myself and we got about a dozen all told. It's great fun and a very pleasant lazy way of spending an afternoon, rather like watching a cricket match! One day Frances and I went over the estuary in the ferry to get blackberries, and when we came back to cross over again we xxxxx *(met American service men)*. They gave Frances quite an ovation and before we'd got very far were singing in chorus 'She's got ginger hair, I never cared for ginger hair but she's got …' and so on. Frances was rather abashed I think. It's getting rather a nuisance the way people will pass remarks on her hair and ask facetiously if she'll give them a curl and that sort of thing.

In letter 127 (5 October 1943) John wrote: At beginning Aug I authorised RAF to pay you everything possible and last month I sent a Power of Attorney which will enable you to realise everything of value that I possess. Sorry you have been embarrassed for cash, I would have arranged things otherwise if I'd thought of imprisonment. I often contemplated death but strangely enough never capture. I'll know better next time! I wonder if you are settled now and have enough funds – I doubt the latter. Really delighted to hear of you enjoying some leisure at last. … I now have yours of 22nd Aug, 2nd Sept but not xxxxx I wonder if you have bought the house at C St Giles. From your description I share your opinion entirely. It's not what we wanted but if you see no other alternative you have my absolute approval should you buy it. The thought of you and Frances homeless worries me a lot. Life isn't very easy for you, my darling and I can do just nothing to help. You can be sure though that I shall endorse every action of yours and you have my very fondest wishes for success. Having the example of High House before me I'm not banking on your having a home already but eagerly await news. I can't say how delighted I am to hear that you have had something approaching a holiday but I don't suppose it was very restful or beneficial. Two months ago I ordered all my credit to be paid to you and the weekly allowance to be increased to the maximum. Let me know if and when you get anything.

My struggles with fiddle are no better as ever – particularly over the questions of space. I manage to average 3½ hrs daily – here and there but I would do much more if I could find a regular haven. I am really going at it with all my might but everything seems to be against me. Kayser studies are a boon and I get a lot of pleasure and instruction from a book you sent months ago. It has an awful title 'Old Master for Young Players'. You sent Book I, could you send Books II & III please. Also would you acquire, before I return, a good bow. My present one will do here but it's an awful one. Also if you could keep an eye open for a good instrument do so, with luck one can sometimes pick up a reasonable fiddle for a mere song. You may think I'm making too much of a fuss over this fiddle, when you have so many more pressing worries, but apart from letters from you and thoughts of you – it almost fills my whole life here.

In letter 130 (15 October 1943) John commented on his father's behaviour: Am very distressed to hear of my Father's attitude towards you borrowing. However, I've executed a Power of Attorney which gives you absolute authority to do as you please with everything of mine. It has been sent to you via the Red X together with the PO withdrawal form you sent. Please cash at will all my few savings certs., withdraw all my PO Savings and our joint one and sell my trifling investments if you need the cash. Many weeks ago I ordered my RAF allowance to you to be increased to the maximum and all back credits to be paid to you. Should that order have gone astray, the Power of Attorney will enable you to extract every available cent from RAF. If you wish to use the Power of Attorney, it has to be stamped I believe and I suggest you get 'our' Solicitor to do the necessary. You will then be in absolute command of the Mr & Mrs JRMV joint resources and your disposal thereof has my blessing in advance. If poss. I'd like you to get out of debt to ASV and to as many others as you can. I await eagerly details of your home creation efforts. Bless you for doing so much. Had a pleasant surprise today xxxxx. Had a delightful gift from Miss Hoare (unfortunate name) via Christine Knowles – 10 pieces of fiddle music. Please thank her sincerely (they were sent off beginning Feb.); she is very kind and this is a well chosen gift. Still having trouble with my fiddling. My instrument came to pieces two days ago and a brand new one which I was lent lasted 24 hours. They are of such poor construction that they split at all joints when stringing up. I've got another old one now which if not of good tone is at least sound. Had Leslie's letter – only 7 weeks in transit. Holding as you will do, my Power of Attorney, you'll have to fill in my Income Tax dope yourself – so there!! I love you as always. Kiss Frances. John.

Weeks passed with no news for Ursula of the property purchase, but she was making plans regardless to improve the house. Nothing much further has transpired about the house. I suppose the solicitors are doing something about it. It looks as though it will be a few weeks yet till we can move in. Mother is going to look after Frances for me for a week when we finally do get possession while I go up there, do a spot of redecoration and see the furniture in. I shall need to stain some of the floors for with our total lack of carpets we shall have to have stained and polished floors to display our few rugs to advantage. When we have visitors we shall [have] to bow them into the rooms backwards dragging the Persian rug with us to give an impression of continuous carpeting [*sic*]!! *Mail both ways seemed to be subject to long delays, each anxiously awaiting news of the other. But by 23 October 1943, in letter 84, there was at least more to report over the property sale:* Things have begun to move at last as regards our house. Mr Burges has sent me the contract to sign and it is all due to be completed by 30th Oct-ober. So I am arranging for the furniture to be moved on the 4th or 5th of November and I am going up a day or two before to do the painting and staining of floors. I do hope everything works out to schedule. There have been so many odd bits of furniture stored in various shops in London, which all have to be rounded up and delivered. I am also having a spot of bother about the piano. The Blind School have given an estimate for the repair amounting to £9.10 and now of course Mr

Herne is jibbing at paying it. *(This had been an ongoing battle which Ursula was about to lose!)* I have given him a time limit and shall then get Mr Burges to write him a solicitor's letter, though I have grave doubts as to whether we shall be able to force him to pay in the end. I should hate to have to pay it myself just now, but I <u>should</u> like to have the piano in working order ready to accompany you! The thought of having our own establishment at last is very exciting.

I do hope you will make some of our joint funds available to me as soon as poss. I won't spend a bean unnecessarily, but by the time I've paid for the moving in and essential black-outs etc I shall probably be down to rock-bottom and it would be nice to have some reserve for emergencies. I do love you so much, darling, and I'm just longing to have you home safe and sound. Do look after yourself. I'm afraid the winter will be pretty bitter in your part of the world. Frances is as full of beans as ever. I took her to church last Sunday but it wasn't a great success and we came out quite soon. She stared solemnly at the stained glass windows and then said in a loud voice 'Oh, look at those dollies.' Her other comments were equally inopportune and penetrating. I'm afraid it's Sunday school or nothing for her. I expected to be up in town today wrestling with the house-decoration, but the Solicitors apparently couldn't get it all fixed up for 30th October as at first arranged, so I'm still waiting. What <u>do</u> Solicitors do all day long? Felmersham is definitely not picturesque, it is only 12 years old, and it is hard for a semi-detached house to look picturesque. I was very glad to see from your letter that you approve of buying a house even tho' it hasn't all the land we wanted – we couldn't have afforded it. I was also very pleased to see that you have ordered an extra allowance from the RAF for me. I will give you more exact descriptions of your new home-to-be when I get there – I have thought and dreamed and wondered and calculated such a lot about it since I saw it over 2 months ago that I really can't remember any more what is fact and what wishful thinking.

John's continuing grim existence was described in letter 132, dated 25 October 1943: No fresh letter to acknowledge. Yours to 14th Sept here. Hope mine are getting through at long last. Managing to do quite a lot of fiddle practice now, sometimes in the strangest of places and most awkward circumstances. Have even spent a few hours in total darkness sitting on a pile of spuds in a shed, 'grinding out scales'. Am still having trouble with instruments – my own has been reassembled by enthusiastic amateurs here but is not strung up yet. I pray that the glue will hold. Have been unable to taste for 2 months – throughout a wretched cold which is going but slowly. Life is awfully dull – your letters and photos liven it up a lot and I'm eagerly awaiting news of house purchase. *And five days later:* Alas, nothing from you to acknowledge – little news to report either, except to reaffirm my dislike of this place in particular and captivity in general. I wonder where you live now and if we do in fact have a home of our own! I keep very busy here. My fiddling hours have gone up – sometimes 5 a day. I take a book keeping class and attend two others on music – one on History, the other concerning the Orchestra; in addition I'm sticking to Dutch and also am reading a little. All this in addition to the regular routine of parade for counting twice daily, fetching and eating food, washing up, washing and darning clothes – cleaning barrack etc. How I pity you poor women! I can't complain of time on my hands, but the monotony is grim and deadly. *On 10 November 1943 John wrote:* Very happy to have, today, yours of 6th Oct and glad to know that you've had some from me at long last. xxxxxxxx I'm always mild in comparison in my comments of local conditions which frankly a xxxxxxxx. My father tells me he has stopped sending tobacco and cigs until 'contact is renewed'. Most donors seem to increase gifts when supply route is threatened in the hope that at least a portion will get through. *And again on 15 November:* Life here continues to be unpleasant – the climate is awful and very little rain suffices to convert our crowded compound into a quagmire which is constantly churned by thousands of pairs of feet. In one respect I prefer it to Luft III though. I'm living with an excellent crowd of fellows (Frank Pepper's crowd) all of them POWs since 1940. The company is a great improvement on the Dutchmen only.

From letters in the last half of November, John expressed his frustration with his violin and the lack of mail getting through: I persist in my

fiddle study by the grim exercise of that quality of mine which you
term 'mulishness'. It is only recently that I have felt any real wish to
desist – chiefly because conditions for practice are absolutely and
undeniably xxxxx. I manage nowadays to average 4 hrs a day,
7 days a week, but those hours are spent usually in the most acutely
uncomfortable conditions with all sorts of noises going on around or
in painfully cramped, damp space. In addition I have been handicapped
by lack of strings, a wretched bow and finally, to crown it, my fiddle
came to pieces – through constant dampness the glue holding it
together gave way. We have attempted to re-assemble it but so far
without success and I'm using an awful old thing which no one else
wants. However, I do get a little fun out of it – particularly with those
pieces you sent – 'Old Masters' etc. I've finished these now and am
about to start on the stuff kindly sent by Miss Hoare. The Kayser
studies you sent are a boon and have improved me a lot since they
came. … No mail from you alas. There has been a noticeable falling
off recently. Hope you are getting mine now. I'd give a lot to be able to
write more often. Life not much different here – no severe cold yet but
awfully wet weather. A wooden hut, the xxxxx has been allotted to us
as a theatre – and we number 2,000 – any show will have to be done
many times for all to see. In one respect only is this camp an improvement on the last – facilities for organised education are slightly better
and we have 4 small rooms available for classes. These of course are in
constant use. I have no hope of a better place for fiddle practice and
may have to desist when weather gets really cold. I miss the photos of
you and Frances which Ba used to take. I often gaze longingly at those
I have. Will 1944 see us together? … A very bad month for mail – everyone is faring badly. Hope you are hearing from me more often now.

*Ursula had sent off parcels quarterly to John, but in letter 87 on
7 November 1943 she wrote:* I saw in the paper this week that a Red X
transport ship has been lost off Marseilles recently, and I am rather
afraid that the last parcel I sent to you may have gone down on it.
I can't bear to think about it! – those 2 pairs of long stockings that
I took so many hours to knit, and about 4 lbs of chocolate lovingly
saved for you. Still, if you go without a parcel for 6 months, you'll

know that it wasn't for lack of dispatching from this end. I do hope you'll manage to make your soap and toothpaste and shaving stick spin out as long as possible, just in case the parcel really is lost. I have written up to Chappell's today to get them to send you some more violin strings – how sad to think of you playing on banjo strings! – or aren't they very different? *(And on 25 November John told his wife:* Had the sad news today that the parcel you sent me in June safely arrived at the last camp and was forwarded xxxxx was looking forward to the blanket and slippers particularly and am running short of tooth paste and shoe blacking. The last month has been putrid for weather, not particularly cold but so wet! One result is that my senses have again vanished after 2 or 3 months service. I don't expect to be able to taste again until next summer at the earliest. My own fiddle has been glued together again and is behaving quite well.*)*

Meanwhile, the house purchase neared completion and on 14 November 1943 Ursula was able to tell John: I am going up to town tomorrow, Monday, hope to get the indoors distempering and floor staining done on Tuesday and Wednesday and the furniture is due to arrive on Thursday. That's what I hope – but there's a slight hitch because I haven't yet heard from my Solicitors whether or not the Vendor has agreed to let me move in before the actual completion of the purchase. I've had your letters of 25th July & 20th August this week – you can't imagine what a lot it means to me to know that you have full confidence in me over this house business. I have felt so wretched and uncertain sometimes not knowing what you would think about things. But now that you say you definitely want just a house in the country from which you can carry on at Touche, I feel that our new home at Chalfont just fits the bill and I'm ever so keen to get moved into it. I have ordered some fruit trees and bushes for the garden. I'm giving you a Cox's Orange Pippin and a Blenheim Orange for Christmas and you're giving me 4 gooseberries and 4 currant bushes. My people are giving me a pear and a greengage.

On Monday I set off up to London, altho' there was no news from our Solicitors as to whether I could have possession of the house on the Tuesday. I just hoped for the best. I got up to town at 5 pm and

rang up the Solicitor who said he'd had no news, so I rang up Mr
Horswell, the Vendor, at his home to ask if he'd mind my moving
in next day. He said he didn't care only I must conform to what his
Solicitors stipulated. Next day I went up to Walter Burges's office,
and Mr Blackman, who's handling it, was very helpful, tried ringing
up the other solicitor in Bristol who was out (he would be!), so I rang
Horswell, who was also out, but eventually we got him and persuaded
him to ring his solicitor and instruct him to accept the £475 instead of
the whole of the balance (£1,350), which of course I couldn't pay down
since the Building Soc. is lending us most of it and by 4 pm the whole
thing was settled and I set out for Chalfont St Giles; had to wait for
slow train and when I got there at 6.30 pm it was dark and cold, and I
tried at one pub after another for a night's lodging; to my horror they
were all full. I was in despair and I'd almost resigned myself to
sleeping on the bare boards in the dark-unblacked-out of our new
home when I nearly collided with a man on a bike turning in at his
gate. On the spur of the moment I asked him if he'd got a bed to spare
and it turned out that he had, and he and his wife took me in and
were most kind. They gave me bed and breakfast for the 4 nights
I was there, so I was awfully lucky, as usual! Later in the evening I
went to the Horswell's to deliver the cheque, and they said they would
have put me up. They are most kind and friendly.

Next day, Wednesday, I got to work on our house, gave the sitting
room 2 coats of cream distemper, and stained the kitchen & dining
room floors with solignum where there had been carpets or lino
before, with the paint etc I'd sent up from Devon. On Thursday, the
furniture arrived – gosh I was thrilled to see it and know we'd got it
out of London safely! The dining table is even lovelier than I'd
remembered, simply gorgeous wood and the sideboard beautifully
fitted out. Nothing had been damaged in transit at all! In the midst
of the unpacking who should walk in but Barbara! She had 2 days off
and badly needed some of the winter clothes which were stored with
mine, so came to collect them. On Friday I got more unpacking done
and measured up all the windows and bought the necessary curtain
rods from a very good ironmonger in the village. I've brought the
curtains back here with me and am making the blackout on Mother's

machine. I travelled down on Saturday *(to Devon)*. When I got back here I found Frances in bed with a temperature of 103! She'd got the flu, today she's much better, but now Mother has gone down with it and I've had a hectic day with Frances convalescent and Mother in a high fever! I wrote to the Red X and told them your violin was in a bad state, and they've written to say they've sent you a good one with extra strings, but it may take 4 or 5 months to arrive. Do you want me to draw £100 from our joint P/O a/c, if I can, to pay back your father or shall he wait? Irene & Bill now have a son. *And finally, on 28 November.* My darling Johnnie, this is a memorable day, for today we moved into our new home. How I wish you were here this evening to sit with me beside our very own fireside, monarchs of all we survey! As it is I feel slightly doleful, yet very glad and thankful to have achieved this much ready for your homecoming. Of course the main part of the work lies ahead, everywhere I look something or other is waiting to be done, but at least we have taken possession and our belongings are around us. I'm writing this in the dining room, by the fire in the Triplex which I fondly hope is heating my bathwater, but as I haven't yet mastered the various knobs and handles on the thing I may well be heating up an oven fit to roast an ox instead! Anyway, our new copper kettle is singing on the hob and I propose to have a cup of tea soon.

We decided to come up on Friday. The journey wasn't too bad, and we eventually got out to Barnet by 6.30 pm. We had a very pleasant evening with your Mother and Ann, your father was firewatching so we missed him. Leslie seems to be flourishing and has astonished everyone by turning down a commission. Irene's baby is called Gordon William Valentine Birnie, and is doing well. This morning we set out from Barnet in good time and Frances and I arrived out here at lunch time, a horrid cold wet day. I got the fires lit, unpacked the black-out which I'd sewn in Salcombe on Mother's machine and sent off in advance, and put it up (one parcel hasn't yet arrived so some of the windows have temporary black-outs in spite of all my staff-work!) and also put in the electric light bulbs which Peter had sent in advance for my birthday present. Then I had to go out and buy in the rations and some food while Frances stayed in the house playing blissfully with her long-lost toys. Now Frances is safely asleep in her own cot, and I shall have to go the same way soon. I've no idea what the time is, for I haven't been able to connect up the electric clocks yet and none of the other timepieces are going either!

By December letters appeared to be getting through and John wrote:
I now have your letters, complete I think to 6th Oct. I do hope you're getting mine at long last. I've been writing to you steadily for 6 months and had no reply to anything. It almost seems a waste of time. Delighted to hear that the Blg. Society will advance money on the house and hope the purchase will go through. I'm very excited at the prospect but just a little anxious for the financial side. We're assuming a bigger liability than I ever dared contemplate and I can only hope that we'll pull through somehow. Conditions here continue unpleasantly. We have had a month of incessant wet – rain, sleet or snow; and the muddy state of the camp is indescribable. Fortunately our coal ration is just about adequate and we manage to keep warm and dry indoors. Will be glad when it freezes permanently so that we can walk about with dry feet. If the house purchase goes through I hope you'll give me a detailed description of it. Is it detached, how far from Station, how big garden etc. etc. I hope you manage to get our furniture from David Hayes and the piano from the other bloke. I wish we hadn't left that other suite of furniture in that warehouse by the river in 1940! I'm afraid you'll have a lot of hard work settling down and also you'll be sadly short of cash for ordinary removal and 'starting up' expenses. As a helpmeet I'm pretty useless I'm afraid, especially when I'm most needed. Best of luck in everything, my beloved – you'll need it, I know. I'm thoroughly browned off here but not mad yet. Your birthday will occur in 3 days time. Would that I could be with you then to wish you well personally and in my own fashion. However, I shall think of you more than ever on the 8th (if possible, for you're always in my thoughts). Do you ever contemplate the first gorgeous moments of our future reunion – and the subsequent bliss. I can assure you that I do – often. Please give your parents my warmest thanks for the generosity in lending us all that cash to enable you to try for a home. I wonder, though, how we can

possibly repay them. Am afraid that I shall never see my June parcel.
I was looking forward particularly to the slippers and blanket – there's
nothing to be done about it though.

On 10th December John wrote again: Definite news of house purchase
is still wanting but you had to wait and so must I. I hope to goodness
you can cope financially but how we'll manage when I have to live on
the same joint income baffles me. Your birthday *(8 December)* also saw
the commencement of the big freeze-up. Everything outside is solid –
and a blessed relief, too, from that awful slush of the past 6 weeks. An
appalling climate! It's bitterly cold now but hard underfoot – no great
depth of snow yet. Coal ration adequate. Cold at night – I could do
with that blanket in the missing parcel! To mark the occasion I made
one or two resolutions on your birthday, one of which was to do some
fiddle practise in the very early morning – before the rest of the camp
awakes. I've done it twice now, it is extremely cold, but it ensures that
I shall be fully occupied for every minute of the day. I've never been
so absolutely busy in all my life. My fiddle is standing up to the hard
wear it gets. Most days I do nearly five hours, my average for a 7 day
week is over four, which I hope to increase. The active expenditure
of time is far greater for I tour the camp, going from u/s lavatory to
potato cellar, to cook house etc. looking for a vacant spot, hovering
about until it is vacant and then putting in furious practise until
dispossessed. Very disheartening at times and I often feel like
throwing in the towel, which reminds me – please definitely include
light underwear and socks in next parcel. Have had no fags
or tobacco for 3 months – stocks still good but not unlimited.

*By 20 December John knew that the house sale was nearing completion
and also that Ursula was staying with her parents in Little Close.*
Delighted to hear of the approaching completion of the contract
for house purchase. I hope everything has gone smoothly but I shall
continue to write to you at 'Trifle Oppressive' until I hear definitely
that you have moved. I'm afraid you have a bigger job ahead of you
than you realise but my faith in you is so profound that I know you'll
manage, but, believe me dearest, I'm fully conscious of and grateful

for your struggles. I wonder what the outcome of the piano dispute was and also if you managed to collect everything intact from David Hayes. I'm dreadfully sorry that you have to 'harp', as you term it, on the subject of my increasing your cash resources. I don't mind you 'harping' on it – I'm fond of music anyway – but I do wish the mail situation was better so that you could know that I've done all I can. … Heard results today to Music Exams sat at Luft III. Have passed the simple one – Grammar of Music and a cert. is waiting at Royal Schools of Music, London. Try to collect it, please. I failed the paper in Harmony – the first exam failure of my life. The only fellow to pass was he who was trying to instruct us. The frost has failed and we're back to the awful slush again. My early morning efforts at fiddling have resulted in an awful cold – the 2nd already this winter. See if you can get any recompense from Red X for my June parcel which has been lost. It's an awful shame that all the labour on the blanket and money in the slippers should be wasted. I don't expect they'll listen but you could try.

In letter 91 (5 December 1943) Ursula had been in the house for a week and sent John a detailed description of it including the amazing Triplex stove, which seemed to be able to do everything! And she told him that There is a space between cooker and sink for a refrigerator, but alas when I asked your Mother about the one she said we could have, she said it had been sold to someone else! *Ursula listed all the decorating she had started and was planning to do; future furniture that would be needed and plans for making some basic furniture out of old packing cases etc. In her last letter of the year she was down in Devon and described the first joint Christmas for the Griffin family for seven years.*

"I just want to be alone"

'I just want to be alone'.
John practising in the incinerator room in Heydekrug, March 1944. John's final practise room.

Chapter Seven

1944

John's first letter of the New Year (no. 144) described his delight that Ursula had finally managed the purchase of the house. Hearty congratulations on your energetic procedure in getting possession of house and tackling the work of decorating etc. Pity I'm so bloody useless! Hope you won't overdo things. Please send full details of house and garden, I'm dying for news of it and so keen. Thanks <u>so much</u> for getting another violin and strings sent. You certainly do everything you can for me. If you can possibly repay ASV without crippling yourself financially, I'd like you to do so. Please send Irene my congrats. I shall be able in future to write only once a week and will do so each Sunday so you can keep a check. This is my first this year and I'll write next on 9th Jan. Four years ago today, my darling, you and I were married. I love you more, if possible, than I did then. The climate here continues to be indescribably awful. We get spells of severe weather when everything is solid, mingled with periods of the most terribly damp slush which nobody can withstand. I'd give a lot for the missing parcel. The low temperature adds another difficulty to my fiddle practise. Please don't imagine that I'll ever be able to play. Musically I'm naught but a clod and I suffer acutely from harmonic amnesia (loss of melody). Nevertheless I struggle along, undaunted. *And a week later he wrote again as promised:* No mail from you, alas, since last year. I [am] eagerly and anxiously awaiting news of progress with the house. I don't know if I shall ever be free again but should I return I'd like to give Frances a grand present so that she will be able to associate my appearance with something pleasant and possibly get to love me on the strength of it. If, when my day of liberation approaches, would you search around for something she would really treasure, buy it and keep it hidden until I come on the scene. *(I found it very moving that he should have had the sensitivity and discernment to think that there might be a problem when he returned. In the event he was correct, although I don't remember it; apparently both he and I were very jealous of one another and made life miserable for my mother for some months.)*

The weather here continues atrociously. Lots of slush, fair amount of cold – most unpleasant. I keep very fit though. Had a cig parcel from 'The Wardens' (bless them) my first for about 4 months. … Waiting (always waiting!) eagerly to hear if you have been living at Chalfont and details of everything you've done. So far winter has not been severe but most unpleasant on account of damp. Some months ago I saw British MO re my nose and he suggested 'washing it out' daily with quantities of solution of boracic and salt. It has worked wonders, I get rid of a lot of nasty coloured mucous every day and my tasting although not always in working order, is very much better. My only exercise is an occasional circuit of the compound but I feel very fit despite the ever present torture of the climate. … Almost a blank year so far for mail from you only 1 letter and so I'm still in the dark as to where you are living and how you are coping. Having no winter at all here. The bitter cold was short lived and we're back again to fearful slush. I've managed to get a new pair of boots out of the Red X Store xxxxxxxx. We have here the worst climate imaginable but I'm extremely fit strangely enough although I have precisely no exercise. Ever since we've been here the Red X Food Store has been well stocked and the usual issue is 1 British and 1 Canadian parcel on alternate weeks. We thus get, I consider, ample sugar, tea, a little cheese, jam, prunes and other delicacies. What I miss is bulky food e.g. Bread and veg. I'm certainly xxxxxxxx I love you so much dear, John.

Ursula returned to Felmersham from Devon on 11 January. Frances and I got back home after quite a pleasant journey. Frances made friends

with some American sailors who fed her on peanuts, which she loved,
and chewing gum, which she swallowed whole in spite of all our
admonitions, much to their amusement. When we got back here,
at about 7 pm we found an enormous pile of mail waiting for us,
35 letters and 5 parcels! I have been very busy for the last 3 evenings
coping with it all. ... I am very agitated about your next parcel, due to
go off at the end of this month. Honestly I don't think it is worthwhile
sending you a lot of stuff, the prospects are looking so much brighter
nowadays. I haven't had any mail to speak of for ages, so I don't know
if you have asked for anything special, except the walking shoes which
I am hoping to get for you. I haven't had time to do any knitting these
last couple of months, as you can imagine! There will be chocolate in
it anyhow, two month's ration – and not mine either! When we were
in Salcombe the good soul who serves in the small local grocer's shop
heard about you, and as it was near the end of the sweet rationing
period and she hadn't used hers, she handed it over to me to spend for
you. Soon after, a friend came to see us and also heard about you, and
by the next post she sent me her sweet ration and her husband's, and
I've bought chocolate with that too. People really are awfully kind!
PS. 12th Jan. Just received Power of Attorney and POSB £150
withdrawal notice. Many thanks. Will use latter to pay ASV, but won't
need former, I hope.

In her next letter, no. 97 (16 January 1944), she told her husband: I have
received a letter from the RAF stating that you had been promoted
to Flight Sergeant on 1.5.43 and to Warrant Officer on 1.8.43. My
allowance is increased by 2/6 for F/Sgt, and 4/- for W/O, making 6/6
weekly in all, and they have issued a new order book for this amount
and also sent me a warrant for £9.6.0. for the arrears in this increase.
I reluctantly wrote and informed Touche of this change in our estate,
so I suppose I shall get a corresponding amount deducted from my
allowance from them. I suppose that your RAF pay has also gone up,
which is a pleasant thought, though I suppose the backlash of
income tax will spoil most of that. But I am very glad indeed about
the promotion for your sake on your return, for I suppose you won't
get out of the RAF right away. Warrant Officers have rather a pansy

uniform, haven't they? *Ursula also mentioned John's brother Leslie:*
An airmail letter card from Leslie arrived this week, written just
after Christmas. He says they had a remarkably good Christmas
dinner served right up in the front line – he seems to be in the thick
of it just now. *Leslie's whereabouts could never be described and when
he was in Libya Ursula told John that he was between Uncle Tom (in
South Africa) and Sidney (a relative in Portugal)! And later, when he
was in Italy, that he was making his way towards home.* You may have
heard from your parents that Leslie has got his commission at last.
You remember that it was offered him and he would have had to go
back to base for 6 months to train, and he turned it down flat. So
now he has been given his commission in the field, a jolly good show.
He has been wounded in the knee but I gather it is not serious. *Ursula
also brought John up to date with news of his sisters.* Irene and her baby
Gordon are staying in Barnet just now, indefinitely I believe, as Bill
has a resident job in a hospital so that there is no point in Irene living
in digs nearby. There seems to be a certain amount of hard feeling
because Irene feels it is her turn for an innings at Gable End, whereas
Bunty of course cannot possibly move with three children (the third is
due this month), and it is felt that Stewart ought to have fixed up
something else for her instead of going off and leaving her literally
with the baby. Grandpa and Grandma also feel that Gable End will
hardly be a rest cure for them with another infant there. Altogether
I am extremely thankful that we have an independent abode now.

*Every letter brought John up to date on what was happening in their
house.* I have been busy making up the new curtains for the sitting-
room. The material is hessian dyed brick-red (no coupons, that's
why), and I have also got a design for embroidering them in wool to
make them look a bit more expensive and I have now started on that
Herculean labour – I doubt very much if they will be finished before
you arrive! … I have executed another of my inimitable pieces of
carpentry, this time a corner hanging cupboard for the spare room. I
will say this much for it, it does serve the purpose intended, and I have
hung a curtain in front so that my carpentry is not exposed to view.
… I have bought two more fruit trees. You will think that fruit-tree-

buying is becoming a real vice with me, but this is really the end of it. There were two pieces of blank wall in a good sunny position that simply asked for a fruit tree to be trained there, and since the sooner we plant them the sooner we shall get fruit, I thought I might as well do it now. I have actually signed the agreement for the house! It has taken five solid months to get that far! Now I have to go up to town to sign the Mortgage to the Building Society, and the Horswells have to sign the Agreement, and then the house is legally ours. How glad I am that I didn't wait down in Devon till the deal had gone through.

On Friday I sent off your seventh parcel, not very thrilling but I trust that the chocolate at least will be welcome. I wonder very much whether it will ever reach you, I shouldn't be surprised if you were on the move six months from now. Sorry to learn about further troubles with your fiddle, but glad that a decent one is on its way to you via Red Cross. Of course you must not give up practising! I have also ordered six A strings for the violin to be sent to you from Chappell's, and have obediently written to thank Miss Hoare for the music she sent via Miss Knowles. I am perturbed when you mention that you sometimes feel like giving up the fiddle, though considering all the difficulties and the impossible conditions for practise, I can only wonder and admire that you have carried on so long. I suppose the weather may defeat you for the worst winter months, obviously you can't practise if you're frozen stiff. But oh, I do so hope that you will take it up again when it is a bit warmer. I will send you some more music too if you could give me any idea what sort of thing you'd like. I should think some Haydn and Handel would be nice, and I must send you the Mozart piano and violin sonatas book for I have got a copy, it would be lovely to play those together. How I wish I could get the piano repaired so that I could start practising too. At the moment there is no pleasure in playing it at all, even the pedals don't work, so I really must have it done and it was supposed to be taken for repair this month. I must write and remind them again. I hope the good fiddle which the Red Cross are sending you will arrive soon.

Last Monday Roy came out for the day as arranged. It was very nice to see him again. I hope he has written to you to give you his impression of your house. He has volunteered for a chaplaincy;

I gather he is very unhappy with the new vicar recently planted on
him and simply must get away. He doesn't know which service he'll go
into – can you imagine him a Sq/Ld? Yesterday Eileen Johnson came
for the day, She has no news of Frank, I'm afraid he must certainly be
written off, and now, poor girl, her young brother has gone the same
way, about a fortnight ago; of course there is still hope she may hear
from him. *(And eventually Eileen did hear that Frank was a POW.)*

Brighteyes is still abroad, he hasn't been home at all, but apparently
has been able to console himself for he has written to Peggy
announcing he doesn't love her anymore, so she's very cut up too.

Last Tuesday was a momentous occasion for both Frances and
me – her first dancing class! She had been looking forward to it most
eagerly. There was no trace of shyness at the dancing class, no clinging
to Mother's knee; she boldly marched into the middle of the hall with
the others (all somewhat older than she) and thoroughly enjoyed
herself. At first she just stood and gazed at the teacher and the other
girls (and one small boy) but soon she got the idea and tried to copy
them. Of course it was all very elementary, but apparently thrilling
to Frances. The crowning glory was when they sang and mimed 'Baa,
Baa, Black sheep'. At '3 bags full' they had to hold up 3 fingers, and
Frances was so absorbed in making her thumb hold her little finger
down that she missed most of the rest! However, she mastered her
little finger in the end. She also had an argument with the teacher as
to whether it was 'none for the little boy who cries down the lane'
or (our version) 'one for the little boy who lives down the lane'. She
compromised in the end by saying that the little boy would have had
one if he hadn't cried. Ever since then she has been pestering me to know
if it's time for the dancing class again. I consider it a good 2/6 worth.

Finally, John wrote in letter 149 (13 February 1944): I am tremendously
excited at the thought that at last we have a place that we can call our
own (even if we do owe 90% of the purchase price) and I am very very
keen to know all about it, its size, locations, rooms and their layout,
neighbours, garden etc etc. Please, in due course, send me every
possible detail of it and of all your heroic labours in fitting it up and
furnishing it. I gaze from afar in amazement at your manifold

activities and am deeply grateful for all you do and thirst for news of progress. This is the first letter I've addressed to the house because I did not know before if you had actually moved in. Home creating nowadays must be like making bricks without straw. Frank Pepper hasn't heard from his wife for over 4 months and is very depressed. Could you find out from Olga if there's any particular reason for the silence. I'm certainly luckier than he in having you for a wife. I hope your gloomy forecast re. my Sept. parcel proves wrong. It would be hard to lose 2 consecutive parcels. I'm running short of boot polish and ran out of toothpaste weeks ago. What is the final outcome of the piano business? ... I read again and again all your details of the house, carefully studying your sketches and generally enjoying the thought of having a home to my name. Delighted to hear of the labour saving and apparently economic system of heating and cooking and glad to know that electrical appliances figure to a certain extent. Of course there are gaps in the letters (non-arrivals I mean, not erasures) but I gather you've contacted D. Hayes for odd items of furniture. Try to get as much from him – let cash be your only bar if rationing can be overcome. Hope Frances enjoys her dancing lessons. Good idea anyway. This month has been our coldest yet but not exactly unbearable. I'm not feeling too bright, my last cold lingers, taste, of course, gone and nose bleeding a lot. However, I've escaped the xxxxxxxx. In my room every single man has had either flu or bad cold xxxxxxxx. We long for the end of this wretched winter and hope for big events in the spring and summer.

John's no. 150 (postcard) of 20 February 1944 was sent to Miss Frances Valentine: My dear Frances: I am afraid that it is already too late for this card to arrive before your birthday but at least it will tell you that I haven't forgotten all about you and hope you had lots of presents and that among them was one from me. Perhaps I shall be home in time for your next birthday and be able to give you something myself. Mother writes a lot to me about you and I'm so pleased and proud to know what a good little girl you are. While I am away, I hope you will look after mother well and see she behaves herself always and is [a] credit to her daughter – she wants some looking after, I know but you must do your best. Have a happy birthday, Frances. Love, Father.

Ursula was beginning to get to know her next door neighbours, the Horswells (who had built the house) and lived next door. Yesterday Frances and I went out to tea. Mrs Horswell's daughter, Gwen, has invited us to tea with her at Chalfont St Peter at least three times and each time one or other of them has fallen ill and the visit has had to be postponed. But this time we brought it off. The party was actually not at her house but at the Dogs Home (don't laugh). She is very friendly with the three girl veterinary surgeons who run the Dogs Home, just down her road, two of them are married and have small girls too, and the whole house is run in the wildest Bohemian disorder, and smells vaguely of goats. The children had a grand time, played noisy games and danced, and I enjoyed myself too, for the vets are intelligent and interesting, if slightly unusual in their housekeeping methods. *And there was another dancing class:* The class is going to present 'Snow White' at the end of the summer term and Frances is to be a rabbit! All those in the youngest class are to be small animals of various kinds, and Frances's great moment comes when she and another rabbit come upstage and comfort Snow White who is crying. She did this with great compassion last week. I get a great kick out of listening to her conducting dancing classes with her toys at home: 'Now then, children, spread out , point your toes' and so on. ...

On the business front Ursula went to London to sign the mortgage papers for the house and have the documents attested by a solicitor. The Horswells have now sold their house, and expect to move out by the end of March. The purchaser is a gent by the name of Brown, an elderly bloke who is going to live there with his valet! I shall be sorry when they go, they have been very friendly and helpful. There is still no news about the house; that is to say, nothing from the building society intimating that they would like some money. Both the Horswells and I have signed the agreement, so I wonder what they are waiting for now. Wonderful people, solicitors!!! *(In her letter 103 of 27 February Ursula had finally received the book for the mortgage pay-ment records and arranged for a banker's order to pay the monthly amount of £6 16s 8d.)* I have had three postcards from you since last I wrote, dated 10th and 25th October and 10th November, and a letter of 21st June!! … I'm very upset that your Father has stopped sending smokes. Does he mean by 'contact is renewed' that you don't devote enough of your mail to Barnet? I must find out tactfully whether he has started sending again; if not, I will do so. Thank you so much for your postcards darling. Your remarks on the weather do not seem to be appreciated for they are often censored. I do hope your fiddle is holding together now and that the new one arrives soon. I have started practising the piano again though there is not much pleasure in it with the instrument in its present sorry state. I have heard of a piano tuner and repairer in Chalfont St Peter and have written to him.

By 20 February (letter 102), Ursula had a new activity: A slight change has come to our household. At the beginning of the week I wrote to Fulmer Chase, the maternity home for officers' wives, to ask if they ever need a temporary home in the district for their expectant mothers, and if so to offer them accommodation here. The objects of this move were three: 1) to help the said E.Ms. since I have had personal experience of what it is like in digs at that crisis in one's career; 2) to provide myself with occasional company which, however, had the advantage of being strictly temporary; and 3) to make a spot of cash. I had no answer from them until on Friday a gentleman by the name of Clarkson Webb called on me. I had pointed out to Fulmer Chase that I couldn't start till next week – however, Mr Webb didn't know that and he was in a bad spot, as his wife was ill in bed and their only maid had temporarily deserted them because her husband had come home on leave, and the poor man was trying to cope with three or four of these wretched young women, including taking them by car, generally in the dead of night, to Fulmer when their labour started. So of course I said I would take one for the weekend, and again after Barbara had gone, and so on Saturday, with practically no notice, I found myself a boarding-house-keeper! The lady in question is a Mrs Kay, who has still a fortnight to go, so she is coming back to me when Barbara goes. The Webbs charge their E.Ms. 3 guineas a week so presumably I shall do the same, and if this goes on I shall be able to pay for having the house repainted much sooner than I expected! Of course it is much easier to cater for three than just for Frances and me and altogether I am quite enjoying my new role; she comes from London and is glad to be out in the country for her last few weeks, so I feel it is a good arrangement all round. ... Mr Webb still undertakes the transport of the maternity cases, and as soon as my E.M. shows signs of trouble, I trot her over there and they take her to Fulmer by car. If it happens in the middle of the night, as I suppose is likely, I shall have to trot over and call him. Oh for a telephone! I am going to apply for one, but haven't the faintest hope of getting one fixed during the war. Mr Webb is arranging a bell-pull out of his bedroom window so that I can get him out in the night if necessary without rousing the whole house. Seems queer for me to be doing the serenading, but that is how it is these days!

A week later, on 27 February, Ursula wrote: It is the queerest thing how Frances and I have managed to live here quietly and undisturbed for three solid months, and now all in a single week we have been besieged from all sides by people wanting to come and live with us! First our Expectant Mother, Mrs Kay, had to be farmed out somewhere else in the village *(while Ba was staying)*, and in addition no less than four people have come asking for rooms! Our neighbours had apparently noticed that Frances and I appeared to live alone in the house and deduced therefrom that there must be room to spare. One came and asked me if I would take in an officer and his wife, another was a middle aged business man and his wife, then came a man enquiring for rooms for a friend with wife and six year old daughter, and yesterday a girl looking for rooms for her aged mother and father. This is mostly owing to our vicinity to London, of course, and I regretfully had to turn all the applicants down. For one thing I have neither bed nor bedding for more than one – the Utility bed which I have on order will not come for several months yet, and even then I shall have to buy another mattress. And until we get ourselves some eiderdowns we haven't enough blankets either. Anyway I am quite satisfied with my one E.M. at a time, and consider her a priority case. All the same, it is rather funny how they all came in a rush.

Probably when Mrs Kay goes into Fulmer Chase, there will be no more applications. However, her baby isn't due for another 10 days, and knowing how unreliable first babies are, I can't make any arrangements in advance. Ba left early on Friday morning, and Mrs Kay arrived back for lunch, and now the household has resumed its routine; Mrs Kay gets up pretty late, 9.30 or so, which is really an advantage because I can get a lot of the cleaning done beforehand; she potters round in the morning, we have lunch at 12.30 and afterwards both she and Frances retire for their rest, then get up and we go for a walk or shopping together. Tea at 5, when that's cleared away I read to Frances till her bedtime; Mrs Kay retires soon after 9 pm and peace is restored. *The saga of getting the piano repaired continued. In spite of a solicitor's letter, Mr Herne obviously refused to pay for the repairs that Ursula was convinced that he had agreed to. Ursula had written to a local piano tuner.* Yesterday he turned up, and had a look at the instrument. He said he couldn't do the major repair, all the refelting and so on, but he took the action out, adjusted it a bit, repaired the pedals which had ceased to function altogether, and tuned it, and found out that the chief cause of the awful rattling and reverberating which I had suffered from was the fact that the action was only loosely screwed into the frame, or perhaps had come loose in transport. Anyway, when he tightened it all up, it sounded far better, in fact quite bearable, so I have decided not to have anything done to it for the time being. The cost of repairs is up about 300%, so if we can carry on till after the war we can get it done probably better and certainly much cheaper. And now it is at least possible to play it with pleasure and that is the main thing. So I was let off with 10/- instead of £10, and feel very relieved.

It was lovely having Ba here for a few days. Frances now says her prayers at night kneeling beside me while I sit on a chair and 'hear' her. When Ba was here she performed this office and one evening was wearing a dress with buttons down the front. Frances's attention is apt to wander a bit, and she said 'God bless Mother, God bless Father, God bless Grannie, God bless button, God bless another button, God bless another …' and had to be hastily recalled to the business in hand. She also confuses Heaven with Hendon, and we get into rather deep theological water sometimes. I think Roy ought to come forward

and do his stuff, but when he was here he did nothing about it at all!
Poor Ba, she is in a pretty low state; she had apparently fallen quite
seriously in love with a fellow called Jock, who went missing five weeks
ago. Poor girl, I know what it feels like, let's only hope she may be as
lucky as I was, though somehow I feel she won't be. I feel so desperately
sorry for her, if only there was any mortal thing one could do.

In early March Ursula finally learned of the lost June parcel, which had
… arrived at the last camp and was forwarded, then the rest is blacked
out. I gather that it is missing, but I hope not for good, I can't bear
to think of all the work that went into that rug, and the warmth you
would have derived from it, being lost. The slippers too were nice
ones. I do hope it will turn up eventually, but can't tell from your
mutilated postcard what has happened to it. I was so glad to see from
your card that your fiddle is repaired and hanging together, and I do
hope the better one from the Red Cross will arrive soon in good
condition. … Now I have done another thing against everybody's
advice and my better judgement, viz. I have agreed to take in a young
mother with baby, instead of sticking to expectant mothers. The latter
are far less trouble of course, since they are not ill and rest a lot of the
time and there is no extra work entailed. But last Tuesday I found a
letter waiting for me on the mat from a Mrs Hodson, a young New
Zealander xxxxx who had just had her baby daughter in the Fulmer
Chase Maternity home and had to spend a fortnight in the post-natal
home Fircroft and was due to go back to London to her in-laws,
neither aspects of which she looked forward to. She wanted a home in
the country indefinitely with her small baby and was rather desperate
since she has no friends in this country. Altogether I felt sorry for her,
knowing what it is like to come out of a nursing home and find people
not too anxious to take in a young mother with baby – remember
your frantic searchings for digs xxxxx so I rang her up, and the next
day we went over to Fircroft, the post-natal home and met Mrs
Hodson and her baby. She is a charming girl, about my age I should
say, and sensible, wide-awake and intelligent. In short, I agreed to have
her, and now of course I am looking forward ever so much to having a
wee baby in the house again. There is a lot to be said for E.Ms. the fact

that they are so temporary and no trouble and so on, but on the other hand for these very reasons it is much easier for them to find a home in the country for a week or two than it is for a mother with baby, and since I am willing, in fact glad, to have a mother and baby, I think it is better I should and leave the E.Ms. to others, who are better equipped with telephone and car. So my Mrs Hodson is coming as soon as Mrs Kay goes. There are advantages in having Mrs Hodson too, being more permanent the income will be steadier (I suggested £2.10 a week) and I shan't be terrified of leaving her alone for ten minutes together while I go out shopping, as I am with Mrs Kay, lest she should pop!

In letter 105, dated 12 March, Ursula wrote to John: A lovely letter and a postcard from you this week – it is amazing how my spirits and temperature go up when I see your dear hand writing! I am so grateful to you for your generosity and for your complete trust in me and my handling of our affairs – the latter I find particularly inspiring since I know, and you must know too, that I am not too hot on the mathematical side. However, everything seems to be well under control so far; this week I have proudly banked my first earnings as 'landlady'. This landlady business seems to be much the surest way of making cash, there is a terrific demand for accommodation. At one time I thought I would like to get rich quick, so I wrote a song about the RAF, very patriotic and all that, called 'Good Show, Bomber Command'. You can imagine it was pretty bloody, but it didn't seem to me to be much worse than the rest of the slush which comes over the radio. However, the music publishers didn't agree with me apparently, and simply wouldn't see what they were missing by not publishing it. So it is doomed to obscurity, and long after I am dead will perhaps be discovered and acclaimed for a masterpiece. It has four verses and a chorus, and when you come back we will render it as a piano and violin duet and give ourselves a good laugh!

I have had other hare-brained ideas for raising cash, but the only one that brings in the goods is letting the spare bedroom! My Mrs Kay began to have slight pains last Friday and decided she would be safer in Fulmer Chase, so Mr Webb carted her off in the evening. Mrs Hodson, the New Zealander, with her month-old baby, were due to come on the Monday, so I heaved a sigh of relief for a quiet weekend, as I had already decided I must do the redecoration *(of the dining room)* before mother and baby arrived, so I set to work on Thursday evening after I had got Frances to bed, and proceeded to scrape off the paper with a special tool I had bought for the purpose. Some of it came quietly, but mostly it was tough, and by 11.30 pm I had only done about a third of the room. On Friday night I resumed the good work, and was looking forward to a weekend on my own to finish it, when on Saturday morning bright and early another E.M. turned up, said she knew Mrs Kay and so deduced I had a room to spare, and could I possibly put her and her husband up for the weekend, as the wretched man had 48 hours' leave. Of course I could hardly refuse, leave being what it is, so I had a hectic time turning out of the double bedroom into the single room, and doing a lot of baking. The gentleman in question, a Lt. in the army, turned up for tea. This afternoon I decided to ring up Mrs Hodson to find out if she was coming tomorrow, for if so I should have to distemper the dining-room tonight, but luckily for me she isn't coming for a few days because her husband has a chance of leave, so that gives me time to get my breath back and finish off the dining-room. *Later she told her husband:* It certainly doesn't pay to do distempering by artificial light; the result next morning looked simply awful, so I had to go and buy another pot of distemper, and spend Tuesday afternoon applying a second coat. Maybe with this wartime paint you really need two coats anyway. Now at all events, it looks pretty good, and the room looks infinitely larger and lighter without that dull dingy paper.

I then had two days to get my breath back and then early on Friday morning Mrs Hodson and her wee baby Carol arrived, and since then life has taken on quite a new aspect. I agreed to take her and the baby in the first place more because I was sorry for her as a stranger in our midst and all that, but now it looks as though it is going to work out splendidly, and I am thoroughly enjoying her companionship. She is a B.Sc. in biology, keen on gardening, plays the piano at about my standard, likes all the same things to eat and is altogether adaptable and pleasant to have in the house. The baby, being only 6 weeks, doesn't make much impression yet, she is quite good except that she insists on having her 6 am feed at 3 am. However, that is Mrs Hodson's wrinkle, and when the baby cries I just feel sorry for her, turn over and go to sleep again. Frances is simply thrilled with having a baby in the house. She insists on watching the bathing and feeding every day, and yesterday Mrs Hodson let her hold the bottle for a little while, while the baby was sucking it, and Frances was just thrilled to bits. Now all her toys have become infants and I am constantly being admonished to be quiet because Bunny is sleeping or Teddy is having his bottle or Golly is on the pot. It seems amazing that Mrs Hodson has only been here three days, so well have we fitted in together. Another great asset of Mrs Hodson's is that she owns a sewing machine. She is keen on dressmaking and smocking too, so that we have lots of things in common. As to financial arrangements, she is paying me £2.10 per week, and is quite content with it. So that ought to help a bit towards paying off our debt to my people, if she stays here for some time. I do hope she will, but of course it all depends on her husband; if there is any chance to be with him naturally she will go. They have been married 4 years and have had altogether about 3 months together! He is hoping to get leave in a month or so and will come here. She tells me he loves making and mending anything in the carpentry line, so maybe he will do a few odd jobs for me!

Ursula's letters were typed on both sides of very thin blue paper. When a remark of hers needed to be censored the ink completely blotted out whatever was typed on the other side. On at least five occasions this happened and the British censor hand wrote in the margin the sentence that would have been lost! The first time this happened was in her letter 106 (19 March 1944). There is a chance that my Father may take a job after all, he has applied for one somewhere in the frozen *('north viz Scotland which seems simply', hand written by the censor as it was on the other side of the sheet where the info about Mrs Hodson's husband was censored.)* It seems awful to me now that they have that delightful home in sunny Devon. I suppose they would let the house, but I'm sure Mother will hate doing so. I'd hoped that Daddy had made up his mind to settle down at last, but apparently the urge to work is still in him. *The arrangement with Mrs Hodson continued to be satisfactory to both.*

Of course I am taking care to save every bean I can towards paying off my parents. Tomorrow Mr Hatchett is due to start the house-painting, which really is a necessity; once that is paid for, all my savings will go to pay off our debt to my people. Mrs Hodson ought to help a bit towards that. I like her more and more as time goes on, we have managed to fit our timetables in together pretty well; of course the garden is constantly festooned with nappies and twice a day the dining-room is turned into a nursery (because the fire is there), but I can never forget all the kindness I received both from Mrs Sandford and Mrs Howie when I was in the same spot, so I'm glad to be able to help her. I think it is quite good for Frances too not to be the only pebble on the beach. When I tick her off for some misdemeanour, she always has a long explanation of why she had to do it, because it is Wednesday (or alternatively because it isn't Wednesday) or because Gonging (the creature of her imagination who seems to be responsible for everything both good or bad) is coming to tea tomorrow or some other fantastic story.

There have been a lot of discussions and talks on post-war housing recently, and the more I hear about the dim prospects, the more thankful I am that we have a house of our own. I had an airgraph from Leslie last week, cheerful as usual, though of course he can't give any information when he writes. I laughed a lot at your description of yourself as 'musically a clod' and your 'harmonic amnesia'. You can't think how I am looking forward to playing with you (and not only that, of course!). The other night we were saying prayers and had just finished when Frances said 'I 'gotten to say Bless Grandpa.' 'Alright, say it now.' 'Oh no, I can't be boddered' and she proceeded to get into bed! Pat and I get on very well together. I wasn't really conscious of being lonely before, except when assailed with longing for you which of course no one but you can ever assuage, but I am sure I should miss Pat very much now if she were to leave. Her husband xxxxxxxx hopes to get leave soon and spend it here. The house painting is going on well, if not very fast; Mr Hatchett suits himself about when and how long he works. I hope it will all be done before your people come out after Easter. I'm dreading that day!

All through March John received mail usually written at least three months earlier. In No. 152, 5 March 1944 he wrote: No mail so far this month but some tobacco from the faithful Miss Hoare. I'm greatly struck by the kindness of so many total strangers. I wish I could get a parcel (clothes etc.) from you. Haven't had one for 9 months now and supplies of socks and boot polish running low. No toothpaste at all. Can't say I'm overjoyed at my promotion – anything that comes merely through passage of time isn't worth having. Frank P still not heard from wife. Am still slaving away at fiddle; such drudgery and such miserable conditions for practise and NO progress! *But a week later.* Yours of 12th & 19th Dec here – to my great joy. Once again I thoroughly enjoy all the details of your activities in house and garden and of course was filled with renewed admiration (not that it ever flags, believe you me). Very glad to hear of your profitable day visit to Barnet. I hope you conveyed your gratitude, even if you didn't feel any. My people like to be thanked. Now that you are well and truly established and slaving [...] to get things in order, I long more and more for my liberation – I'm so confoundedly useless here.
Thank goodness the winter nears an end. Although it hasn't been unbearably cold we've had snow in 5 consecutive months (and are still getting it). The real thaw began a short while ago and the camp is in an indescribably xxxxx it really is most unpleasant – just like the entrance to a field which grazes a large herd of cattle. The coming summer promises to be xxxxxxxx. Hurry up the end! As to my fiddle, I'm losing the urge. I'm hopeless and conditions are so beastly that I sometimes feel near hysteria when baffled either by inability to cope or by obstacles to my being allowed to play. However, I'm just driving myself on not with any hope of succeeding but because of unwillingness to admit defeat. If ever I get a place for practising in which I can stand up, have enough room to wield a bow without hitting roof or wall, do not have to put up with obnoxious odours, decaying veg, banging, shouting, ribald comments, bad light, rivals etc etc I shall feel in paradise. God! How I hate this life! However, the thought of you is a never failing source of comfort. ...The camp is drying up a bit after the awful period following the thaw and I have recovered my good health and sense of taste. Since I've been a POW

my zest for farming has diminished and has been replaced by an
absorbing interest in music. Of course I spend hours per day on my
fiddle, read a certain amount on the subject and listen to records
whenever possible. There are many and varied recordings in the
camp. My hope is that you and I can go into the subject seriously
when we're together. It has certainly made a tremendous difference
to my existence here and my interest grows instead of flagging as
with other activities which I have from time to time taken up.

*At the end of March John commented that letters were taking three
months on average to arrive.* I wish a clothing parcel would turn up.
I haven't had one since early last July, 9 months ago. We are still in
the grip of winter and experiencing more snow than ever before with
drifts literally of several feet in height. At the beginning of this month,
it thawed and the camp eventually dried and drained itself to a
tolerable condition. Subsequently it became bitterly cold and 2 days
ago started snowing in real earnest and is still doing so. In some ways
the camp is better than when we arrived. Sanitary conditions are
vastly improved and if somewhat crude are at least satisfactory.
We also have a small theatre – each show has to be done 13 times to
allow all to see it. Internally, we are well organised and every inch of
available space used for something or other. The site and climate will
never be improved, of course, but the worst feature of the present
xxxxxxxx. I am very fit, still grinding away at the fiddle, conditions for
the practise on which grow steadily more difficult as overcrowding
increases. Being at my wits' end for room in which to fiddle I braved
the scorn of the camp today and used a brick built dustbin cum
incinerator (it wasn't burning). It was pretty cold but otherwise
satisfactory if smelly. *And later:* My latest venue for practise, an
incinerator, is a success although cold and dirty. At least I am isolated
and don't worry others. I am still hopeless but persistent. I won't drop
the fiddle if it is humanly possible. *And again:* My practise in the
incinerator is a great success – I get almost absolute solitude (dirt
and cold also) for about 6 hours per day, but alas I make no progress.
And in May Am still practising violently – in my incinerator. In the
opinion of the camp I'm 'round the bend' (or mad) a common disease

here. However, I'm fairly convinced that I'm sane enough despite my taste for curious practice rooms.

Nearly three weeks since your last letter and no prospect of the next for some time, according to our official statements. The mail situation has steadily worsened during the past year. Three months is the average time taken now compared with 6 weeks. 30th Jan is the date of your last letter and I'm thirsting for news of you, the house and Frances. Have received another 4 books from Stockholm (sender unknown). They weren't worth reading so I gave them to the library. I'm still sitting for a few hours in the incinerator. It is still very cold and I've developed chilblains and another wretched cold but thanks to that excellent treatment of the M.O. my senses are preserved intact. I shan't touch the Argotone you so kindly sent until this other treatment fails. Its success so far is 100% and it has made a great difference to my life here. I'd love some more photos of you, Frances and the house, I often look through those I have and offer a prayer of thanks to Ba without whom I would not have them. I hope you are well and succeeding in all your labours with house. How I wish I could help. Hope no bombs fall near you. If so, you'd better retire to Devon and keep yourselves intact for me! Frank P still not heard from wife.

Has everyone gone to sleep in England? We wait patiently but old Jo (Stalin) seems to be the only active body nowadays. Please give someone a shake. ... Is there any chance of action from Britain this decade? (apart from R.N. & RAF). The stories of strikes (even apprentices – God Almighty!!) and stagnation in Italy make dismal reading while old Jo goes steadily marching on. 'The Kriegies' friend' we call him. Some of my 4 year colleagues are almost losing faith – one or two their reason, alas. Are still getting regular supplies of Red X food, but despite increased mouths to feed we have suffered 3 cuts in spuds during the winter. However, we aren't on our knees yet. I believe Frank P has now had 1 letter from his wife in over six months. Winter is now definitely over but spring is very timid. What little grass can be seen from within the wire has turned green but there are no other signs of vernal awakening. How the hell did Irene's old man get out of the service? Could he give me any hints? Has Bunty's third turned

up yet? What brand? I think of you incessantly, dearest, and yearn
so ardently.

*Ursula went to Devon for Easter in April, writing to John of the peace
and plenty.* There are fields simply carpeted with primroses, and
hedgerows blue with violet and now the bluebells are pushing through
too and will soon be in full bloom. Yesterday morning, Easter Sunday,
Frances and I went for a walk in the woods on the other side of the
estuary to pick some primroses for Grannie. Frances was very
absorbed in the serious business of trying to pick long stalks and not
just break off the flower head, but I was diverted by the sweet picture
she made, her golden curls bent down near the pale yellow primroses
while the spring sunlight streamed through fresh green leaves to light
up her hair. *When John received this letter on 25 June 1944 he replied:
'I loved your description of her on that sunny March morning. I wish
I could have been with you.' However, Ursula soon returned to
Felmersham and wrote on 16 April:* Yesterday was your birthday, and
I kept thinking of you all day long and wishing terribly hard that
you were here, and hoping that we shall celebrate your next birthday
together. Surely it must be over by then, if not long before. I long
above all things to be able to make you happy, and to try to make up to
you a little bit for all you have had to go through. The last time I wrote
was from Salcombe where Frances and I were enjoying a peaceful
Easter holiday with my parents. We came home again last Thursday,
to find everything alright at home, and Pat (Hodson) very relieved to
have us back again. I think it had been a bit much for her looking after
the baby and the house; and her in-laws, who I imagined were staying
here helping her, only came for 2 nights and apparently didn't do a
thing for her. Anyway, it is all more or less in running order again
now, and I can hardly remember that we have been away at all. The
house *('painting is finished', hand written by the censor again)* but the
gates haven't come back from being repaired yet. The Horswells have
now left next door and I am very sorry to see them go, they were such
kind neighbours. Mr Hubert Brown hasn't yet taken up residence.
There followed a description of all the flowers in the garden. I have tried
to mow the lawns, but our lawn mower, the little one from Lido which

Mother gave us, is a temperamental sort of machine and only cuts
when it feels like it, and then not very close. After struggling with it
for a bit I went across to old Mr Wallace who lives opposite and asked
him for a spanner to try to adjust the thing. It ended up with him
bringing his own good mower across and cutting half the lawn for
me! It really looks quite nice now, only I haven't been able to trim the
hedges as we have no shears, as yet. Shears are hard to come by; I was
thinking of giving you a pair for your birthday but haven't been able
to find any. So I shall have to try to borrow some. Also the step ladder
for the loft, which I ordered and paid for at the end of March, has not
yet been delivered, so in the absence of the Horswell's step ladder I
have no means of getting up to it. I hope mine will come soon. Your
clothing parcel is now assembled and due to go off next Wednesday.
It contains *(among other things)* the blanket to replace the rug which
went astray, and I do hope it will arrive safely, though I wish you
could have left long before that. However, the future is very obscure
still, so I thought I would be on the safe side and send it.

Frances had a second birthday when we got back here, consisting
of a couple of parcels waiting here for her, and our present, the
famous grocer's shop. Pat had made her a cake, iced it and put on
F.M.V., and also gave her a discarded feeding bottle complete with
teat, which Frances thinks is marvellous and uses constantly for
feeding Bunny or some other luckless toy. She was very thrilled with
her grocer's shop too, I filled up the various little jars with real
groceries for a start, a few lentils, beans, a bit of rice, flour, cornflakes,
broken biscuits and so on. She got the idea at once, announced that
she was Miss Pusey (our grocer), and proceeded to mix the contents
of the various jars together into one glorious mess. This afternoon we
had a couple of U.S. soldiers to tea, xxxxxxxx quite pleasant for a chat.
*In her next letter Ursula said she had bought a violin that was supposed
to be quite good.* The bow needs some repair and I am going to have
that done. It is complete in a case with mute, spare bridge, tuning fork
and so on, and I do so hope you will like it. I feel such a fool knowing
nothing of fiddles, but anyway it wasn't devastatingly expensive (£4).

John's youngest sister Ann came to stay: She brought me one piece of good news, that a Swedish friend of your father's had visited you about 6 weeks ago and had found you in good health and spirits. *(John wrote to his father regarding this on 19 March 1944 saying 'it was grand to speak with someone from outside the barbed wire' and that he had asked for a violin bow!)*

I was ever so cheered to hear that, it seems to bring you so much nearer to have news of you in March, since most of your letters are about 3 months old when I get them, I was particularly glad too, because in your last postcard, dated 6th February, received yesterday, you mentioned that there was a lot of 'flu in the camp, and I was just beginning to get nervous when Pat pointed out that you couldn't have got it because you were fit and well 6 weeks ago, or if you had you were better. The atmosphere in the house gets quite tense at 9.15 every morning, when the postman is due, and when we hear him we drop everything and dash to the door. Of course Pat gets far more letters than I do, four or five a week, but then her husband seems to be in action most of the time, so I am not envious. ... Mon. 24/4/44: Many thanks for yours of 15th December – congratulations on Grammar of Music Exam result, I'll certainly try to collect the certificate, well done! Do hope the Swedish friends will be able to send you a decent fiddle bow.

John's postcard written at the end of April said: Nothing from you since the beginning of the month. How I miss it! Very cold here. I have felt colder all this month than during the whole winter – there's no sign of spring yet either. Yesterday was my seven hundredth day of confinement. How many more I wonder? Have received 10 books from Sweden, sender unknown. Unfortunately all were thrillers or Western Stories so I've handed them to the library. Still no sign of your parcels of last June, Sept or Dec and no tobacco or cigs for months. My fiddle has been repaired by a chap here and is very good now. Wish I could do it justice. *And a week later:* ... a month since I had any mail from you. Am longing for some daily. Had 2 small tobacco parcels from Miss Hoare (bless her) but no other for months. Frank P never gets any so I have pooled all my present stock and future receipts with him and another unfortunate. Shocking weather here – rain, mud and wind. Had a game of football today – my first exercise since last autumn! What little landscape that can be seen from here is as bleak as in mid-winter. No leaves on the trees yet and the fields bare. The mail situation is shocking nowadays. It's impossible to keep up any correspondence with you, yet there's so much I want to know about you and the house. My patience is being sorely tried! April was the worst month ever for letters.

However, by the middle of May, in letter 162 to Ursula: Yesterday was a gala day for me: 12 letters – 6 of them from you, dated at regular weekly intervals from 6th Feb to 12th March. What a treasure you are – each letter is long and full of interest for me whereas everyone else gets only those horrible and very limited letter forms. Thank you, darling for writing at such length and so regularly. I hadn't heard from you for over 5 weeks. I wish they'd come as regularly as they are despatched. ASV's tobacco has started arriving again so don't worry on that score. If you can, I would suggest having the piano renovated while we have the cash. Once again I stand amazed at your terrific energy and purposefulness – this time at your P.Gs. You certainly do your bit to help others. E.M.s. must be a bit of a worry though and while seeing the disadvantages I favour the Mother and Babe proposition. I hope you get suitable people though. I know how I would have appreciated someone like you in April 1941. I still go faint at the recollection of my worried state then. The cash aspect is pleasing – but don't, I implore you, undertake this venture for that alone and please spare yourself – don't overdo things. Very sorry to hear of Ba's trouble. You talk of Frances saying her prayers. I wonder if you have my letter telling you about my beliefs. *(John had written to say that he had finally decided that he could not accept Christian beliefs.)*

I hope to convert you someday but what about Frances if we two don't agree? Still no sign of clothing parcels – my last one received was sent off in March 1943. Let Red X know, would you. The June '43 one got to Luft III but failed to make the grade here. The skates arrived 2 days ago – MINUS BOOTS. I try hard to keep gloom out of my letters to you. Frank P. is now in his 5th year of incarceration. I feel very sorry for him – he rarely hears from Vera (once so far this year) and gets no tobacco from anyone. Love to both as always, John. *In the previous camp the POWs had managed to keep abreast of news fairly well, but it was much more difficult in Heydekrug. At the end of May John wrote:* We're getting xxxxx nowadays and all anxiously awaiting action somewhere. Are you hoaxing us? Am a bit anxious about Leslie these days. Hope he is safe.

In letter 113 (7 May 1944) Ursula was able to write: At last your letters addressed direct to this house are beginning to arrive. I have yours of 27.2 and the P. C. you wrote to Frances for her birthday, which thrilled her very much. It is so nice to think that now you know a little about your future home, and I do so hope that you are satisfied with it; I am, although of course there are always things I want to do to improve it. Anyway I think we ought to be happy here. Perhaps we should be happy anywhere providing we were together, but much more so in a little home of our own. It was my turn for cooking, not going to church (on alternate weeks I cook on Saturday and go to church on Sunday, and on the other Pat goes to church). So I did a vast bake, because we seem to be having a lot of people coming next week, including I hope Barbara and Vera Bowack. Then I had a visit from a local Red Cross bigwig, asking if she could help me with my parcels to you. We discussed the question of my doing a spot of work for the Red Cross locally, so I may find myself charring in a hospital soon! Perhaps you will hardly believe it, but sometimes I actually envy you! I envy this unparalleled chance to tackle a new subject and extend the scope of your mind.

This resulted in an amazed response from John on 24 September 1944: It took me a little while to recover from the shock of knowing that you 'almost envy me'. My dear Ursula, you little know this life then. I admit that we have time on our hands but that is sadly interrupted. Apart from that I see no sign of the 'unparalleled chances' of which you write. The life is mean, sordid, humdrum from day unto day ad infinitum. Beauty is absolutely lacking – I miss that as much as anything. Facilities for study are almost impossible – our billets are so dark, noisy and terribly overcrowded. Food is monotonous and not over plentiful (to say the least). The petty trials of temper are so many (and so petty). Toleration from others of any personal peculiarity is non existent because monotony and close proximity magnifies all things. Tempers are so friable. Altogether it's an unlovely life and I haven't dared to repeat that remark of yours to others for fear of defaming your character which I take care to stand high in the opinions of my fellow POWs! I have always painted you in your true light – that of a perfect wife, ideal companion and a woman of personality, character, enterprise and ability.

In early May Ursula wrote: On Friday I went into Gerrards Cross to collect the films which Pat and I had developing there, and I hope to enclose some of the snaps with this. Unfortunately my camera is still leaking light rather badly, so the photos aren't too good, but they may give you a slight idea of the house. That was my one and only film, and I am afraid it is very unlikely that I shall get hold of another. In a week or two the Polyfotos of Frances ought to be ready. I am awfully sorry to hear of Frank Pepper's total lack of mail. I am going to write to Olga and will enquire tactfully about Vera. She must be a pretty low sort of toad, the future doesn't look too bright for them. The chief event of the week was the purchase of a pair of shears – quite an achievement these days, I can tell you. They only cost 5/11 too, and seem to be quite good. As a result I spent Saturday afternoon clipping the edges of the front and back lawns. I had a letter from Grunfeld this week, enclosing a copy from Nilson describing a visit from a Swedish representative of some sort to you. I suppose this is a different chap from the one your father told me about, is it? You live in quite a social whirl!

Frances is very keen on laying the table for me, and she doesn't do too badly at it; gives us large forks for desert occasionally and that sort of thing, but on the whole she is pretty good – for her age. She is awfully sweet with Carol too, and makes herself quite useful to Pat in collecting and assembling the requisites for Carol's bath. In one of the photos I am sending herewith you will behold your daughter sitting in a cardboard box, deeply engrossed in the intricate business

of putting a nappy on her Bunny Rabbit. She has even learnt to fold
Carol's nappies into double triangles. I am sending all the snaps at
once, instead of spreading them out over as many letters as possible,
because I am afraid mail communications may get even worse when
things really get moving. The main preoccupation at the moment is
the news that Pat's husband Frank is coming on leave next week. Pat
is in an absolute fever, has gone clean off her food, and spends all day
making herself new clothes to greet the occasion. He hasn't had a
week's leave for over 6 months, and has been in one or two notable
actions, so there will be great celebrations. The baby is to be
christened on Sunday 21st May, their wedding anniversary, and I am
to be one of its godmothers. So I am busy making myself a new dress
too, with some material which I bought last summer and never had
time to make up.

In letter 115 (22 May 1944) Ursula wrote: This letter probably won't
contain much sense because I'm writing it at the dining table still
littered with supper things, at which Pat and her husband Frank are
sitting smoking their cigarettes and making rude remarks at me.
They have volunteered to do the washing up for me, chiefly because
I have looked after their baby all day while they went gadding off to
Windsor, so I am making the best of it. (They will keep talking!)
This week has been pretty hectic. It started off with Vera Bowack
arriving on Monday evening with Desmond FitzGerald, an old friend
of Norman's, for supper. I am wondering if perhaps Desmond may
some day take Norman's place. Vera stayed for the night, and left next
day after lunch on the same bus as Frances and I. We were going to
the dancing class. Then Barbara came for two nights. I wanted to meet
her, as I knew she had some awkward luggage, but didn't know quite
which train she was coming on. However, I worked it out that she
might arrive at the bus stop at 8 pm or 8.27. At 7.50, when I wanted
to get out my bicycle to whizz down and meet her, I couldn't find the
garage key anywhere. I searched frantically, but it was nowhere to be
found, so in desperation I seized the triangular file and proceeded to
burgle the garage by filing through the padlock. I got down to the bus
stop soon after, but she didn't arrive on either bus, so I decided I must

go back and see that the children were alright, and then go down again and meet the 9 pm bus. This I did, and was half way down to the Pheasant again when I met her trudging up the hill, an enormous brown paper parcel under one arm, a cake tin with holes in the lid on the other, and a strange lady walking beside her carrying her suitcase on her bicycle. This kind woman had gone right out of her way to help Barbara, who had succeeded in arriving on a bus that wasn't even down on the timetable! It turned out that Ba had brought Frances a kitten, a wee ginger job, five weeks old, with blue eyes and white spats.

Yesterday was the Hodson's fourth wedding anniversary, and the baby was christened down at St Giles church. I was godmother, and managed to find a small silver bracelet in Gerrards Cross for half a guinea which I presented to the infant. We had a teaparty to celebrate the occasion, at which were present Frank's mother, two sisters and a girl who lives with them, and on Pat's side Matron from Fircroft (since all Pat's relations are in New Zealand). We had a posh cake, decorated with some of the flowers I saved from our wedding cake. It was rather amusing about that too. Pat was sent several cakes for Christmas and she gave away most of them but kept one specially for Carol's christening. When the great day drew near she asked her mother-in-law to send out this parcel, which she hadn't unpacked, and when it arrived here it turned out to be not a cake at all but some other tins of food! So I had to set to and bake a cake after all. Anyway the christening went off according to plan. Frances is thrilled to bits with her kitten, and I am afraid she is going to throttle the poor little creature with her excessive passion. I have to intervene constantly to save its life, but the kitten seems to like it and always goes back to Frances for more. It is as yet by no means clean, and I am trying to train Frances to wipe up after her cat, but she is not too good. … I am sending you this week the photo of the front of the house. Sorry about the splodge of light right across it there must be a leak of light in the bellows of my camera, as *('so many of my snaps suffer', kindly handwritten by the censor)* from this defect. However, I hope the photo will give you some idea of our establishment; Frances stands in the gateway, from which the actual gates are still missing, awaiting repairs. My Aunt Con writes that Miss Hoare, your benefactress, has just died of heart failure, I'm so sorry – for your sake too.

Ursula's letter 116 was written on 28 May. My own darling Johnnie, there is still no mail from you – I have a nasty feeling that letters are going to become scarcer and scarcer until they practically cease to arrive as the war draws to its climax. However, if the fact that mail is getting rarer means that the war is drawing closer to its end, I can put up with it quite stoically. Of course it is far worse for you to be cut off from news of home. I believe I have told you in earlier letters that at the end of our garden there is a piece cut off, which geometrically should obviously belong to us, on which Mr Horswell built himself a massive series of outhouses, about 10 ft tall and consisting of various sections, the rest of the ground he used for a chicken run. I have been coveting this bit of land for a long time, so at last I plucked up courage to approach our new neighbour, Mr Brown. He turned out to be quite docile, to my surprise, and said at once that he would consider my request either to sell or rent the land to us. I really haven't the faintest idea how much the land is worth; it is not large, but the building is probably worth something, though not to anybody else, since I shouldn't think it could be taken away.

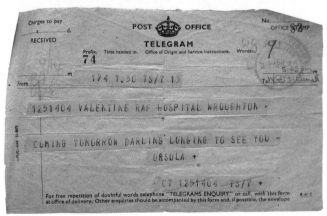

Telegram exchanges between John and Ursula 22 April 1945.

Chapter Eight

After D-Day

On 11 June John wrote to Ursula: Unhappily I am still without mail from you and am fearing that I'll have to go on very short rations of it in the future. The stirring news of the past week has thrilled us all but doubtless it will lead to further mail delays. However, I'll willingly go without your letters if our reunion is hastened by the same cause. Optimism is rife here as a result of our wonderful invasion but I'm not indulging to any great extent. If I could be home in time to celebrate your birthday I'll be surprised and that is the most I hope for. Since my capture I have started several varied intellectual pursuits, but all have petered out after a few months with the sole exception of the violin, my interest in which grows steadily stronger. With the warmer weather I'm able to practise a lot more and it now occupies all my available time everyday. I do nothing else nowadays, not even reading. I've started playing duets with another fellow and for want of proper material he and I play 1st and 2nd violin respectively of a few Mozart quartets for strings. Mind you, I don't play well. I scratch badly and am rarely in tune and eventually a bar or two behind or ahead but its good fun to see who gets to the end first. Seriously, though, I am improving but it is a very difficult instrument to master and I've a long way to go yet. I wonder if I'll be able to continue with it after my release if you or H.M. King will allow me time; I intend trying. It has been and is a real blessing to me here and if I believed in God, I'd thank him for it. I've been in this camp for a year now and dislike it more as time goes on.

Hope and expectation of the war ending feature more and more in letters from now on. On 6 June Ursula wrote: Tuesday June 6th The great day has arrived at last; I hope you will have heard about it as we are hearing. There must be considerable rejoicings in all the prison camps. Here we feel a mixture of tenseness and relief, relief that at last it has started, but tenseness because it is going to be pretty awful from now till victory. There is so little that ordinary housewives can do to help. The ordinary daily round has seemed an awful anticlimax today, but of course Frances went to her dancing class as usual. I suppose that even when the armistice is signed I shall still keep on washing up and sweeping and dusting! My day will come later, so don't be surprised if on your return the house looks far from clean; I shall probably have gone on strike at last! I do hope you will like the Polyfoto snaps of Frances that I am sending herewith. I actually had a postcard from you this week, but as it was dated 23rd January, the news wasn't exactly hot. Anyway I was glad to gather from it that you had got yourself a new pair of boots from the Red Cross, for of course the shoes I sent wouldn't arrive for ages, if ever. I have no idea what to send in your next parcel; sometimes I feel all hopeful and think it doesn't matter whether I send one or not because you ought to be home before you could receive it, but other times I am in more cautious mood and realise that it is better to be on the safe side.

Two lines of your postcard were blacked out, so that it doesn't leave very much over for me to reply to. You say you are fit, and that is the main thing. Also you say that you love me, and that is more important – not really more important I suppose, for if you were ill, life would be a nightmare, but it makes everything worthwhile for me. You have seemed particularly near to me this week, so that two or three times I wanted to down tools and just cry for longing for you – particularly on the 30th May, terrible anniversary. Remember how wretched we used to feel if we were apart for more than a month? And now it is two solid years – grim years, they have seemed pretty arid to me, though I can do more or less what I like with my time, so what they have been like for you I can barely imagine. We shall just have to blot them out with the happiness and intensity of our living when you come back.

On Thursday I took Frances to the cinema for the first time to see 'Snow White and the Seven Dwarfs', as this story plays such a large part in her imagination as well as her dancing class just now. She grasped the main points of the story, and though she was duly impressed by the wicked queen, the huntsman and so on, she wasn't really frightened and doesn't seem to have suffered from bad dreams on that account. *(On the contrary I was scared stiff of the wicked queen and for years afterwards if we went past the little road leading to the cinema, I would crouch down with a feeling of dread!)*

In letter 118 (11 June 1944) she said: Nothing very much has happened this week, that is in our private domestic affairs; outside, very big things have happened which you will doubtless have got to know about. There are such a lot of things I should like to write to you about which are forbidden, things that are happening in the world just now. I'm afraid my letters must seem awfully trivial to you sometimes, but I am not allowed to write about any but purely domestic matters, and nothing very exciting happens in the domestic round! The main thing at home was that Mr Brown, our new next door neighbour and I have come to terms about the sale of the piece of land at the end of our garden, with the outbuildings thereon. The price agreed on is £20, which I think is probably quite a bargain from our point of view, and he is apparently satisfied too, since he doesn't use the land and couldn't sell it to anyone else. *(There followed a description of the extensive outbuildings and plans for keeping poultry and rabbits.)* As for the £20 purchase price, that of course is going to set me right back where I started from in my attempt to save something towards the £200 we owe my people, but I do think you would approve of the purchase. I shall have to think of some quicker way of making £200! *And in letter 119:* Quite a lot of your remarks about the camp were censored out of your letters so I gather they weren't too complimentary. In this letter (12th March) you write very despondently about the fiddle, and it nearly makes me weep to think of all you have to contend against and of your courage in carrying on. From the later letters I gather that you managed to pull out of that

particular slough of despond, as I suppose you do out of so many that
you never mention. God, how I long to make you really happy again!
It is awful to think that you haven't had a clothing parcel for 9
months, but I'm afraid there is nothing I can do about it here. What
rotten luck that two consecutive ones should have gone astray; it
wouldn't have been so bad if there had been one between. There is to
be a service at St Paul's for prisoners of war, and I have written for
tickets for Ann and me.

Later in June, in letter 120: I have had one postcard from you this
week, dated 16th April; glad you have had letters from Fred Don and
Eileen Johnson, but most of your friends don't write although they
would like to because we have been constantly told that each prisoner
should only receive one letter a week all told from all friends and
relations, and so people like Freeman and Bish don't write because
they are afraid it may hold up my letters and your people's. Perhaps
it isn't actually so, but that is why they don't write, not that they have
forgotten you and anything of the sort. Anyway, I will certainly write
and thank Fred for his letters to you – he always was a good and
cheerful correspondent. I'm glad to hear from *('your postcard that you
have at last found a good place to practise – though it seems hard that
you should be incinerated as well as incarcerated! You will doubtless play
all the more freely too if you know that you are not disturbing others.
My piano practice goes xxxxx as regularly as possible',* hand written by
the censor) but often there is gardening to be done in the evenings,
specially watering the tomatoes and peas and beans, which cuts into
the hour, 8–9 pm when I can get down to it. It is not really possible
to do any by day because of Frances.

I have now got myself some voluntary work to do in a convalescent
home near here. I have arranged to go every Friday afternoon and do
more or less whatever they want. I started last Friday by getting tea
and cutting bread and butter for the men and the staff, and afterwards
darning about two dozen pairs of socks for them. xxxxxxx and helps
to give the illusion that one is doing something for the war effort – if
only it could be something more effective, but I really don't see how
that is possible out here. In the evening I had consented to collect

from house-to-house for Queen Alexandra's Rose Day. It is a job
I hate, but gave me a legitimate excuse for meeting some of our
neighbours on their home ground. One is a Mrs Kent, who lives in a
very picturesque wooden house, in a thickly wooded garden which
I have often admired. It seems her husband used to work in the
oriental section of the British Museum, and he decided to take up
Turkish and she learnt it with him for fun, and gradually they have
become acknowledged experts, and she does a lot of translating
out of Turkish. *(I still have the copy of Fairy Tales from Turkey, one
of my favourite childhood books.)* I do always hope that as time goes
on we may develop interests and activities in common in which I can
really work with you. I hope that our music may become one such
bond, in which of course the children can join too, and perhaps
others may develop. I feel life will be so full and rich for us, when
once this ghastly period of waiting is over and we can get down
to xxxxxxxx.

On 25 June 1944 (letter 166) John wrote: I was overjoyed yesterday to
have yours of 26th March – in sequence. For one thing I haven't heard
from you for over a month and secondly by way of reaction from all
the good news of the last weeks I was in a very depressed state. Your
letter restored my good spirits as does everything that comes from
you. Unhappily I still await my missing parcels (clothing). A year has
now elapsed since I last had one. Not many go astray. I have just been
singularly unlucky. Thanks for sending details of household ex. I have
absolute confidence in your ability to manage our affairs; in fact you
seem to be managing things so excellently in every way that I intend
leaving everything to you for ever and sending you out to work while
I stay at home and look after Frances! I am as fit as ever – a little tired
perhaps since I've been working harder than ever at my fiddle – over
43 hours last week. Practise conditions are worse than ever since the
loss of our theatre. *(There was a fire and the theatre was burned down.)*
My attempt at duet playing was abruptly terminated after only a week
or two's runs by the loss through fire of our theatre. The bands and
choir which used to rehearse there, now do so in my former practice
room – the spud cellar. The weather being good I spend my days in

the incinerator which has room only for one. The latter has been a
great success as a practise room for I get absolutely no competition
there. The only snag is the sneers and gibes of the rest
of the camp, by whom serious doubts are cast upon my sanity. I hope
they are wrong but I sometimes wonder, because derangement is
unfortunately not unknown here xxxxx I wish I could forsee the
events of the next 6 months. Sometimes I even visualise liberation –
but not often.

And in letter 167 (2 July 1944): The past week has been an outstanding
one for me because of the arrival after an interval of a year of a
personal parcel. It was the Jan one and was in excellent condition. I
am afraid that I've given up as lost those sent in July and Oct of last
year. It's most unfortunate especially as the former did get to Luft III
but, of course, am powerless to do anything about them. The big item
in this most welcome parcel is the shoes, which fit me exactly and are
a splendid pair. I'm afraid they must have set your finances back a bit.
I have removed the partially worn out rubber soles and heels from
what was left of my former pair and am having them nailed on to the
new ones. The abundant consignment of chocolate was most
acceptable although having been closeted with a bar or two of soap
for so many months some of choc had slightly soapy flavour.
However, it isn't serious and the choc will serve the dual purpose of
cleaning the teeth at the same time enchanting the palate. I wonder
how many more parcels you'll send me and how many of them I'll
receive. …

*Ursula received no letters from John for weeks and in despair wrote to the
POW Department in London. This was their reply:*

Prisoners of War Department,
St James's Palace,
London SW1
4th August 1944
RAF/M 2444

Dear Mrs Valentine, re: 1251404 Warrant Officer J. Valentine
Thank you for your letter of August 2nd. We hope you will try not to
worry about your husband who is a prisoner of War at Stalag Luft 6.
Although we have received no official information to this effect, we
feel sure that in view of the rapid advance of the Russian Armies this
camp will have been transferred to another part of Germany, but you
should continue to send letters to your husband addressing them as
before and they will, no doubt, be forwarded

The first clothing parcel you sent this year did not leave this
country until the beginning of February and as parcels at that time
were taking quite five months to reach their destination, it is unlikely
that your husband could have received it by the time he wrote to you
in May. We are sorry that so many of your parcels appear not to have
reached your husband and hope that it is only due to his transfer from
one camp to another and that the parcels will eventually catch him up.
It must have been very disappointing for your husband to receive the
skates which were sent through our Stores Department without the
boots, but the boots were despatched in your July parcel and we hope
they will soon arrive. Once parcels are despatched from the Packing
Centres, they are the charge and responsibility of the Postal
authorities and we regret that we can do little to trace them.

We certainly advise you not to send the parcel which you now have
ready until a further announcement has been made by the Post Office.
They have advised that the next of kin of Prisoners should for the
time being refrain from sending parcels owing to the dislocation of
transport on the continent.
Yours sincerely, pp E.M. THORNTON, Director

*No further letter from John arrived until that of 30 July 1944; the missing
ones presumably announced this impending move.* We are slowly getting
used to the new camp. Its advantages are twofold, firstly the view of
the surrounding countryside which is the best I've struck yet and
secondly the privilege of being able to roam at will anywhere in the
large camp instead of as heretofore, being cooped up in small
compounds. The disadvantages are overcrowding, crude and limited
toilet facilities and the incomplete state of the camp – e.g. we have no

lights or facilities for cooking Red X foods. However, it being summer
we cope without much bother. I have a place in which to practise
which is about the only thing I look for in a camp nowadays. Needless
to say we have had no mail nor parcels since coming here nor do we
really expect them – although I'd give anything for a few letters from
my beloved wife from whom I have had nothing for 2 months. I have
met an Army Sgt who was with Leslie until Feb of this year and knew
him very well. His name is Jeans and he seemed to think quite a lot of
Leslie. Jeans has been POW since Feb and hasn't had a parcel yet but
as I had to leave all my spare kit behind at Luft VI, I have been able to
help him out only to the extent of some tooth paste. I'm keeping very
fit but don't think I have the stamina that I once had – any prolonged
effort tires me and I'm usually quite exhausted after a day in which
I've managed to do a fair amount of fiddling. Amongst the things I
refused to leave at Luft VI were all the photos of you and F and all
your letters – both of which provide me with refreshment when I feel
in the need. I expect my mail to you will be suffering the same fate as
yours to me but I shall continue writing in the hope that something
may reach you. Doubtless you've been worrying about my fate during
these momentous months in the East just as I've been worrying about
yours since the menace of the new weapon reared its ugly head.
Would that we could interchange telegrams to let each other know
that all was well. Times must be exciting at home these days.

*The 'new weapon' John mentioned was the V-1. Germany had built a
number of military installations, including launching sites and depots,
in order to carry out the planned V-1 'flying bombs' or pilotless aircraft.
The first of these was dropped on London on 12 June 1944. Because of
their much greater range and unpredictability, not only London, but
surrounding areas were vulnerable. The worst day for London was 5 July
when 104 V-1s fell. Ursula decided to temporarily leave home and join
her parents in Devon.*

The next letter from John was dated 6 August 1944. xxxxx I have been
very worried of recent weeks about your safety from the new weapon.
I know you're a long way out of London but I've no idea how far

north these things travel. I hope that, if your area has been within the danger zone, you have 'hopped it' to a more salubrious spot. Although we've only been here a week or two I shan't be sorry to leave. The camp is devoid of many of the rough comforts and conveniences which we had previously regarded as minimum necessities. However, we cope just because we must. I wonder if you've been able to take Frances for a holiday this year. It's years since I heard from you.

Ursula wrote on 20 July 1944 (letter 122) from Little Close in Salcombe. You will see from the address that we are down staying with Mother again. Pat and her baby are here too and we had an awful rush getting away. We had to walk two miles to the nearest station with her heavy luggage and the baby's pram! and then go back to do the packing from 11 pm onwards! So you can understand that there wasn't much peace or time for letter writing. However, we weathered the journey alright in the end, and are now living here in peace and plenty. We are expecting to stay for a couple of months, if not more, and Mr Horne, the estate agent in the village and a good friend of mine, is going to let the house furnished for that time. He says he will see to it that the tenants leave when we want them to. He advised strongly against leaving it empty in case it should be taken over, so I only hope everything will be alright. It was very difficult to decide what was best to be done, but Frances's wellbeing counts above everything and really I am getting terribly excited and anxious too as events move nearer towards you; I don't suppose you will ever receive this letter. I wonder where you will be three months from now? I suppose it's just possible you might be home, glorious thought! It was an awful wrench to leave the garden just as everything was producing; there's a lovely crop of raspberries, of which we ate all we could hold in the time at our disposal! Mr Palmer, who lives next door, says he will keep an eye on it for us and put in a half-day's work when necessary.

And 10 days later she wrote: I am filled with dread and anxiety about you as the battle front gets nearer to you. It's getting quite unbearable. God keep you safe, my dearest. The house is now let for 2 months. I have been occupying my leisure time and trying to make up to my conscience for not having more work to do, by dressmaking – the material for all these has been waiting for ages and I've just never had time to make them up! There doesn't seem much spare time even here, for I help Mother in the house in the mornings, take Frances to the beach in the afternoons, and in the evenings we play bridge or Mah-jong! What a lazy life! Still, I'm saving some money and I suppose that's something. I am supposed to send off a clothing parcel to you next month but haven't the faintest idea what to send or whether you are ever likely to receive it. I haven't had a letter for about a month and feel awfully cut off from you somehow. How I long to have you safely home again my darling! God keep you safe and bring you safely home at last. Frances sends you a big kiss – she says she hopes you will bring her a boiled egg and I tell her that's most unlikely!

In letter 123 (31 July 1944): I'm afraid my letters to you have been a bit irregular since I've been down here, not because I think of you less, but partly because, with the war situation changing so fast and so favourably, I don't really think you are ever likely to receive these letters – at least, I hope not! Pat and her baby have now left us as she wanted to find somewhere where her husband could go if he got leave. Also with the prospect of the war ending soon, she couldn't have come back to Felmersham, so she scouted round and has been very lucky to get rooms on a farm about 10 miles from here. I have had two letters from you at least, a p.c. of 4th May and letter of 14th. So glad you'd had some mail at last. There are going to be an awful lot of letters wandering round Europe when the war's over and the boys come home! … The main occurrence this week has been a visit to an auction sale of furniture in the village. I bought quite a lot of things, the chief item is a wardrobe for the spare bedroom. I paid £16 for this wardrobe and consider it a bargain, though getting it home will be a problem; meanwhile, it is standing in the garage here. Among other things I also bought an enormous feather bed for 19/- which I am going to cut up into a quantity of pillows and cushions, which we badly need. It set me back over £26 but they are all useful acquisitions for our home.

On 13 July it was announced that Heydekrug was to be evacuated.
The POWs were marched to the station and herded into cattle trucks.
The journey to Thorn (Torun in Poland) took thirty-six hours, with
many delays when their train was shunted into sidings to make way
for troop trains. But they only remained there until 8 August when once
again travelling by cattle trucks they went to at least one other camp
before arriving in Fallingbostel (in Lower Saxony). With each move
the POWs had to carry everything they wanted, so many possessions
inevitably had to be abandoned. In letter 170 (20 August 1944) John wrote:
xxxxx The new camp is not bad – no worse anyway than previous
ones although congestion is once more the order of the day. We have
quite a pleasant view of the countryside and are permitted to walk
over the whole area of the vast camp instead of being strictly confined
to our own pen. I have, alas, been unable to find anywhere to practise
and it looks as if I shall have to give it up for the time being. It's a
great pity, after all I've put into it but I've no alternative as yet. As a
matter of fact I've done very little since I left Luft VI a month ago but
I have realised with absolute clarity, how little progress I've made
since I started. I couldn't play even the simplest of tunes if I tried –
which I haven't. All my fond hopes of playing with you I've sadly but
firmly relinquished. One glorious surprise of the last week was the
receipt of a letter from you dated 28th May. Several are missing, the
previous one being 26th March but it was nevertheless grand to hear
from you again. I hope the others come and also the snaps you mention
as enclosed therewith. The one of Pat Hodson and offspring arrived.

Please continue to write to Luft III although we are not there. Our
camp houses a mixture of Army and RAF NCOs. The Army boys get
regular mail in quick time. Many of them have July letters now!!
During the past month, when the war news has been so thrilling I've
been profoundly depressed. One reason of course was my inability to
occupy myself with the fiddle. To crown it, I developed a foul cold and
cough followed by a spell of vomiting and sickness. I felt extremely
weak for a day or two but am feeling a lot better now although a little
'tottery' after my enforced fasting. I've never before been so xxxxx as
I am now and I hate it intensely. Naturally, during the long hours on
my bed, I've thought of you a lot and have stuck up a row of photos

of you and F to look at for encouragement. *And in letter 171 (27 August 1944):* Another week without mail – we are also without food now but are hoping daily for fresh arrivals from Geneva. Our stock was exhausted this week with an issue of half a parcel per man. I am still very idle and am loathing it too. Since we came here I've done only 1 hour's practise – I find the days very long and boring without the preoccupation of my fiddle. The weather has been glorious, though, and I've managed to get quite sun tanned. My malaise which I mentioned last week has entirely disappeared but there is quite an epidemic of it in the camp. Flies in their thousands are the cause. The war news gets better each day and optimism abounds in the camp. I steadfastly refuse to believe in an early end for fear of bitter disappointment later. I yearn for news of you. Your Heaven sent letters are complete up to the end of March – 5 months ago – since when I have had only 1, written at the end of May. What particularly worries me are the alarming possibilities of the new weapon. I've no idea if they penetrate to your part of the world or to that of my parents; I'd give a lot to get mail of as recent a date as the Army boys in the camp get as a matter of course xxxxx I hope you are still keeping the scrap book of newspaper cuttings which you mentioned a long while ago. We get very little news as you may imagine and for all I know of the day's happenings I might as well be in the grave. I wonder if we shall be together before the year is out? Most people here think so but to me it sounds too good to be true. Frank P thinks his wife has left the A.T.S. Do you know if it's true and if so why? Louis den Boer, my Dutch friend, had the sad news last week of the death of his fiancée. A terrible blow at this stage of the war. He was very upset at first.

Letter 172 was dated 3 September 1944: I was absolutely delighted to have 2 letters from you this week written 23rd and 30th April. I was really thrilled to hear of your birthday gift to me. I can't tell you how much I appreciate the thought although when I consider my present state of inefficiency I can't help thinking that your kindness xxxxx be wasted. I hope you're not nurturing false hopes that you've become the wife of a virtuoso. I'm awful, bloody awful to be more exact. I'm afraid that nature had made me a plodder and that even if I stick at it

I'll never be anything else at the fiddle. Anyway, I know that I'll treasure your instrument more than any other I may own. The Red X fiddle hasn't arrived yet but my own (a German one) has been repaired quite well and I'll try to bring it home together with the bow so kindly sent from Sweden. News of my birthday gift made me pluck up courage to practise. xxxxx I'm so glad to hear of Ann's visit, I hope my parents come some time. Am eagerly looking forward to the photo of you, F and the house. I wish with all my heart that I could oblige you in the matter of caring for you and helping you in all your worries and anxieties. I wonder if the parcel will ever arrive – you definitely haven't 'boobed' in your choice of contents. With the current news, I often get quite optimistic but such spells don't last long and I relapse into my usual passive resignation. I can see that we have a difference of opinion regarding one major aspect of life – the religious one. I'm convinced that Christianity is one vast edifice of superstition – with possibly one fundamental truth, but you seem to be true believer which I never was and never will be, nor do I now wish to be having seen the light. However, I love you more than ever, which is almost impossible. Keep well and beautiful.

In letter 173 (10 September 1944) John wrote to Ursula: Another two letters during the past week – 1st and 10th April – I think all are here up to end April bar one. I also had one from Roy Cowdry and 2 from my father's Swedish friend Mr Wernekinck to whom I shall be able to spare a card. He is the gentleman who so kindly sent the fiddle bow and toothpaste. I love every letter I get from you; I become more and more amazed at your tremendous stock of ideas and energy – particularly that which you devote to building up our home. I'm delighted to hear of your Easter visit to sunny Devon and hope you've been able to manage at least one more trip this year. Despite the grand war news of these days I've been more miserable here than ever before as a POW. To begin with optimism is so rife that one can't help feeling unsettled. Everyone speaks as if the end of the war were only a week or so hence but despite all hoping, each day is so painfully like the previous, while the following always proves to be a mere repetition ad nauseam that any blaze of cheerfulness subsides into smouldering

gloom. Secondly I can't find anywhere to pass the time with my fiddle.
I do a little practise each day but not nearly so much as I wish and
that in the most unpleasant surroundings. Thirdly the camp is in an
unfinished state – no light and other essential conveniences xxxxx.
Until now my life as a POW has been one of activity, but now with
opportunities for employment so limited, time hangs heavily on my
hands – boredom and depression make their appearance. I have your
letters and photos right from the start though and get a great deal of
pleasure from them. I'd love to receive some of the more recent snaps
that you've been sending. I'm sorry that this is such a gloomy missive
– but perhaps you'll never get it so no harm will be done. *And in letter
174 (17 September 1944)*: No mail from you, dearest, I'm still in the
dark as to how you have fared from May onwards. We eagerly follow
the daily progress of events (and of the Allies) but the time passes very
slowly – more so than ever before. We have a library going at last.
Unfortunately our Red X food issue has suffered a permanent cut of
50% – a general one I believe in all British POW camps. We have been
on this scale for a few weeks but strangely enough I feel it very little
and am as fit as ever. My practise troubles continue though. I only
manage 2–3 hours daily and those in the most distressing of
circumstances but I am doggedly resolved not to give in now even if
lack of ability forces me to do so when I become a free man once more.

*Ursula wrote from Devon in early September in a very hopeful frame
of mind.* I suppose it is really a waste of time writing to you any more!
In future I hope we always communicate by word of mouth. But as
I have already bought this letter card, I may as well send it. This
morning I received your letter of June 25, heavily censored as usual,
in which you propose letting me go out to work while you look after
Frances. No B. likely!! You'd just play your fiddle all the time. No,
when you come back, I'm going to sit back and put my feet on the
mantelpiece! The news is amazingly good, it really won't be long now.
… I wonder how much news you get to hear these days – enough to
cheer you up, I hope. Sometimes I even let myself imagine your
homecoming – but not too often, it doesn't pay! Life here is quieter
now that Peter has gone back, but tomorrow Barbara comes down for

a fortnight, and I think when she goes back we shall probably go home too, all being well. The tenants have left Felmersham now, but I'm not letting it again; the risk of damage doesn't seem worth it for so short a time. I'm anxious to get back but it doesn't seem wise just yet. I do hope it will all be intact for you.

In her letter 127 of 2 October 1944, Ursula told John: Still no mail from you – over a month now, and I expect you are faring just as badly if not worse. I'm hoping there may be some waiting for me at home. We are going back tomorrow, travelling up with Barbara who has been having a fortnight's holiday and she's going to spend a couple of nights with us. We have had a lovely long holiday down here, but I feel it's about time we went back and I started to get things into order. Pat Hodson has now rented a wee cottage down here, near where she was staying, so I'll be able to get rid of all her things eventually and have the house to ourselves – all ready for you, so do hurry up! Frances is very keen to be back at Chalfont in spite of the counter attraction of the beach and the ferry-boat. I'm so glad she loves it and feels it is 'home' already, and I do hope you will too. If only I knew where you are now, it's awful not having any news except that you have left Luft VI. I'm afraid you'll have had to jettison a lot of stuff but hope you've hung on to the fiddle.

In letter 175 (24 September 1944) John wrote: Your letters of 16th April and 7th May are here, completing the series up to the latter, with that one, too, were 3 snaps over which I have pored eagerly and avidly. It was a real treat for my eyes to see your beloved likeness again. Would that I could have photos of you more frequently. How our Frances grows! Her size astounded me in that snap of you holding her. It quite took my breath away for a second or so, for I still imagined her to be the wee toddler of the photos of last year! I was delighted to see something of the house too (the back view) and hope that more pictures will arrive. Most of all, though, I loved those of you, for after all you are the one who means more to me in all the world and I'm usually dependant [sic] upon memory for my pictures of you apart from the earlier snaps which I know so well. I hope none was lost

from this letter. I still scrape away at the fiddle when and where
possible. How hard it is to improve! I want years of practise yet before
I can be worthy of accompanying you. I'm still as keen as ever though
and determined not to give it up until I have your candid opinions as
to my prospects of eventual success. I had long cherished hope of
being home for your next birthday (more ardently than I can tell) but
I have now relinquished it. *And on 8 October:* The only events of note
during the week were a titanic inoculation and a vaccination. The
former caused no trouble apart from a tender arm and the latter is
still in a state of minor inflammation. Having had no fresh supplies
since we left Luft VI my stocks of tobacco and cigs are running out.
Also the staff of life is now on slightly shorter commons. We have at
last got electric light in the billets and the evening hours in the
flickering light of a lamp of pyjama cord and margarine (horribly
smoky) are over, thank goodness. They were sore on the eyes. Most
of the Army fellows here get their mail in 2/3 weeks (9 days is the
record). Our 5 months' delay makes us very jealous.

In his letter 177 of 15 October 1944, John sounded more upbeat: Four
letters from you – 14th and 21st May, 19th June and 4th Sept!!! Series
now complete to end May. How I wish they would arrive as regularly
as written. I was delighted to have them – each has been read four
times already and the photo most carefully studied. How beautiful are
Frances and her gracious mother – I love them both so much. The
gent. whom Grunfeld says I met is my Father's contact. What service is
Carol's father in? The censor always obliterates all references. Of
course I don't mind them using our bed! But I'm excessively jealous
all the same. Your 'feminine society' not quite so undiluted as our
masculine. Please tell your Aunt Con of my sorrow at hearing of Miss
Hoare's death. I really am grateful for her kind gifts and hoped one
day to be able to meet her and say so. If you are to be disappointed
if I do not audit your a/c I shall do so gladly and thoroughly. My aim
when I get home is to make you happy in any and every way possible.
You certainly deserve a little attention from me after all these years of
neglect. Bless you for all you've done and the positively heroic way in
which you've acted single handed. I urge you to invest every cent (if

poss.) in building up our home – so don't laugh at me please. I'm
delighted (hugely) at the purchase of the extra land and outhouses.
Congratulations darling. Could I have a description and sketch of the
complete garden now. Thanks to your earlier sketches and the photos
I have a fair idea of the 'property'. Your letter of 4th Sept. was a great
relief. I'd been worrying a lot about you and F during the bomb
months. I note it was written from Devon. Have you been there long?
What have you done about the house? I forgive your crack about
further writing being a 'waste of time' because I think you meant it.
Had you intended it to be sarcastic I'd have been mortally hurt, but
I see that like so many others here you were unduly optimistic about
the duration of the war. I wasn't, but that hasn't prevented me from
being very depressed these last weeks. They have been and still are the
worst of my captivity. I cannot see the end yet and am still unable to
while away much time with my fiddle.

Ursula's next letter was from Felmersham (8 October 1944). Here we are
safely installed in our own little home again, and how glad I am to be
back! We travelled up on Tuesday with Barbara, catching the 7.30 am
train, and we got home soon after 4 pm. Barbara started to unpack a
bit while I dashed out to get the necessary minimum of food into the
house. I had ordered coal a week or two before, and was very glad to
find that it had been delivered, so now we have a bit of a stock to help
us through the winter. Frances was overjoyed to find all her toys and
precious possessions again, but was so tired after the journey that I
hadn't much trouble in separating her from them temporarily and
putting her to bed. Of course the house was in a considerable uproar,
because we had stuffed a lot of our belongings, Pat's and mine, into
the nursery and locked it up before we went away 3 months ago. I
spent the whole day carrying things from here to there, unearthing
our special treasures which I had put out of the tenants' way and
generally reorganising the house. Frances helped me manfully,
struggling up and down stairs under large loads. The tenants have
left the house in surprisingly good condition. The garden has been
kept in good order by old Mr Palmer, from next door, and there are
plenty of winter greens coming on. Mr Palmer has harvested the

potato and shallot crops for us; we ought to have enough spuds to last most of the winter at our present rate of consumption. How lovely it will be to have the house all to myself at last, all ready and waiting for you! I am torn between the desire to revel in the privacy and convenience of being on my own, and the desire to earn a spot more money by having someone to live with me. My reading of the military situation takes alternately optimistic and pessimistic turns, and it is hard to decide what to do.

This is the last letter marked 'GEPRUFT 113', so apparently the last letter to reach John: U. No. 129 Felmersham October 17th 1944. My own darling Johnnie: we have been having a very pleasant weekend with Ann staying here. Frances went to Sunday school for the second time on Sunday, Ann and I took her down, then went on blackberrying and came back shortly before 4 pm when she was due to emerge. But the class had apparently ended early and there was no sign of Frances. We hurried home, and found her waiting quite composedly in the front garden! She wasn't nearly so upset as I had been. I asked her what she had been taught at Sunday school, and she said they had read a story about Baby Nosey. After further questioning I discovered that it must have been Moses in the bullrushes!

I remembered to send a card to your Mother on her birthday and a cable to Leslie who is in hospital again but not too seriously, I gathered from Ann. It will be a good thing if it keeps him out of the fray for a bit, he has had more than his share. I do wish I could have some word from you, it is nearly two months now since I heard, and I have no idea whereabouts you are. I do hope the mail situation is not equally bad with you, though really with the war in its present stage I suppose it is hardly to be wondered at. Well, it won't matter if it means that you will be back the sooner, but I should just like to see your dear writing again. All my love to you, my darling husband. Yours for always, Ursula.

Letter 178 (29 October 1944) was on a printed form marked Stalag Luft 357, but John had crossed out 357 and replaced it with III. Do you remember what happened 5 years ago tonight? I have been thinking of it a lot, wishing that we were able to celebrate the anniversary together. I hope you regret your acceptance of my offer as little as I regret making it. My only regret is that I didn't do so earlier. Your letters of 4th and 11th June are here and also 19th Aug. Series complete to 17th June. I still seize every opportunity of fiddling xxxxx but I'm badly in need of good tuition for I get little or no help from fellow POWs. I'm delighted with the Polyfotos of Frances and have perused them often. Could you honestly gratify me with a similar collection of likenesses of my beloved wife? She is the one for whom I care most in the world and I can't tell you how deeply I'd appreciate gazing at some new and decent photos of her. Please dearest – please – do this for me. You suggest that your letters might be 'awfully trivial' to me but I assure you positively that they are not. I enjoy every single word of the two typewritten sides and congratulate myself on having a wife willing to write so regularly at such length. Other fellows get those awful brief little forms which, like this, barely contain room for a greeting. Congratulations on your purchases of furniture etc. in Devon. You certainly never relax your efforts for our home. As to life here – it is grim in the extreme. Every move I've made has been for the worse. The only advantages of the camp are its large size and pleasant (fairly) surroundings. I won't catalogue its disadvantages because the censor wouldn't pass them.

In the book No Flight from the Cage, *author Calton Younger described the life: 'We were shut in from 5 pm to 8 am, the room was fireless, and the little light that seeped over the mud wastes and between the grey shafts of rain was interrupted and dispersed by lines of clothing laundered in cold water, scrubbed with nail-brushes to an even beige, hung to dry though there was little chance of its ever doing so. The occasional parcel came but soon the stock was exhausted and we reverted to the unsatisfying round of swede soup at midday and a brace of potatoes in the evening. ...'*

Meanwhile, conditions in John's camp only worsened and on 12 November 1944 he wrote: I wish this could be a more cheerful letter than it is, but local circumstances are very, very trying. However, I'll begin with the brighter points. Your letter of 18th Sept. heads the list. Many earlier ones are still awaited. Next comes the arrival of the violin sent off a year ago. The case was smashed and the fiddle slightly cracked; all the same it is a good instrument, much better than the one I had. It is very ancient and battered in appearance but has a lovely rich tone and I prefer it infinitely. Unfortunately I get fewer opportunities of playing as the days go by and sometimes don't touch it at all in a day. Those long regular hours of Luft VI are regrettably impossible here. I just do what I can when and where I am xxxxx to life here nowadays, nothing pleasant can be said. I find each day one long torture xxxxxxxx we have had only 2/3rds of a Red X parcel in the last month but we have just received notice from Geneva that some parcels are on the way which will give us weekly issue of ½ for some five weeks. We eagerly await the first xxxxxxxx clothing parcels have been arriving slowly but steadily for some time now. Many recent ones have been received – July August and even Sept., I hope to get one soon for I've had only 1 in the last 18 months despite your regular quarterly dispatch. Whenever poss. will you send some large shipments of tobacco (Players' No Name) and cigs to enable me to build up a stock again. I hate smoking dog ends. A tobacco parcel from ASV came and I utilised half of it to buy a pair of indoor slippers and a shirt and long pants to serve as pyjamas. So I'm set for the winter as to clothing. Would you also send a good book of scales and arpeggio exercises. Judging by the almost exultant tone of your letter of 4th Sept. you have suffered a bitter disappointment this autumn. Poor darling, I can and do sympathise. Just at the moment reunion seems as far away as ever.

Presumably many letters were missing – the last two to reach Ursula were the following postcard to Frances and one more letter.
To: Miss Frances Valentine, Felmersham
My Dearest Frances: this will be too late to reach you for Christmas but I hope you had a lovely time and were lucky enough to receive lots of presents from Father Christmas. He usually rewards good girls and Mother tells me that you are a very good one. I hope she is a very good Mother too and had plenty of nice presents as well. You must be a big girl nowadays and will shortly be going to school I suppose. I am

longing to see you and to know how you have changed from the little
baby I left behind so long ago. Give my love to Mother. Do look after
her, won't you – she is so nice. Love from Father.

*Letter 181 (17 December 1944) was the last of John's letters that Ursula
received.* In case my last letter is delayed or lost I shall repeat that I
have increased my pay allotment to you to the maximum consistent
with my new rank and ordered all accumulated cash at 3/3/44 to be
sent to you. This of course won't affect Touche's dole to you. I have
also asked for a copy of my pay account for some years to be sent to
you 'for Income tax purposes'. Just hold on to it when you get it. The
rest of this letter will be purely selfish requests and I hope you will
excuse them and fulfil all those you can. *(John gave a long list of
requirements – clothing, toiletries and tobacco. With all the moves from
camp to camp much had been lost or had to be left behind.)* Red X food
is still difficult to get – supplies most irregular but for 3 weeks now we
have had half a parcel each week; none now in stock. The Red X has
considerably cut down the soap and tobacco content of each parcel
and as we only get ½ a parcel and that not regularly, we are very short
of these commodities. Conditions here don't improve and we look like
having a bleak Xmas. Haven't had a shower for a month now – no coal
sent yet. However, I usually cheer myself up by thinking of you and
F waiting for me. My fondest love to you both, John.

In No Flight from the Cage *Calton Younger described that Christmas.
By this time all the prisoners were suffering from malnutrition; their diet
had been swedes – often rotten – and the occasional potato for months.
A neighbouring camp, 11b, had been established longer and so had a
stock of Red X parcels. 'They gave us 2,500, enough for four men to share
a parcel. Toby and Ron shared a whole tin of corned beef, Dick and I a
tin of spam. We had potatoes and swedes, and afterwards, plum-duff
made from potatoes, which had been grated, then squeezed in muslin
so that we were left with a sticky pink suet, and prunes. When it was
all over we had thundering bellyaches, and took to our bunks. From the
barracks men went tracklessly through the snow, which was still falling
slowly, to the latrines which soon gave off a thick aroma, a rich foulness*

that held the soul of Christmas puddings!' My father never talked about his POW experiences except for one incident, which Calton Younger described: 'One man had bartered cigarettes for some dehydrated vegetable, and, with sublime ignorance, ate it dry, then drank several cups of tea. Probably he thought he had the same bellyache as everyone else, but it was not the same. He literally burst, and died.'

All the following letters from Ursula were sent off to Germany, but as they are not stamped GEPRUFT presumably never reached John while a POW, so when he did receive them is uncertain. No envelopes were kept so their passage through the postal system is unknown. The following is from Ursula's letter 130, dated 13 November 1944: The Post Office tells us that letters posted this week ought to reach prisoners in time for Christmas, so here I am, on a wet and cold November evening, trying to visualise Christmas, remembering what it used to be like with you, picturing how lovely it will be in years to come when we are together. The only Christmas I try not to think about is this coming one. I had had just great hopes that this might be THE Christmas of our lives, radiant with the joy of reunion which I am sure will outshine even the bright happiness of our wedding or the lustre of our golden wedding in years to come. But apparently it is not to be, and I can hardly bear to think of you and all the other boys; it seems a hollow mockery to wish you a Merry Christmas, and yet I do hope that it will be cheerful for you, particularly that you will get something good and extra to eat and drink, and I am sure you will know that I shall be thinking of you with all my love every minute of the day. All my love, darling and a special kiss for Christmas – wait till you come back, I'll kiss you cock-eyed! ... At last I've got hold of some photos to send you; these were taken by Barbara when she had her holiday at the end of September. I do hope they reach you at Christmas time, my darling, it seems a miserable enough offering – how I wish I could send you something more representative of my love and longing for you. *On 20 November she wrote:* This morning the Hodsons descended on us to collect their belongings, Pat, Frank and baby Carol. They hired a car and piled everything into it – it was a sight to see! Frank is on embarkation leave, due to go to the uttermost ends of the earth, I am afraid, and of course Pat is very glum about it, but maybe it won't be so long for them either now. *And a week later:* Frances and I got home from our visit to Gable End this afternoon at 4.30 pm, and the first thing to greet me as I opened the front door was the longed-for sight of letters from you, three of them, dated 2nd and 30th July and 27th August and a postcard of 6th August. After the desert of three letterless months, this is indeed an oasis! I was extremely glad to hear that you have received the January parcel and that the shoes are a success. Pity about the soap and chocolate combining! That is the Red Cross packing centre's fault, not mine. You must have been glad to meet Jeans, who had been with Leslie at the beginning of the year. You will doubtless have heard from your people that he is on the shelf again, it looks as though it may be a longer job this time and of course we are hoping he may be sent home, he certainly deserves it. Bunty heard today that Stewart may be home after Christmas for interviews prior to being shot off somewhere else; the obvious thing is for you to return too, to a grand family reunion! I do hope you have got some food parcels and that your stocks are built up again now that the cold weather has set in. I just dread to think about it, when we have so much over here. I am gradually laying in stocks of things that will do you good and build up your strength again; I'll soon have you as fit as a fighting cock again. You mention that Frank P. thinks his wife may be out of the ATS. I'm afraid I know nothing about her. I wrote to Olga as you asked to enquire about her when Frank hadn't heard for such ages, but I suppose Olga didn't welcome such enquiries from outsiders, for she never replied to my letter and I don't suppose it's any good writing again. There is only one way I know of to get out of the ATS, but I hope for Frank's sake that she has found another, if it is true she has left. How very sad for Louis den Boer that his fiancée has died, the Dutch must have been going through a terrible time altogether. I do wish you were able to tell me where your present camp is, but I suppose that is not allowed. Two of your letters had chunks censored out, which Frances thought outrageous, and when I asked her what she suggested doing about it, she said the Germans were very unkind and ought to be smacked.

In letter 134 (5 December 1944) Ursula told John: The postman brought
me a letter and a postcard from you, dated 10th and 17th September,
much the most recent I have had. He also brought the Prisoner of War
Journal, from which I learnt that we can now start sending next-of-
kin clothing parcels again. This threw me into an uproar because I
hadn't got anything ready for your parcel, supposing that we would
not be allowed to send any more at all, so I had to get cracking about
that. I am very undecided about what to send you, the parcel surely
won't arrive for several months, if at all, so it seemed to me that the
best thing would be to send a clean shirt and pullover and socks for
you to come home in! I must get the parcel posted before we leave
here, on Thursday week, 14th December, for our Christmas holiday
in Devon, so I hope the Red Cross people hurry with the things I have
ordered from them. Your letter of 10th September was rather a sad
one. I gather that life in the new camp leaves much to be desired, and
I can well imagine that now that the end of the war is drawing nearer,
the feeling of suspense and frustration weighs more heavily on you all
than it did when there was no end in view and you all lived on blind
faith. It is very hard to imagine the actual day of liberation and of
reunion, to think that it will be just an ordinary day of 24 hours,
probably not even fine weather and that most people's lives will go
on just as usual. I remember feeling like this about our wedding day,
hardly believing that it would really dawn, yet it did, and we were
safely married according to plan, thereby starting an era of great
happiness for us both. So too this other day will come eventually and
our happiness will start all over again, even better than before and
after a bit we shall look back on this separation as a bad dream, a
shadow in our lives which accentuates the sunshine to come. I get
quite hot and bothered when I read your generous praises of my
home-making efforts. Really it is quite undeserved. It is natural for
a woman to fuss around the house to make it as nice as possible. Wait
till you see the results, that will be the test, and sometimes I feel all
cold inside lest you should be too disappointed. But this little house
ought to do us fine for a good few years and we are very lucky indeed
to have a house at all.

I have now got a seat fixed on the back of my bicycle for Frances.

Peter got me the seat for my birthday present and I fixed it on the other day and we went for a pleasant spin together. Then I thought I had better have the brakes adjusted, as the back brake didn't work at all and I didn't like to trust to one with a double load on board. So I had the brakes done, but in the process the man must have loosened the screw which fastened the seat to the saddle pillar, so that when I got on to the bike with a bit of a jerk, the seat came loose and Frances was deposited on the road with a resounding thud. Poor kid, it shook her up a bit but she didn't make much fuss, and I didn't suggest her riding again till I could get the seat properly fixed. *(I remember the fall vividly, and lying on the ground gazing up at the sky!)* On another journey the chain came off, luckily quite near St Peter's, so I scooted back into the village and left the bike to be repaired. When I went to collect it the man was very gloomy about the method of fixing the seat to the pillar, said it wasn't really strong enough, so I straightaway took it into the local blacksmith and had it welded on, so now I think it is quite safe. We called for it on the way home from dancing this afternoon and rode home quite gaily. It will be a great asset to be able to get around on it. All my love to you my darling, just keep going through this winter and afterwards life will really start again. Ursula.

The following is a letter from Asea Electric Ltd to Sune Busch Esq., copied to A.S. Valentine, Vasteras, Sweden, 7 December 1944.

Dear Sune, I got the other day a card dated 12th September from Mr Valentine, who is in a prison camp in Germany. He writes as follows: 'Your letters of 9th April and 2nd May arrived together. I was delighted to have them so that I could send you my most grateful thanks for the kind gifts of a violin bow and tooth paste. Both reached me some time ago. The bow is excellent and I use it a great deal. It means a lot to me here. I assure you, I appreciate it deeply as well as the tooth paste of which I was greatly in need. Very many thanks for your kindness. I saw Mr Soderberg a second time (29th May) and asked him if any kind friends could send some violin music – not elementary nor yet advanced – something between the two. It may be that the end of the war approaches but if not I should be again most grateful for any help you can give me in that way. With kind regards and renewed thanks.'

I have previously sent him some chocolate, a violin bow, tooth paste and so on, and I will now arrange for some suitable music and some other things to be sent to him so that they if possible could reach him for Christmas. I understand that his parents will be very glad to know that he seems to be well off.

Kindest regards. Yours sincerely, H. Wernekinck.

This letter of Ursula's, no. 135, written from Felmersham and dated 13 December 1944, together with the following 'letter cards', passed British censorship but were returned marked: 'THIS LETTER FORMED PART OF UNDELIVERED MAILS WHICH FELL INTO THE HANDS OF THE ALLIED FORCES IN GERMANY. IT IS UNDELIVERABLE AS ADDRESSED, AND IS THEREFORE RETURNED TO YOU.' No envelopes were kept so all other letters from No. 130 13 November onwards presumably never reached John in the camps; but since they have been preserved I assume that he must have received them at some point, perhaps after his repatriation.

My darling Johnnie, I sent off your ninth clothing parcel yesterday, which should have gone in August but that the sending of parcels was stopped owing to transport difficulties. It contains the usual toilet items and as much chocolate as I could collect (about 6 lbs all together I think, mostly from the Red Cross). I do hope this consignment reaches you moderately soon and in good condition. I have now got a new map of the location of POW camps from the Red Cross, and think I have a better idea of where you are. Does the scenery remind you of the witches' scene in Macbeth? Frances and I are off down to Devon tomorrow for Christmas and the New Year and expect to be home in 2–3 weeks.

Prisoners of War Department
St James's Palace, London SW1
14th December 1944
RAF/M 2444

Dear Mrs Valentine, re: <u>12521404 Warrant Office J.Valentine</u>

Thank you for your letter, which we received on December 12th.

The map of the Prisoner of War camps has already been sent to you and although you will not find Stalag 357 marked on it, it is situated at Oerbke near Fallingbostel, which is in square C.4.

We know that the censorship of all letters for RAF Prisoners of War at Stalag Luft 3 delays their delivery very seriously and think that you can quite well try sending letters to your husband to Stalag 357 omitting Stalag Luft 3 from the address. We cannot, of course, guarantee that they will reach him any more quickly, but you may think it worth the attempt.

We hope you will soon hear from your husband again.

Yours sincerely, p.p . E.M.THORNTON, Director.

Letter 136 (19/12/44). Frances and I have now arrived safely at Little Close, and are finding it much warmer than at home. The sun is shining and it almost looks warm enough for a bathe – but not quite! Daddy and I went to an auction sale last Friday, which is as exciting as a day at the races for me. I managed to buy a bookcase and some very useful kitchen and garden tools and some china. The problem now will be to get them home, but I think Daddy will pack them up for me scientifically. So we had a good day together and are well satisfied.

Letter 137 (1/1/45). A happy New Year to you. The happiest of your life – and of mine, my dearest. I am sure you were thinking of Frances and me specially last night, as I was of you. We have been having a sharp frost here, so it must have been far worse at home and I am feeling very nervous about the pipes, although I drained all the water out before I left. There is always some left in the bends and stretches you can't reach. However, there is nothing to be done till the thaw, so I may as well relax. I dread to think what it is like in your part of the world. I do so hope my May parcel has arrived with its extra blanket. We have been having a very quiet peaceful time since Christmas. I had a nice letter from Mrs Howie, Mr Hazard, Aunt Mary, and Vera Bowack. All my love, darling, it can't be long now!

And on 6 January she wrote: Johnnie, my darling, Many happy returns of our wedding day, my dear husband, and may all the future ones be celebrated together! I wonder if you have been able to make today in any way different and pleasanter than all the others. I hope that perhaps a letter or parcel may have arrived opportunely. I haven't had a letter from you today, though one dated 18th Oct. came two days ago. This afternoon I have been putting the finishing touches to a bookshelf which I have been making, under Daddy's expert supervision, out of a packing case. It is to go in our dining room and I am painting it cream to tone with the walls. I'm getting more and more ambitious ideas about the animals I want to keep after you've come home and we've settled down. I'd like to have Chinchilla rabbits, Siamese cats, a goat and of course a dog. But I'm not tying myself down with all that till we've had our fling and paid our visits on your return, and maybe you'll have something to say about it! Keep well darling, these months must be the hardest of all for you. I love you so much.

Letter 139 was written to John on 14 January 1945: We came back *(to Felmersham)* last Wednesday, 10th January, and were amazed to find about 6 inches of snow lying over all the countryside here. Frances was very thrilled at the sight of it, the first real snow she has experienced. It only lasted a couple days and has now practically all gone – thank goodness. I was very relieved to find everything in order in the house. I had been so afraid of the pipes freezing or bursting or something so I wrote to Mr Hatchett before our return and asked him to come in and get the water system working again, which he duly did. We got home about 4 pm having started at 7 am and found quite a collection of Christmas parcels waiting for us. On Saturday part of the stuff I had sent up by rail from Devon arrived, including the parts of the bookshelf Daddy and I had been making out of packing-case wood. So yesterday afternoon I set to work to put it together and make it fit its appointed niche, which was no easy matter with our primitive tools. (Incidentally I hereby warn you that you will probably receive carpentry tools for every birthday and Christmas from now on until we have the necessary minimum equipment – starting with a vice and a jack plane!) We had made the bookcase with grooves for the shelves to slide into, but had purposely left the shelves too long as I hadn't got the exact measurement of the alcove and of course it had to fit snugly. So now I proceeded to measure it up and was of course afraid to cut the shelves too short for that would have done for them altogether, so I cut the first one a shade too long and then of course had to shave off bits to get the right size, an easy enough job with a plane, but with only a saw, screwdriver and triangular file, it was awful! The second shelf was better and the third one accurate, but it all took time. The bookshelf I bought at the sale in Devon will probably go up in the nursery, painted 'morning blue' to match the other furniture, for Frances's library is growing fast and presents quite a problem now.

You asked in your last letter for a plan of the new plot of ground, here it is. *(Ursula drew a pencil sketch at the side of the letter.)* There has been no further word from Mr Burges about the purchase *(of the piece of land at the end of the garden)*, it is really hardly credible that such a small purchase could have taken so long – he obviously just doesn't bother about it. However, there is no real hurry, as long as old Brown doesn't peg out in the meantime, which he looks quite capable of. The outhouse nearest the house is fitted with rabbit hutches on one wall, and I should really like to keep some high-grade rabbits like Chinchillas or Rex or even Angoras!! We shall need to fix up a bench at the back of the garage for our carpentering etc; I think there would be room unless we propose to buy a super-limousine, which I take it is very unlikely. I hope we shall be able to have a small car someday, though I shouldn't think it would be possible for some years. There are so many things I want for us – a standard lamp in the drawing room, a radiogram, a sewing machine, a new or at least a better piano; I suppose we shall have to get out a priority list and save up for them in that order. And of course, a refrigerator, don't forget that! And I'd like to have a slight binge of some sort with you too, if you are agreeable! I was able to put £10 in the bank owing to the Christmas holiday. It is also nice to have paid back £100 to my people; it was my ambition to have the whole £200 paid off before your return but I'm afraid that will be out of the question.

All letters sent between 14 January and 4 March are missing.

15th January 1945
5, Lauriston Road,
Wimbledon, London SW19

Dear Ursula,
We were very glad to hear from you the other day, and to know that
you are all well.

I have just heard from Krakenberger to the effect that he has sent a
Christmas parcel containing 5 English books and a table-tennis set to
John, who I hope and trust will have received these gifts safely and in
time for Christmas. Unfortunately the choice of things which can be
sent from Switzerland has recently been greatly restricted so that the
only things which are permitted for despatch are books, sports articles
and musical instruments. Should you have any suggestions to make,
seeing that you know John's likes and dislikes very much better than
we do, I should certainly be pleased to hear from you on the subject.

With all good wishes, and kindest regards. Yours sincerely, H
Grunfeld.

Ursula's letter 140 (4 March 1945) is mostly a description of daily life:
I suppose I may as well prepare you for a shock – the chief being that
I have a large and ever increasing number of white hairs! The effect
is not yet generally grey, I am glad to assure you, nevertheless there
are plenty of white hairs. I am doing my best to combat incipient
wrinkles, and my figure is no better than it was, so altogether you
must be prepared to put up with an old hag! Incidentally how is your
trouble? You haven't mentioned it at all lately and the last time you
said you were getting so much better results with salt and water, and
I should so like to know how it is doing now. We must certainly get
it seen to once and for all when you come back – though if it means
your leaving me going into hospital I shall cry! Once I have got you
back I am sure I shan't be able to bear to part with you even for a day!
We have received a very thrilling invitation, to go and stay for a long
weekend with the C.O. *(Air Vice Marshal Don Bennett)* and his wife

at Barbara's place of work. The wife is a great pal of Barbara's, and I shall be so interested to see it all, and Ba's hut, and meet some of the people she is always telling us about. The Red Cross has returned the pair of pyjamas I sent in your last parcel, because they weren't striped! The rest of the parcel is on its way, however; I do hope you have received some of the earlier ones, for I expect the chocolate they contain would come in useful. I am terribly worried about the conditions you are having to put up with now, my dearest, and I pray that you will be able to hold out and keep fit somehow, for the longed-for end really can't be so far off now. We shall be so happy once this nightmare is over!

In letter 141 of 10 March Ursula wrote: This week has been truly eventful on all fronts, home and abroad. You will doubtless know all about foreign ones and have felt even more strongly on the subject than I, if possible. Darling, it can't be long now, it really can't; in fact, this letter will probably reach its destination to find its bird flown – home to the nest! We started off by going to tea with Mrs Kent, the lady whose translation from Turkish I have been helping to type. They had seemed ideally happy until just a few months ago when he suddenly went off the rails, and poor little Mrs Kent still seems hardly able to realise it. I'm so sorry for her, and it gives one an awful jolt to think that such things can happen to anyone. Another surprise on that day was a visit from a Mrs Pearcy, a woman of 40–50, who is proposing to open a small school, two hours in the mornings only, in the village. She is not a qualified teacher, but has had considerable teaching experience and assures me she knows lots about modern methods. She proposes to charge 1/- an hour, i.e. 10/- a week, which is not cheap, but I am seriously considering sending Frances to her after Easter, and a couple of hours regularly in the mornings would suit her fine – and me too, incidentally!

And in letter 142 (25 March 1945): Frances and I returned last Thursday from our visit to the Bennetts, which lasted 10 days and which we both thoroughly enjoyed. We crammed a tremendous amount of fun into our ten days' holiday, and I am feeling very much refreshed for it. Among other things we had two dances xxxxx went to the cinema 3 times and the theatre up in town once, and played squash 4 or 5 times as well. We popped over to Barbara's canteen whenever possible and lent a hand there, and met all the people whom she has described to us so often. They are a cheery lot, and the hut has a very pleasant friendly atmosphere. It is certainly a much nicer life for Barbara than her ambulance station. The dances were great fun too, Ly arranged dinner parties beforehand, and Ba came with us as well; we arrived rather late and left too early for me, otherwise it was grand. I'm afraid my thirst for dancing will be quite unquenchable when you return, so I hope you will be prepared for it. It is such a joy just to get into evening dress and glide round the dance-floor after so much unalloyed domesticity!

At the weekend the Bennetts had a distinguished visitor in Wilfrid Roberts, MP, chairman of the Liberal Party. He made me feel more than ever that I would rather join the Liberal Party than anything else. I wonder what your views will be, I am longing to discuss it all with you. I was rather perturbed today when I came out of church to see a notice posted up about the electoral register, saying that those who wanted to claim to be included must do that before yesterday! So I wrote off hurriedly, under yesterday's date, and hope very much that I shall be in time, or that as a householder I shall be automatically on it, for it would be simply terrible if after waiting nearly nine years for a vote I were done out of it after all! I also enquired whether I could vote for you, and whether your name were on the register so that you can vote for yourself, which would be far better! On Friday Frances and I went to a meeting of a discussion group in St Peter's where they had got the chairman of the local District Council to talk on housing, and a very good meeting it was, with questions afterwards lasting nearly an hour. There have been arrears of washing and cleaning and correspondence to clear up, so that I feel I haven't caught up with myself yet; however, it will sort itself out in time. You must be feeling a lot more cheerful these days, so am I, and I sincerely hope you will be home long before this letter could reach you. Oh my darling, what a glorious, glorious day that will be! All my love to you my darling, Ursula.

This is the last typewritten letter – showing signs of British censorship!
On 19 April Ursula received a letter from John, but in another hand,
announcing that the camp had been liberated by the British.

J.R.M. Valentine, 19th April 1945

My Dearest Ursula,
The camp was liberated by a unit of the British Army on the 16th
April; unfortunately only one third of the fellows were still there, the
Germans having evacuated the rest a few days earlier; I managed to
stay behind because I was in the sick bay recovering from diphthria
[sic]. I was moved from the camp today to an Army hospital where
this letter is being written.

    I have got over the illness with the exception of the usual after
effects, the worse of which is a temporary but more or less complete
(paralisce [sic]) of my limbs, I dont [sic] know when I shall be
brought back to Britain nor when I shall be able to see you. But I am
anxiously longing to be with you and Francis. During all these years I
have missed you terribly and the day of our reunion will be one of the
great days of my life. I will let you know as soon as possible on my
return to Britain. With Fondest love to you both, John X X X X.

Before this letter reached Ursula the public had been learning something
of the terrible conditions that prisoners had been enduring. Richard
McMillan, war correspondent with the British 2nd Army wrote on
Tuesday 17 April: British tanks and infantry are now driving into the
Stalag belt. We are in what is known as 'Prison Camp Germany'. All
our commanders are carrying lists of dozens of Stalags in the area.
Many thousands of British and American troops are known to be in
them. … One man commented 'No letter-cards have been issued to
us for weeks. I was in the march from East Prussia and, like everyone
else, by the time I got here last month I was more dead than alive. …
The fires of battle are still blazing fiercely in Fallingbostel but crowds
of liberated prisoners are parading the streets shouting and singing
and wild with joy. There was an extraordinary scene last night when
thousands of these lean, hungry men sacked the German town. Nearly

every man came away carrying on his shoulder a great packing-case of preserved meat or canned vegetables. The Germans had plenty of food here. They had deliberately starved the men.

Telegrams followed:

21 April 1945
Valentine, Felmersham, Bottrells Lane, Chalfont St Giles
ARRIVED IN ENGLAND LETTER FOLLOWING.

22 April 1945
Valentine, Felmersham, Bottrells Lane, Chalfont St Giles, Bucks
CONVALESCING DIPHTHERIA DETAINED RAF HOSPITAL WROUGHTON NR SWINDON WILTS. ALLOWED VISITORS DAILY AFTER MIDDAY LONGING TO SEE YOU DON T BRING FRANCES, LOVE JOHN.

22 April 1945
12514404 Valentine, RAF hospital, Wroughton
COMING TOMORROW DARLING LONGING TO SEE YOU – URSULA.

And then came Ursula's final letter no. 143, written from Felmersham and dated Sunday 22 April 1945. My own darling Johnnie, How marvellous that I shall be seeing you tomorrow – possibly before you get this letter. You can't think how I've longed for this moment – tho' I daresay you have too. Poor darling, diphtheria on top of everything else, what a terrible time you've had, it's really a miracle that you have come through it. I can't write much now, my heart is full to bursting point and besides I've got everything in the world to do so as to get away early tomorrow morning. Luckily for me, Mother and Daddy have been staying here for the past week, so they are taking Frances down to Devon with them, where she will be as happy as a sandboy till we can fetch her back. So I can stay with you till you're fit to come out – may it be soon!

   Till tomorrow, my sweetheart, isn't it unbelievable! Always yours only, Ursula.

Ursula described arriving in Swindon and finding a B&B and then setting off for the hospital. Although John's letter was written by someone else and mentioned paralysis, this had not really sunk in. Nor had the implications of the later cable saying not to bring Frances. As she walked down the ward to meet John the nurse asked her if she knew of his condition. When she replied 'no' she was told that he was almost completely paralysed but could just move his head. He was over 6ft tall but at this point weighed only 6 stone. After the emotional and shattering reunion, Ursula missed the correct exit from the hospital and found herself in a yard full of cut-off plaster casts – like a macabre exhibition of statuary was her description! She then couldn't remember where she was staying and walked up and down rows of identical streets looking for her B&B for what seemed like hours.

John remained in hospital for some months. He was soon moved to the RAF Cosgrove hospital near Wolverhampton and Ursula stayed with him until he recovered from his paralysis in July. During this time Frances was looked after by the Griffin grandparents at first and then with Bunty and the Valentine grandparents at Gable End. Ursula then returned to Felmersham with Frances and resumed almost daily letters to John. When his health improved John was allowed home on occasional short leaves. The lasting result of his diphtheria was permanent damage to his knees, diagnosed as osteo-arthritis, and he received a war pension. John also had continuing problems with his nose and throat and nearly died after an operation (for a tonsillectomy?) in late 1945. He was finally invalided out of the RAF in the spring of 1946 and returned home to Felmersham. Ursula's social conscience remained as active as ever and when the war ended she started to work for SSAFA (Soldiers', Sailors' and Airmen's Families Association). During the latter half of 1945 and until John returned home permanently, Ursula's letters (seventy-three in all) often refer to the problems she encountered in her SSAFA work. Later on she changed to working for DPs (displaced persons), which continued for many years.

The family expanded with the birth of a son in August 1946 and two more daughters in April 1948 and May 1951. John never achieved the results on the violin that his herculean efforts deserved. After he fully recovered his health he returned to the violin and took lessons. Frances

*began to learn the cello when she was eight and after a couple of years
they did play some simple piano trios together. In later years John
abandoned the violin for the clarinet and having lessons on this from
the outset, made rapid progress. His love of music remained with him
for all his life.*

*The family moved to a larger house in Jordans, Buckinghamshire,
in 1948 and the nearest they got to their dream of farming was a much
larger house with nine acres of land, bought in 1953, where they kept pigs,
geese, hens and a pony. John remained a Chartered Accountant for all his
working life. In 1949 the family went to Sark for a holiday and both John
and Ursula fell in love with the island. They came across a semi-
underground German dugout on the cliff above the lighthouse and took
out a 75 year lease on it. This became the family holiday home and in
1959 they built a room, kitchen and bathroom above it, the architect
designing it being Philip Floyd's brother Michael, by then a close family
friend. In 1963 it was extended to become a small bungalow to which they
retired and remained for the rest of their lives. John never spoke about his
wartime experiences but felt very comfortable in Sark since the islanders
had endured five years of occupation and he felt able to empathise with
them; the only time he ever wore his medals was for the 50th Liberation
Day celebration on Sark!*

*After John was invalided out of the RAF in April 1946 he wanted to write
more fully to the parents of his pilot, Philip Floyd, which he finally did in
November that year. Through this he became close friends with Philip's
younger brother Michael and it is to him that we are indebted for a
photocopy of the following letter, plus photocopies of John's letter from
the POW camp and Ursula's letter to them.*

Felmersham, Bottrells Lane
Chalfont St Giles, Bucks 4/11/46

Dear Mr Floyd,
You will probably remember me by name for I had the honour to be
your son's navigator on his last and fatal trip to Germany.
    I saw your letter of appeal for text books in *The Times* and it

provided me with your address. Ever since my return from Germany
I have wanted to write to you but I was prevented from so doing
primarily because my wife lost your address when moving here in
1943. In addition I hesitated to obtain your address through R.A.F.
channels for I did not wish to reopen a subject which must have been
very painful to you. However, since your letter and the reference to
your gallant son I am taking the risk of writing in the hope that you
would be interested in his last journey. Please forgive me if I probe
a wound that is not yet healed and do not bother to reply.

As you know, we were among the force of 1,000 machines which set
off to bomb Cologne on the night of 30th May 1942. It was a beautiful
clear evening with a full moon and perfect visibility. All went
smoothly until we were approaching the target area. We could see the
flak ahead and the flashes of exploding bombs. We were about 13,000
feet up and suddenly caught in the intersection point of a score or
more search light beams. Their predictors must have been following
us without our knowledge for there was no warning or trial beams.
We were suddenly illuminated and obviously the focus of attention of
a single unit or battery of lights. We had experienced this before and
your son, without worrying in the slightest, gave us an exhibition of
his prowess as a pilot such as he had done on previous occasions. He
dived, climbed, twisted, turned, stalled and even almost looped but,
try as he could, was unable to get us out of the cone. By this time, of
course, it was not only lights that were worrying us. Being so firmly
caught by the lights we had become the target of a considerable
volume of artillery and shells had been exploding all around. We had
been hit several times but fortunately no one was injured and the
flying qualities of the machine were not impaired.

Finally your son decided that more drastic measures were required
and ordered me in my capacity of bomb aimer to jettison our bomb
load. This being done, he put the machine into a steep dive and we
careered madly downwards. We had to descend to 9,000 feet before
we were clear of the lights which were extremely persistent. However,
he pulled out of the dive when we were no longer illuminated and we
endeavoured to set a course for home. It was only a matter of seconds
before we were caught in more lights and then saw to our horror that

we were within range of relatively light A.A. fire which was being 'hosepiped' at us from all directions. I remember most distinctly your son saying most calmly that he thought 'we had had it' but of course he didn't give in without a fight. He started climbing and trying to dodge streams of tracer ammunition flying in our direction but a few moments later the mid upper gunner reported that an engine was on fire. A bullet had pierced the container of the engine coolant material which had drained off with the result that this engine quickly overheated and burst into flames.

Conditions were now desperate but your son was completely unruffled. He coolly ordered the crew to bale out and applied himself to steadying the machine until we were all clear. We were of course losing height at an alarming rate and to behave as he did required the steadiest of nerves.

There was a short queue to escape from the front hatch and while waiting my turn I tapped your son on the knee and held out my hand. We couldn't speak for the noise of the remaining engine and the rushing wind drowned everything else. Your son quietly grasped my hand, smiled and then concentrated on his job of pilot and captain of the machine. He knew that it was his duty to remain at his post until all his crew were as safe as it was within his power to make them, i.e. they had left the machine by parachute.

I am afraid that in his thought for us he gave himself no chance. A few seconds after shaking his hand I was dangling at the end of a 'chute and my first recollection was that of our machine hitting the ground and completely bursting into flames. Your son must have died instantly and it is no exaggeration to say that at the cost of his own life he saved those of five others.

You can imagine the grateful and admiring memory that I have of a gallant English gentleman. The gratitude of our wives, mothers and other relations and friends needs no telling from me.

When I reached a British POW camp I reported your son's courageous behaviour to a British officer in the hope that news of it might be conveyed officially or otherwise to this country. He listened sympathetically but regretted his inability to help.

I landed at Mülheim or Oberhausen (they adjoin) in the Ruhr.

I wonder if you have any news of your son's grave and would be grateful for any information you care to give me.

From my first issue of official POW notepaper I sent you a letter (or card) from the survivors of your son's crew conveying our condolences and our respect for your brave son, in whose debt we shall always remain.

If I am not causing you too much pain by this recital, I shall be more than pleased to give you any further information in my power. Please do not hesitate to write.

Yours sincerely, J.R.M. Valentine.

Members of the crew of P/O Floyd's aircraft:

Sergeant J.R.M.Valentine; Sergeant Propert; Sergeant J. Smith; Sergeant Wright; Sergeant Woodrow; Sergeant Randell.

Commonwealth War Graves Commission:

Philip Nevil Floyd, Pilot Officer 107521, No. 49 Squadron, Royal Air Force Volunteer Reserve, who died on Sunday 31 May 1942, aged twenty-one. Cemetery: Reichswald Forest War Cemetery, Germany, grave reference 9.A.14.

The remains of the Manchester, taken by 15-year-old Werner Gerlach on 31 May 1942 from a window in his parent's house in Mülheim. *Courtesy of Anna Ferrie*

Appendix 1

John Valentine's prisoner-of-war camps.

Appendix 2

The following six pages show John Valentine's November 1946 letter to the parents of his pilot, Philip Floyd.

Telephone:
CHALFONT ST. GILES 323

"FELMERSHAM"

BOTTRELLS LANE,

CHALFONT ST. GILES,

BUCKS.

4/11/46

Dear Mr Lloyd,

You will probably remember me by name for I had the honour to be your sons navigator on his last and fatal trip to Germany.

I saw your letter of appeal for text books in the Times and it provided me with your address. Ever since my return from Germany, I have wanted to write to you but I was prevented from so doing primarily because my wife lost your address when moving here in 1943. In addition I hesitated to obtain your address through R.A.F. Channels for I did not wish to re-open a subject which must have been very painful to you. However, seeing your letter & the reference to your gallant son I am taking the risk of writing in the hope that you would be interested in his last journey. Please forgive me if I probe a wound that is not yet healed and do not bother to reply.

(1a)   As you know, we were among
the force of 1000 machines which
set off to bomb Cologne on the
night of 30th May 1942. It was
a beautiful clear evening with a
full moon & perfect visibility. All
went smoothly until we were
approaching the target area. We
could see the flak ahead & the
flashes of exploding bombs. We were
about 13,000 feet up & suddenly caught
in the intersection point of a score
or more search lights beams. Their predictors
must have been following us without
our knowledge for there was no
warning or trial beams. We were
suddenly illuminated & obviously the
focus of attention of a single unit or battery
of lights. We had experienced this before
& your son, without worrying in the
slightest, gave us an exhibition of his
prowess as a pilot such as he had
done on previous occasions. He dived,
climbed, twisted, turned, stalled
& even almost looped but, try as he
could, was unable to get us out of
the cone. By this time, of course, it was
not only lights that were worrying
us. Being so firmly caught by the

2)

lights we had become the target
of a considerable volume of artillery
& shells had been exploding all around.
We had been hit several times but
fortunately no one was injured & the
flying qualities of the machine were
not impaired.

Finally your son decided that
more drastic measures were required
& ordered me in my capacity of
bomb aimer to jettison our bomb load.
This being done, he put the machine
into a steep dive & we careered
madly downwards. We had to descend
to 3000 feet before we were clear of the
lights which were extremely persistent.
However, he pulled out of the dive when
we were no longer illuminated &
we endeavoured to set a course for home.
It was only a matter of seconds before
we were caught in more lights & then
saw to our horror that we were within
range of relatively light A.A. fire which
was being "hosepiped" at us from all directions.
I remember most distinctly your son saying
most calmly that he thought "we had had it"
but of course he didn't give in without a
fight. He started climbing & trying to
dodge streams of tracer ammunition
flying in our direction but a few moments

later the mid upper gunner reported that our engine was on fire. A bullet had pierced the container of the engine coolant material which had drained off with the result that this engine quickly overheated & burst into flames.

Conditions were now desperate but your son was completely unruffled. He coolly ordered the crew to bale out & applied himself to steadying the machine until we were all clear. We were of course losing height at an alarming rate & to behave as he did required the steadiest of nerves.

There was a short queue to escape from the front hatch & while awaiting my turn I tapped your son on the knee & held out my hand. We couldn't speak for the noise of the remaining engine & the rushing wind drowned everything else. Your son quietly grasped my hand, smiled & then concentrated on his job of pilot & captain of the machine. He knew that it was his duty to remain at his post until all his crew were as safe as it was within his power to make them i.e. they had left the machine by parachute.

I am afraid that in his thought for us he gave himself no chance. A few seconds after shaking his hand I was

(3)

dangling at the end of a chute. My first recollection was that of our machine hitting the ground & completely bursting into flames. Your son must have died instantly & it is no exaggeration to say that at the cost of his own life he saved those of five others.

You can imagine the grateful & admiring memory that I have of a gallant English gentleman. The gratitude of our wives, mothers & other relations & friends needs no telling from me.

When I reached a British POW camp I reported your sons courageous behaviour to a British officer in the hope that news of it might be conveyed officially or otherwise to this country. He listened sympathetically but regretted his inability to help.

I landed at Mülheim or Oberhausen (they adjoin) in the Ruhr. I wonder if you have any news of your sons grave & would be grateful for any information you care to give me.

From my first issue of official POW notepaper I sent you a letter (or card) from the survivors of your sons crew

Conveying our condolences + our respect
for your brave son, in whose debt we
shall always remain

      If I am not causing
you too much pain by this recital,
I shall be more than pleased to
give you any further information in
my power. Please do not hesitate
to write.

      Yours sincerely

        John. Valentine

Appendix 3

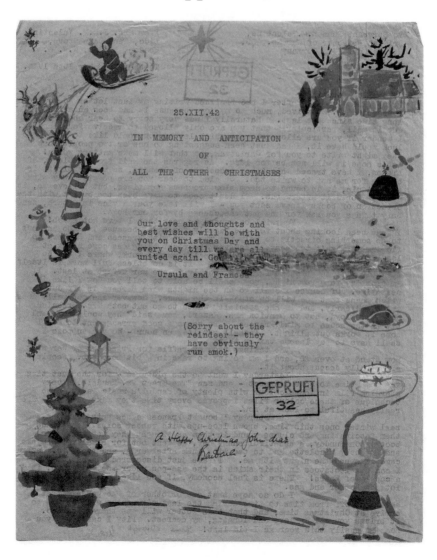

1942 Christmas letter to John.

Index

I

J

K

L

R

S